Philosophy and Orgar

G000122367

This groundbreaking new book explores why philosophy matters to organization and why organization matters to philosophy. Drawing on recent efforts in management and organization studies to take philosophy seriously, this volume features contributions from some of the most exciting scholars writing today at the intersection of philosophy and organization. Accessibly written in an engaging style, the chapters offer several images of philosophy, engage critically with the way that philosophy might inform organization, and illuminate issues including idleness, aesthetics, singularity, things and language, power and cruelty.

This book will be essential reading for students of philosophy and of business and management, and will be of interest to all those who seek to think seriously about the way their lives are organized.

Campbell Jones is Director of the Centre for Philosophy and Political Economy and Senior Lecturer in Critical Theory and Business Ethics at the University of Leicester School of Management, UK.

René ten Bos is Professor in Philosophy and Organizational Theory at Radboud University, Nijmegen, the Netherlands. He has written on ethics and fashion and is co-author (with Campbell Jones and Martin Parker) of the textbook *For Business Ethics*, also published by Routledge.

Philosophy and Organization

Edited by Campbell Jones
and René ten Bos

Routledge
Taylor & Francis Group

LONDON AND NEW YORK

First published 2007
by Routledge
2 Park Square, Milton Park, Abingdon, Oxon OX14 4RN

Simultaneously published in the USA and Canada
by Routledge
270 Madison Avenue, New York, NY 10016

Routledge is an imprint of the Taylor & Francis Group, an informa business

Typeset in Perpetua and Bell Gothic by
RefineCatch Limited, Bungay, Suffolk
Printed and bound in Great Britain by
Antony Rowe Ltd, Chippenham, Wiltshire

British Library Cataloguing in Publication Data
A catalogue record for this book is available from the British Library

Library of Congress Cataloging in Publication Data
Philosophy and organization / edited by Campbell Jones and René ten
Bos — 1st ed.
    p. cm.
Includes bibliographical references and index.
ISBN 0–415–37117–1 (hard cover) — ISBN 0–415–37118–X (soft cover)
1. Organization—Philosophy.   2. Organizational behavior.
3. Aesthetics.   I. Jones, Campbell, 1973–   II. Bos, René ten, 1959–.
HM786.P45 2007
302.3′5—dc22   2006031376

ISBN10: 0–415–37117–1 (hbk)
ISBN10: 0–415–37118–X (pbk)
ISBN10: 0–203–03085–0 (ebk)

ISBN13: 978–0–415–37117–9 (hbk)
ISBN13: 978–0–415–37118–6 (pbk)
ISBN13: 978–0–203–03085–1 (ebk)

Contents

Contributors

Steffen Böhm is Lecturer in Management at the Department of Accounting, Finance and Management, University of Essex. He is a member of the editorial collective of the journal *ephemera: theory & politics in organization* (www.ephemeraweb.org) and founding co-editor of the new publishing press mayflybooks (www.mayflybooks.org). His book *Repositioning Organization Theory: Impossibilities and Strategies* (2006, Palgrave) reads a range of critical and post-structural philosophies in order to critique the political positioning of the field of organization and management theory. He co-organized the conference 'Returning to Dialectics? Towards a Critical Philosophy of Management' (University of Essex, May 2006), which aimed at a rereading of dialectical philosophy and its possibilities for a critique of organization and management.

Janet Borgerson is Reader in the University of Exeter School of Business and Economics. She received her PhD in philosophy from the University of Wisconsin, Madison, and completed postdoctoral work in existential phenomenology at Brown University. She has held faculty positions in philosophy and management at the University of Rhode Island, Stockholm University, and the Royal Institute of Technology, Stockholm, and has received fellowships from the Cranbrook Institute, Harvard University, and the Goethe Institute. Her research has appeared in *Sociological Review, Journal of Philosophical Research, Feminist Theory, Radical Philosophy Review, Organization Studies, Culture and Organization, Consumption, Markets, & Culture, European Journal of Marketing, Advances in Consumer Research, International Marketing Review, Journal of Knowledge Management, Gender, Work & Organization*, and the *CLR James Journal*.

Steven D. Brown lectures in psychology at Loughborough University, UK and is visiting professor at the Universeiti voor Humanistiek in the Netherlands. His interests are around the respecification of the psychogical (e.g. memory, affect, conduct) in immanent, transhuman terms. He is co-author of *The Social Psychology of Experience: Studies in Remembering and Forgetting* (with David Middleton, Sage, 2005) and *Psychology without Foundations* (with Paul Stenner, Sage, forthcoming).

Pippa Carter is a Visiting Fellow in the University of Leicester School of Management, having been employed as an academic until the desire to be idle became irresistible. Her research interests are in the field of critical organization theory, on which she has published widely, with her co-researcher Norman Jackson. She has been especially attracted to the possibility of, and the potential gains from, applying the insights of post-structuralism and of Critical Theory to the problem of organization. Her vision of idleness remains unrealized, but is still an ambition.

Peter Case, Professor of Organization Studies at Bristol Business School, holds higher degrees from the University of Massachusetts and the University of Bath. His academic studies encompass organization theory, multicultural aspects of management development and the organizational impact of information and communication technologies. In addition to receiving invitations to lecture and run doctoral workshops internationally, he has held visiting scholarships at Helsinki School of Economics and the Royal Institute of Technology of Stockholm. He is chairperson of the Standing Conference on Organizational Symbolism and is a member of the editorial boards of *Leadership, Culture and Organization*, and the *Leadership and Organizational Development Journal*.

Ignaas Devisch is Professor in Ethics, Philosophy and Medical Philosophy. He is allied to the Artevelde University College and Ghent University and is also guest researcher at the Heyendaal Institute of the Radboud University of Nijmegen, the Netherlands. He studied at the universities of Ghent and Brussels. He publishes on social and political philosophy, culture and continental philosophy and on medical philosophy. For further information visit http://users.ugent.be/~idevisch

Martin Fuglsang is Associate Professor in Organizational Philosophy at the Department of Management, Politics and Philosophy at Copenhagen Business School, Denmark. He is the author of three books and co-editor of the anthology *Deleuze and the Social* (with Bent Meier Sørensen, Edinburgh University Press, 2006). In connection to the problematics of the chapter that appear in this volume, please also see the following interrelated chapters: 'Business Ethics and its World' in D. Boje (ed.) *Critical Theory and Ethics in Business and Public Administration* and 'The Humanisation of Capitalism and its Faciality' in M. Pedersen and A. R. Kristensen (eds) *Management Philosophy*. He has held a visiting scholarship at Stanford University and most recently a guest professorship in Critical Cultural Studies at the University of California, Santa Cruz.

Stefano Harney teaches at the University of London in the Queen Mary School of Business and Management. His most recent book is called *Governance and Criminality* and is forthcoming from Routledge.

Norman Jackson is a Visiting Fellow at the University of Leicester School of Management. Though lacking such an elegant concept at the time, he can trace his awareness of the *dressage* function of labour to his days at grammar school. A subsequent career in engineering, management and academia served to reinforce this understanding, as well as furnishing an opportunity to study its functioning professionally. He retains an engineering approach to understanding 'problems' and finds in post-structuralism a powerful set of 'tools' for analysing the ills of organization. Much of his work, in league with his accomplice Pippa Carter, has addressed, directly or indirectly, the oppressive urge in the management of labour.

Campbell Jones has worked on contemporary continental philosophy, and in particular post-Second World War French philosophy. More specifically he has read Jacques Derrida, which means also those who Derrida reads and those who read Derrida. Other publications include *Contemporary Organization Theory* (edited with Rolland Munro, Blackwell, 2005) and *For Business Ethics* (with Martin Parker and René ten Bos, Routledge, 2005).

Ruud Kaulingfreks studied sociology and philosophy at Santiago de Chile, Tilburg and Amsterdam. After working for 15 years in art schools he moved to organization studies and became a management consultant. Currently he works at the University for Humanistics at Utrecht. He is honorary professor and a member of the Centre for Philosophy and Political Economy at the University of Leicester School of Management. He has published extensively on philosophy, art and organization theory, in both Dutch and English.

Rolland Munro is Professor of Organization Theory and Director of the Centre for Social Theory and Technology at Keele University. Recent publications include work on wit and reason, melancholy, automobility and the eighteenth-century garden wars. He has long been engaged in writing a book on the Euro-American's cultural and social entanglement with technology, *The Demanding Relationship*, to clarify ideas like motility, disposal, engrossment and punctualizing. He has co-edited three Sociological Review Monographs with Blackwells: *Ideas of Difference* (1997), *The Consumption of Mass* (2001) and *Contemporary Organization Theory* (2005).

Nceku Q. Nyathi is a doctoral candidate in management and a member of the Centre for Philosophy and Political Economy at the University of Leicester School of Management. His current research interests include postcolonial theory, alternative forms of management and organizational theorizing from Africa and African philosophy.

Damian O'Doherty is a Lecturer in Organization Analysis at the Manchester Business School in the University of Manchester. He has published widely in management and organization journals and sits on the editorial boards of a number of leading journals in the field. He has just completed a three-year ESRC funded research project under the Evolution of Business Knowledge programme and is currently writing papers on digital technology and airports.

Alf Rehn is a lover, not a fighter, philosophically speaking. In addition to this he is a professor of management and organization in Finland, as well as a professor of innovation and entrepreneurship in Sweden, and channels his considerable angst into books and articles on various topics, including philosophical ones.

Sverre Spoelstra is a Research Fellow at the University of Lund, Sweden. He has a long-standing interest in both philosophy and organization studies, with much of his research focusing on ways in which philosophy and organization studies come together. His current research interests include critique, Spinoza, wonder, individuation and the multitude. He is a member of the editorial collective of *ephemera: theory & politics in organization* and an editor of the Dutch journal *Filosofie in Bedrijf*.

René ten Bos is Professor of Philosophy and Organizational Theory at Radboud University in Nijmegen, the Netherlands. He has published in *Organization; Organization Studies; Journal of Management Studies; Theory, Culture & Society* and is also the author of *Fashion and Utopia in Management Thinking* (2000) and co-author of *For Business Ethics* (with Campbell Jones and Martin Parker, 2005). He is a board member of the Standing Conference of Organizational Symbolism and also belongs to the editorial board of *Organization*. He takes an interest in and has published on organizational ethics, strategic management, human and non-human animals, managerial melancholia, organizational defacement, epistemological problems about accountancy, problems of inclusion and exclusion, gender, and so forth. For the near future, there are no plans for any decent specialization.

Samantha Warren lives and works in Portsmouth on the south coast of England. She teaches organization studies and research methods at the University of Portsmouth Business School and her research interests centre on the intersections between consumption, aesthetics and organization. Her PhD explored the management of cultures of fun and play and she is also interested in workforce drug testing, visual research methods and sensual methodologies that move beyond traditional talk-and-text approaches to understanding organizational life. Samantha is a member of the editorial collective of the open access journal *ephemera: theory & politics in organizations*, and an executive board member of the Standing Conference on Organizational Symbolism (SCOS).

Acknowledgements

The editors would like to thank all of the participants at the stream on 'How to do things with philosophy' that was held at the Third Critical Management Studies Conference at Lancaster, 7–9 July 2003, where earlier drafts of several of the contributions to this volume were presented. For his contribution to organizing that stream we also thank Shayne Grice. We would like to thank all of the participants to this volume for their tolerance of our many editorial demands. Thanks in particular to Ruud Kaulingfreks and Rolland Munro for their searching critiques of our introduction. We also thank Jacqueline Curthoys at Routledge for her support of this project throughout.

Introduction

Campbell Jones and René ten Bos

Before we trip ourselves up, let us start slowly, with our feet on the ground. We will assume for now that ground and feet exist, that we know what they mean, and that those feet are well dressed for the occasion. Let us begin with a mundane question, then. Not the kind of question that philosophers usually start with, but rather, with the kind of question that we will argue is today essential, even *fundamental*. A question, therefore, of administration, management, marketing and organization. What section of the library or the bookshop might this book appear in?

Suppose that a manager or a business person picks up the book in the business administration section and glosses through the table of contents. He or she will learn that the book is, among other things, about the uselessness and nonsense of philosophy, about singularity and cruelty, about idleness and resistance. What will be the look on the face of this potential reader? Will they be interested and have a closer look inside the book? Or will they simply discard it with hardly concealed condescension? Why, this person might think, should I want to read a book the authors of which have no intention to veil that philosophy might be at odds with normal organizational imperatives such as utility and sense?

On the other hand, suppose that a philosopher picks up the book in the philosophy section. What will be on their face? What will a philosopher who scans the table of contents make of this book? Perhaps this philosopher will think that philosophy is serious and bookish. But here is a book which does not appear to be serious or bookish at all. Can a book which professes to be about philosophy *and* organization really be serious? Picture this philosopher and one can imagine a certain bemusement or even bewilderment. 'What will they think of next? Those fools in the business schools now propose to take over the last bastion of hope – philosophy itself? What disaster has befallen the modern world!'

This is in many respects an impossible book. First of all, it seems to address an impossible audience. It does not only combine insights from the field of organizational theory with philosophy. This has often been done and that would hardly be new at all. Organizational theory has benefited immensely from philosophical insights, but the use of ideas by, for example, Aristotle, Kant or Foucault, does not make organizational theory philosophical. This presupposes a certain understanding of what

1

philosophy is all about. Yet, one of the basic problems of philosophy is that it resists definition.

If you look at introductory books on philosophy or look up 'philosophy' in a dictionary or on the internet, you will usually find the warning that it is notoriously difficult to define philosophy. Scuttling past such difficulties, it is nevertheless a commonplace to say that philosophy has something to do with rational inquiry, criticism, concepts, intellectualism, and so forth. Philosophy is almost always distinguished from faith, established authority and popular beliefs, and is more a matter of reason. This, however, should not tempt us to think that philosophy is like science, first of all because its endeavours do not straightforwardly refer to the empirical world. In this way, philosophy appears as a field of inquiry which has a second-order character, that is to say, it is systematic reflection about a particular practice or way of thinking.

Perhaps it is this second-order character that has led many philosophers to drift off into the lofty realms of 'pure thought'. But what about the mundane world of those who spend their lives in fields, factories and offices? We propose that philosophy should take these mundane experiences much more seriously than it typically has done. We will use the word 'organization' to refer to the structuring of this mundane world. To the list of respectable philosophical research areas such as ethics, epistemology, aesthetics, theology, politics, and so forth, we should add organization. If there is one thing which is shared by the authors who have contributed to this volume, then it is their commitment to such a philosophy of organization.

But what would a philosophy of organization amount to? Would it be something that provides us with a sort of meta-reflection about the way that organizations or people in these organizations think? Would a philosophy of organization contribute to finally making management of organizations rational after all? Would it rather be about the insanity of the organized world? In other words, what would constitute the proper terrain for a philosophy of organization?

NO WONDER

No matter how rational philosophy may seek to become, philosophy does not start with reason. For Plato, it is with wonder where philosophy begins and nowhere else (1954c: 155d). 'It is owing to wonder', Aristotle (1984) writes, 'that men both now begin and at first began to philosophize' (982b 13–14). We find a similar idea in Descartes, for whom wonder is the first of the passions:

> When our first encounter with some object surprises us and we find it novel, or very different from what we formerly knew or from what we supposed it ought to be, this causes us to wonder and to be astonished at it. Since all this may happen before we know whether or not the object is beneficial to us, I regard wonder as

the first of the passions. It has no opposite, for, if the object before us has no characteristics that surprise us, we are not moved by it at all and we consider it without passion.

(Descartes, 1955: 350)

Wonder invokes all kinds of affects: anxiety, curiosity, anger, hope, doubt, confusion. These passions and these affects drive philosophy to reason. So, if we claim that organization should be a philosophical subject, then it is because organization makes us anxious, curious, angry, hopeful, doubtful and confused.

Plato and Aristotle were very well aware that of all human beings perhaps children are the most gifted when it comes to the possibility of being affected by wonders. It is easy to see how questions such as 'What is good?', 'What is bad?' or 'What can we know?' might attract children, but does that also hold for the question 'What is organization?' or 'Why do we organize?'? Are these questions that can be taken on by the indelible naivety which is part and parcel of philosophy?

OK, let us stop just here. The book has hardly begun and already here, at the beginning of what the authors refer to as an introduction, it is rapidly deteriorating into a conundrum. Philosophers! First, they propose that philosophy can be a rational affair and now, just a few paragraphs further, they claim that philosophy is about passion and that it seeks to be naive. But this is exactly what we would ask for the philosophy of organization to come: it should become rational, serious, passionate and naive.

NO WAY

Become naive? Yes, for at least three reasons. First, we would like to stress, as suggested earlier, that organization is a wonder and that organizations perform wonders. We understand wonder here in a quite banal sense. Not only is a wonder something exceptional but also it is something which can be both glorious and grotesque. Most people spend long and tiresome hours labouring in organizations, but the things they consider most important in their lives – being born, falling in love, attracting health problems, and so on – tend to escape organization. They belong to the sphere of the aleatory and contingent. This doesn't stop us from trying to organize. Indeed, we might think of organization as a sort of immunity system forever seeking to keep the world of chance at bay. Management or bureaucracy, it might be argued, is all about sabotaging this world of chance.

Second, and related to this, we embrace a certain naivety in the sense that we do not take the goodness or badness of organization for granted. In standard texts on management and organization, it is always tacitly assumed that organization is good and disorganization is bad. To even cast doubt on this idea means that you will not likely be understood as a serious partner in the discussion. However, we do not think that organization can be easily subjected to this kind of bipolar logics. Organization is not good or bad as such. It is, we suggest, strange. Perhaps, it is the strangeness of organization that will not allow managers to explain to their children what they do all day. This is also perhaps why they keep on asking.

The third reason is related to the notion of *aporia*, which means impasse, puzzlement, a situation where one finds no way out. The term is also used in rhetoric where it denotes 'doubt'. Aporia is what one experiences before the confusing puzzles and paradoxes of our lives and of the universe. It is an experience that confronts us with undecidability. Above, we spoke about the relationship between philosophy and wonder. Now, we understand that this wonder is also a certain experience of naivety, confusion and puzzlement when we face such an undecidability. Socrates and other ancient philosophers tried to evoke the philosophic spirit in their students by attuning them to aporias and not by simply providing answers to these puzzles. Contemporary philosophers such as Jacques Derrida again try to bring this experience of the impossible back to the heart of philosophy.

For us, dealing with aporias is pivotal to organization. It is true that organizations find solutions, make clear pathways and seek control. Yet, at the same time they produce problems, impasses, contradictions, difficulties, uncontrollability and disorganization. These are not mere supplements to proper organization, but are the property of organizations. Those who work in organizations have experiences that are clearly not straightforward and that can be referred to as aporetic. One aspect of aporia seems to be crucially important for the exercise of philosophy, to wit, the idea that it opens up to discussion and disagreement (Rancière, 1999). Philosophy is not about proof, resolution or certainty. We leave that for the police. Philosophy is about taking seriously the experience of aporia and undecidability, about continuously becoming naive, becoming child.

THE CASE

In books that teach about organization, you are sooner or later likely to encounter 'the case'. We do not propose to break from this tradition here. We would like to share the case of what we think is a very strange but also a very important organization, the United States Department of Energy (DOE). This is a big governmental organization which addresses energy issues in the United States and has as its mission to secure the delivery of energy to any single individual in the country while maintaining a safe and healthy environment. The DOE was founded during the Carter administration (1976–1980). To give you an idea how important this organization is, we provide you with just a few numbers: the DOE has more than 100,000 employees, works on a budget of almost US$20 billion annually, controls nearly 2.5 million acres of real estate holdings and owns more than 1600 research laboratories (for more details visit www.energy.gov/organization).

One of the most important responsibilities of the DOE relates to the management and organization of the unbelievably accumulated store of nuclear wastes in the United States (about 36 million cubic metres). But even for such a vast bureaucratic structure, this task is far from straightforward. This becomes evident when one realizes the long-term implications of the nuclear waste sites the DOE has to manage. This is far from simply a technical issue about the decay and storage of nuclear waste. One of the major problems the organization encountered was related to warning markers that were being used at a site near Carlsbad, New Mexico to keep passengers at bay. While these markers are quite understandable for the present generation and probably the next, will they still be understandable to those living, say, ten thousand years from now?

The immense problem of semiotic continuity therefore popped up and the DOE argued that it would be a serious moral responsibility to ensure that they used signs and markers that are understandable for people in the future as well. A special working group, the so-called Futures Panel, was assembled in 1990 and was given the task of envisaging and identifying the range and configuration of future societies that might occur in the United States and that might have an impact on the waste site in New Mexico. The Futures Panel argued that 'it is still necessary to consider possible future societies when designing markers and obstacles to prevent human intrusion', but one should of course bear in mind that the further one delves in the future, the 'less complete these alternative futures are going to be' (van Wyck, 2005: 50).

The Futures Panel therefore produced what van Wyck describes as 'an unbelievable set of probabilistically based future society and intrusion scenarios, keyed to 100, 1000, and 10,000 years in the future' (2005: 50). Among the scenarios conjured up by the panel is feministic world hegemony in 2091 that will interpret the warning markers as tokens of 'inferior, inadequate, and muddled masculine thinking' (van Wyck, 2005: 51). Why this interpretation should necessarily lead to the release of radionuclides is unclear to us, but apparently the panel surmised that feminist world hegemony will not be able to preclude the opening up of nuclear sites. Other future scenarios are related to the cultural relativism allegedly defended by philosophers such as Kuhn and Marcuse whose adherents might inspire an 'anti-technoscientific cultural revolution'. That Kuhn and Marcuse might still be considered dangerous at the end of the twenty-first century might come as a surprise to some.

DOE has also formulated a concrete action plan that ranges over almost 100 years. Here are some details of the planning:

Design and test marker concepts and materials – 1996–2083 (87 years)
Construct test berm – 1998–2005 (7 years)
Monitor performance of test markers and berm – 2005–2083 (78 years)
Test comprehension of marker messages – 2018–2023 (5 years)
Develop final design of markers – 2083–2090 (7 years)
Construct all markers 2090–2093 (3 years)

(van Wyck, 2005: 75)

5

With the DOE case, all manner of philosophical and organizational problems come to the fore, cutting to basic questions such as: what is the durability of a sign? What is its meaning? How can one control the future? What is planning? We wonder why it is that philosophy and theory have such an important role in the DOE's scenario planning. We also note that the problems here are far from being merely technical organizational problems. We believe that the DOE presents just one case and that many organizations have undertaken similarly puzzling actions that might arouse the philosophical mind. In an exemplary way van Wyck (2005) shows us the philosophical relevance of this particular case. He talks not only about the ever-shifting meaning of notions such as responsibility and justice, but also about concepts of 'threat' and 'risk' which have, needless to say, sparked extensive philosophical attention. Most importantly, van Wyck shows us that those who work in the Futures Panel must have undergone some sort of philosophical *experience* in the sense that it must reconcile what is irreconcilable: what is interred near Karlsbad must remain a secret and must yet be disclosed so as to warn future generations about the dangers of the site. According to van Wyck, the entire project operates at limits:

> At the limit of civilization; its place is the desert – the other American wilderness. At the limit of history; its time is the deep future. At the limit of meaning; its witness is unknown, abstract, and indeterminate. At the limit of the symbolic; auguring the *language* of the future is a dizzying confrontation with the aporias that obtain when one steps outside the frame of the present. At the limit of technology; the ability to engineer materials for this unprecedented duration is and remains hypothetical at best.
>
> (van Wyck, 2005: 26, emphasis in original)

Here, we have a fine example of a philosophical aporia that we can begin to understand only if we abandon the straightforward or commonsensical attitude which is oftentimes, also in the DOE, embraced as the only proper way to do things. But what are these 'things'? We feel that organization is never about the thing as such. The DOE case poignantly shows this. Its mission is about wealth and safety but again and again the DOE understands that these are continually in jeopardy and cannot be managed or organized. More generally, the philosophical aporia of organization is that it never can organize what it says it should organize. We could provide many more examples here. Think of ideas of creativity, the quality of services, the way people in organization engage with each other, the plans made for the future, and so forth. This is what the DOE case tell us. We do not organize these 'things' but organize *around* them, something to which we routinely refer with words such as 'managing' or 'facilitating'. The authors in this book have all sorts of naive and serious and always contestable things to say about the pretensions of organization, management, and, indeed, philosophy.

ANALYSIS

This being said, one might suggest that the case we have chosen is not very representative. One might quite rightly insist that there are other cases more pressing, important, or interesting. At the time of writing this, we were tempted to speak of the philosophical implications of the recent discovery that, on a global scale, drugs companies spend US$60 billion annually on promotional activities, much more than they spend on research and development (Consumers International, 2006). Or we could have spoken of the philosophical enormity of global poverty today and of the indifference of average citizens in the rich countries with respect to this problem. There are, of course, many more mind-boggling cases that we could have highlighted here.

We could also have proceeded without any case at all and just make some purely 'philosophical' points about the philosophical nature of the world of work. Ignorance of the world of work and political economy was the charge that Marx laid at the feet of the German idealist philosophers in his critique of *The German Ideology* (Marx and Engels, 1964). This explains his uneasy relationship to Hegel: although a 'pupil of that mighty thinker', Marx proposed to turn Hegel's world of ideas upside down (Marx, 1976: 103).

It would be wrong to suggest, however, that philosophy has always ignored the world of work organization. Already in Plato, we find extensive elaborations on what it means to do work and to function well in a society or in a household. These are topics we assume should concern organization and management scholars as well. The translator of a well-known edition of Plato's *The Republic* refers to this book as a kind of management handbook:

> For, as we have seen, what Plato wanted was an aristocracy of talent, and we must see the principles behind this detail. And if we want a modern brief description of this kind of society, 'Managerial Meritocracy' is perhaps the nearest we can get; it emphasizes the need for qualifications and competence in government, though it leaves out many of the other element in the Platonic solution.
>
> (Lee, 1982: 50)

Of course, we may also see *The Republic*, alongside another dialogue known as *The Statesman*, as a study in leadership (Plato, 1954a, 1954b). This all suggests that right from the outset, philosophy has been interested in what we nowadays might refer to as organization. Now, having said this, we ought to be little bit more careful. That philosophy has always been interested in work, leadership, or in managing a household is true, but should not seduce us to think that philosophy somehow uses the perspective of organization. Philosophy has a long and largely ambivalent history. On the one hand, it stands clearly within the tradition of rationality. On the other, however, it is also at home in tradition that clearly belies such rationality. In other words, there is a philosophy which is largely at odds with the world of rationality and organization.

7

Philosophy is not about organization in the way in which the social sciences — sociology, economy, psychology — can be about organizations. This is also the reason why the social sciences, in spite of all its lip-service to the history of thought, have always scorned upon philosophical efforts to ponder organization. Norbert Elias (1984), the famous sociologist, (in)famously claimed that the social sciences and certainly not philosophy are fundamental. If at all interested in philosophy, then the social sciences only aim to make it subservient to its own cause.

To put it differently, philosophers can appear in the social sciences, but philosophy as such disappears. From Plato to Habermas or Foucault, philosophers have been utilized in organization studies — one might indeed speak of a veritable fashion in the taking up of philosophers — but a feel for *aporia* and *undecidability* is often painfully lacking. Rather than philosophizing with these thinkers about the question of organization, they become a kind of receptacle from which ideas might be taken. We would argue that philosophy has not so much the task to deliver novel ideas and concepts to other disciplines such as organization studies (which would merely reduce it to a 'maiden' science serving a fully-fledged scientific master) as to question the very idea of organization, a task that will not yield any clear-cut answer.

Our defence of the idea that there is or should be a philosophy of organization is not at all intended to domesticate philosophy. It is meant to do two things: first, it should allow organization scholars to cast a glance at a world that belies organization and rationality (which is, of course, implied by our understanding of *aporia*); second, it should also allow philosophers to ponder the desirability of rationality and organization. Some philosophers have done this. Take, for example, Deleuze and Guattari's remark in one of their most famous books that being stratified, organized, or subjected is not 'the worst that can happen' to you, a remark which we suggest lies at the heart of their philosophical effort to understand the relationship between what can be organized and what cannot be organized (Deleuze and Guattari, 1988: 161).

But even when philosophers do not understand their own reflection on organization as pivotal to their own work, then we can still trace its presence. Work, work ethics, the organization of the state, the desire to escape from work, the idea of power or potentiality — all these and many other themes have been important to philosophers. The contributions that make up this book bear witness to this. Partly because of the wide dispersal of these ideas, in this book you will encounter discussions about a nigh-to bewildering variety of philosophers from very different schools and traditions. There are not many books on philosophy in which one finds such disparate authors from such different periods and traditions. Even if all of these philosophers have not been directly philosophers of organization, the task in this book is to make them so. As Žižek, another contemporary philosopher and critic, argues:

> I don't think that philosophy can any longer play any of its traditional roles, as in establishing the foundations of science, constructing a general ontology and so on. Rather, philosophy should simply fulfil its task of transcendental questioning. And

this role is more necessary than ever today. Why? Because, to put it in slightly pathetic terms, today we live in extremely interesting times where one of the main consequences of such developments as biogenetics, cloning, artificial intelligence and so on is that for the first time maybe in the history of humanity we have a situation in which what were philosophical problems are now problems that concern everyone, that are discussed widely by the public. Biogenetic interventions, for example, confront us directly with questions concerning freedom of the will, the idea of nature and natural being, personal identity, to name a few. Our time is one in which we are increasingly confronted with problems that are ultimately philosophical in nature.

(Žižek and Daly, 2004: 53–54)

This does not only hold, we argue, for biogenetics of cloning, nor only for the disposal of nuclear waste. This holds for organization in general. And it is probably not a matter only for our times that organization presents philosophical puzzles. This has always been the case, even if it is today that we live in an unmistakably organized world.

PHILOSOPHY OF MANAGEMENT, THEN?

This sense that philosophy might matter today, either because it always has or because of something about the state of the world at the moment, is reasonably popular in certain circles today. What has been done so far in the name of philosophy in connection with organization?

There is now a biannual Philosophy of Management conference. There are journals called *Philosophy of Management* and the Dutch journal *Filosofie in Bedrijf* (Philosophy in Practice) and online journals such as *Philosophy for Business* (www.isfp.co.uk/businesspathways). In the university there are courses and degrees in philosophy and management, and departments bringing these together such as the Department of Management, Politics and Philosophy at Copenhagen Business School. Perhaps unsurprisingly, there are myriad consultants selling Socratic dialogues and other helpful managerial techniques.

In a way, then, it is not a new idea to bring philosophy into management. We are not just thinking here of the common phrase 'philosophy of management' in the commonsensical meaning of a 'way of thinking about management'. This usage has a long history, dating back well before Oliver Sheldon's *The Philosophy of Management* of 1923. Other than this usage, those bringing 'actual' philosophy into the study of management is also far from new. Philosophy has even held a certain pride of place in areas such as business ethics, although there are certain rather major limits of the usage of philosophy by business ethicists, as we have argued elsewhere (see Jones et al., 2005). Philosophy has also held a particularly important place in organization studies through the way that it has featured, again and again, in discussions of research methods and in particular in debates on the philosophy of social science (see Jones, 2007). In this respect, philosophical issues, principally matters of epistemology and ontology, have long been important in organization studies, from its inception and struggles over method through to contemporary discussions of critical realism (see Ackroyd and Fleetwood, 2000, 2004).

For some, the awakening to the potential of philosophy to inform organizational studies came in the form of the account of the way that any analysis of organization is always informed by various background assumptions, or as it was most famously put, by various 'sociological paradigms' (Burrell and Morgan, 1979). We find critical accounts of the way that a certain idea of philosophy was introduced into organization studies in Chapters 1 and 3 in this volume by Damian O'Doherty and Sverre Spoelstra. Philosophy also made significant inroads in the discussions in the 1990s around postmodernism (see Hancock and Tyler, 2001; Hassard and Parker, 1993).

Beyond these continuous injections of philosophy into organization studies, and these issue-based appropriations, there has been a set of works that take up, either in part or in whole, the ideas of philosophers to understand management and organization (Böhm, 2006; Chia, 1998; Jones and Munro, 2005; Kirkeby, 2000; Linstead, 2004; Linstead and Linstead, 2005; Sørensen, 2004; Starkey and McKinlay, 1998; ten Bos, 2000). When we speak of philosophy of organization, we are also referring to this set of efforts to take up philosophy for organization studies.

We have titled this book *Philosophy and Organization*, and have not given it one of the other possible related titles that are currently in circulation. We have used the word 'organization' rather than 'philosophy of management', not in order to exclude a consideration of management, but rather in order to cast our net more broadly. As has often been noted, there is a tendency to reduce organization to management (Parker, 2002), and the practical concerns and sectional interests that this brings with it. We are seeking to avoid the politics of this reduction, but also to stress the philosophical character of organization.

We have also avoided the expression 'philosophy of management' because of the presuppositions that it makes both about who is of philosophical interest and also who is capable of philosophical activity. As Ruud Kaulingfreks (Chapter 2 in this volume) notes, managers today do often profess an interest in being philosophers. Given the tradition of the idea of philosopher-kings since Plato, it is hardly surprising that managers, the heirs-apparent to the twenty-first century, are interested in wisdom and all of its trappings.

We might recall the way that Plato excludes workers from philosophy, and the continuation of this attempt to exclude workers from philosophy ever since, as has been documented and challenged by Rancière (2004). We should remind ourselves here of workers' philosophy, the thinking of those deemed lacking in wisdom. This is not to reassure ourselves with shallow assumptions about the superiority of all those marginalized, but is rather to remind us that not only those apparently wise are wise. In this volume we find, then, the thought and philosophy of workerism (Fuglsang,

10

Chapter 4) and those marginalized by gender (Borgerson, Chapter 7) and race (Harney and Nyathi, Chapter 8). One further reason for referring to organization rather than management is as a general diagnosis of the contemporary society as organized, and the political consequences of this.

WHAT WE DO NOT WANT

In case we have not already been clear, let us say that we are not entirely happy with the way philosophy has dealt with the issue of organization and management and when it has dealt with organization and management, we are far from happy with the forms that this has taken. The chapters assembled here are offered in the spirit of a refiguration of the possibilities of philosophy and its promise for thinking organization. But what, exactly, is our objection to the previous uses of philosophy? To put it in terms of style and of *ethos*, let us attempt to capture some of this in terms of kitsch and nostalgia.

Kitsch has been defined in various kinds of way. Famous is Kundera's proposal to see kitsch as the 'denial of shit' (Kundera, 1985). It has also been defined as the reproduction of the same in an ever apparently renewed form (Linstead, 2002). Philosophy is often brought into the world of organization and management studies as a kind of ornament, for example, in the form of an isolated quote in which allegedly profound witticisms are discovered. There is also an opposed tendency to bring in philosophers as those with whom serious academics and practitioners should take issue. Routinely, so-called 'postmodern' philosophers are reduced to something they never were: deniers of the truth, anti-democrats, or, more simply, cynics. We refer to these tendencies, which are by no means limited to the area of management and organization studies, as kitsch. We should also recall Benjamin's astute analysis of the phantasmagoria of the commodity form in which the appearance of the ever-new is simultaneously the reproduction of the same (Benjamin, 1999).

Philosophy is also often used as a means to overcome feelings of nostalgia and melancholia. Even if such feelings can become overwhelming in work organizations (see ten Bos, 2003), one of the things that philosophy can do is to provide an outlet for these kind of feelings. Philosophy is often a return to origins or a 'back to basics' for die-hard managers or academics who feel that their work lacks any deeper sense. We also think here of the contemporary popularity, not only among managers and consultants, of philosophy as a form of lifestyle or philosophy of life.

For us, philosophy is neither kitsch nor nostalgia. It is, if anything, the promise of the new that lies hidden in what cannot yet be thought and is therefore always to-come. It is in this sense that this collection of chapters is not nostalgic for a lost past, but rather hopeful for a future. It sees the past of philosophy and learns from it. It sees the past of philosophy and organization and is thankful for the possibilities that the past has produced. But it is also radically transgressive in that it steps out from that

11

past towards a philosophy and organization that is always, and can only ever be, to come.

Given that this is what we want to achieve, how do we propose to get there? To start with, as one final caveat, we should stress that this book does not attempt to be definitive, to provide the final word on the possibilities of philosophy and organization. This is not a handbook or encyclopedia. Moreover, we do not mean to close things down. The idea that we somehow know where we are coming from (the origin, the *arche*) and where we are going (the goal, end, *telos*) has a long and respectable standing in the history of philosophy; it is part and parcel of western metaphysics. For us, however, philosophy is not so much a matter of origins and ends, but, and in line with what we said above about aporias, far more a continuous effort to think and rethink, again and again. But if we do not have the ambition of totalization, this does not mean that we have no ambition.

CONTENT

For the sake of simplicity, the book is divided into three parts. The chapters in the first part, 'Images', offer attempts to conceptualize what philosophy might be and to account for what philosophy might, or might not, offer something for the thinking of organization. Damian O'Doherty (Chapter 1) delves into the emergence of philosophy in organization studies, through a careful account of the place of philosophy in the work of Burrell and Morgan (1979) and in labour process theory. He illustrates the double movement whereby philosophy has been both introduced and denied in organization studies and urges a continual reflectiveness and 'recovery' of philosophy for the analysis of organization. In Chapter 2, Ruud Kaulingfreks argues that philosophy is useless, and that any attempt to find something useful in philosophy will destroy the philosophical. This does not lead him to deny the value of philosophy for management and organization studies but rather, following Heidegger, that the uselessness of philosophy is one of the important things that it can teach our culture of utility. Chapter 3, by Sverre Spoelstra, recovers the place of nonsense and idiocy, arguing that the task of philosophy is the construction of concepts against common sense. He distinguishes this from the idea of philosophy as 'underlabourer' to social science, arguing that philosophy does more than to clear the ground, and is an essentially productive and positive business. The last chapter in Part One, by Martin Fuglsang, illustrates how the production of a concept can illuminate and diagnose a world. Taking the example of the concept of 'immaterial labour', he makes a case for philosophy as the affirmation of possibilities, and hence for critique and resistance, through the production of concepts, to the world as currently organized.

The chapters in Part Two offer a set of 'Engagements' between philosophy and organization studies, in each case arguing against the grain of organization studies and showing the potential of a philosophical engagement. In Chapter 5, Peter Case takes on critical management studies, which is one of the locations in which analysts of organization have turned explicitly to philosophy. Drawing on Austin and Hadot, he argues against the abstractions of critical management studies and shows how a serious engagement with philosophy leads not to distance from the world but instead to an engagement with it. In Chapter 6, Steffen Böhm reads the reception of Critical Theory in organization studies, exposing the ways that Critical Theory has become reduced to slogans and formulae. Against this reception, he articulates the philosophical importance of Theodor Adorno and Walter Benjamin and their contribution, as philosophers, to understanding and changing organization. In a similar vein, Janet Borgerson (Chapter 7) reads the reduction of feminist ethical theory in business ethics and in the study of organization more generally. Showing the way that feminist ethical theory has been reduced to caricatures or subsumed under other, supposedly more foundational, schools of ethics, she opens up the possibility of taking feminist ethical theory as one of the crucially powerful and important foundations of a philosophy of organization. The final chapter in Part Two, by Stefano Harney and Nceku Q. Nyathi, engages with the idea that philosophy is a matter of contesting common sense, in at least two ways: first they point out that, if philosophy is interested in radical thought, then it would be foolish to ignore the radical tradition of anti-racism; and second, by sketching some of the key points in the history of that tradition they point to the grave omissions of organization studies in so far as it has failed to account for race, which is not simply a matter of bad politics, but also a matter of weak thinking.

While Part One offers images of philosophy and its promise for organization and Part Two outlines the prospects for organization studies of an engagement with philosophy, the chapters in Part Three each take one principal theme to offer 'Illuminations' of issues of relevance to organization. The chapters in Part Three are in a sense 'applied' philosophy of organization in that they each show what can be seen in relation to this or that particular issue. In Chapter 9, Norman Jackson and Pippa Carter take up the enduring issue of idleness at work. In the place of Heidegger's question 'Why are there things rather than nothing?', they ask the equally fundamental question: 'Why do we work rather than not work?' In Chapter 10, Samantha Warren and Alf Rehn take up the classic philosophical issue of aesthetics, one of the popular issues of the moment, showing how philosophy can both clarify and muddy the water of the analysis of the aesthetics of organization. In Chapter 11, Ignaas Devisch takes up the conception of 'singularity' found in the work of Jean-Luc Nancy and others, to present problems to the profound issues of individuality and unity, issues so often taken for granted in organization studies. In Chapter 12, Rolland Munro engages with the critique, that has been widespread in recent years in organization studies, of the idea that language is transparent, only to expose the way in which, behind that veil, has been the return of the earlier, and perhaps even more dangerous idea of the transparency of things. In doing so, however, Munro not only 'applies' philosophy to organization but at the same time *does* it, setting out to both break open familiar understandings of words and things but also acting to change the meanings of the practice of philosophy. In the closing chapter Steven D. Brown starts out from the ideas of Foucault, whose work on power has been among the most popular starting points for many interested in philosophy and organization. Like all of the other chapters in this book, he upsets the setup, arguing that Foucault's writing on power fail, but that if organization studies is to move ahead then it must consider other, more productive failures, such as the writings of the philosopher/madman Antonin Artaud.

THEY STUTTERED

So what is this thing, this philosophy of organization? This book contains a lot of answers to this question, and you will perhaps now not be surprised that these are often very different. Philosophy is useless (Kaulingfreks). Philosophy breaks common sense (Spoelstra). Philosophy is a habit of mind and life (Case). Philosophy creates concepts to diagnose the present (Fuglsang). Philosophy involves shifting the landscape (Munro). Philosophy is radical politics (Böhm). Philosophy is realizing that we fail (Brown). But what is it that holds these conceptions of philosophy of organization together?

   We should perhaps therefore provide you with our own understanding of philosophy, a 'definition' if you will. We will do this, as long as you are willing to allow that we ourselves will object again and again to this definition – and to any other one. To define philosophy is just as objectionable as refusing to enter into any conversation about what it might be. We give a definition that fails, and we know it fails. You might think of the definition we will provide, and in fact the whole of philosophy, in the way that Wittgenstein famously describes his way of thinking:

> My propositions serve as elucidations in the following way: anyone who understands me eventually recognizes them as nonsensical, when he has used them – as steps – to climb up beyond them. (He must, so to speak, throw away the ladder after he has climbed up it.) He must transcend these propositions, and then he will see the world aright.
>
> (Wittgenstein, 1961: 74)

Our definition then: philosophy is not a matter of seeing the world 'aright', nor is it a matter of exactitude of correctness, although these are both very important. Philosophy is a matter of interruption, of breaking open familiar universes of understanding and practice. It is not about the smooth flow of communication, but of the breakdown of that communication. Philosophy takes the principle of similarity and coherence to the limit, to the point that even these concepts are rendered unfamiliar and incoherent. Philosophy is not 'to wonder' in the sense that the schoolchild might look out the window imagining other possibilities, nor the frustrated worker's dreams of escape. It is when that wonder becomes fused with the torture of scholarship and the passion of engagement that wonder becomes philosophy. At this point the matter of becoming philosophical breaks from the common sense of wonder and enters into a world of speech and action. Here thought becomes a world, which is the thing that thinking has always dreamed of. Thought becomes word, and the word becomes flesh.

This takes philosophy out of the apparent solitude of thinking and connects it with a world. This connection with a world could be denied in thought, if never in practice. Connecting with a world, thought is put in a chain of possible connections and disconnections. It can attempt to move smoothly with that world, as with the image we find in Epicurus of 'parallel rain', in which none of the individual drops hit the others. But that is the fantasy of isolation, one of the oldest fantasies of disconnected egoism. Alternatively, the drops can mingle, the bodies can be affected by other bodies. In this case, things do not go so smoothly after all.

In this sense, one might argue that the cause and the result of philosophy are not comfort and smoothness but uneasiness. When this disease expresses itself in language, it does not often run with the grain but rather works 'against the grain'. Philosophy does not produce beautiful and clear speech. The connections of philosophy are also disconnections. This is why even the most eloquent philosopher stutters. Philosophy stutters. The philosopher stutters.

When we say this we are thinking of Deleuze's (1998) essay 'He stuttered', in which he argues that great writing – and, we would like to add, great philosophy – pushes language to the limit. This is the breakdown of language, the collapse under the force of the struggle with thinking and expression. One of Deleuze's exemplars here is Kafka, who both in his writing and his characters enacts a stammering and stuttering. The world depicted in Kafka's stories is one of comprehensible incomprehensibility, of meanings continuously breaking down. Kafka's language is a *perpetuum mobile*: 'Kafka's Gregor squeaks more than he speaks' (Deleuze, 1998: 107).

Kafka is not only important for Deleuze but also important for us. It is perhaps not audacious to suggest that Kafka is one of the greatest philosophers of organization. What path might organization theory have taken if it had chosen as its starting point not the work of Max Weber but Franz Kafka?

Kafka allows us to understand philosophy of organization as practical and engaged and also as aporetic and mind-boggling. We see then that philosophy can be a saying that does something. In that sense, there should be no preface to philosophy and organization. Here, we might recall Hegel's rejoinder about the limits of prefaces, which points to the need of the doing of philosophy rather than talking about it. In his preface to the *Phenomenology of Spirit*, Hegel condemns the preface not only as 'superfluous', but also as 'inappropriate and misleading'.

For whatever might appropriately be said about philosophy in a preface – say a historical *statement* of the main drift and the point of view, the general content and results, a string of random assertions and assurances about truth – none of this can be accepted as the way in which to expound philosophical truth.

(Hegel, 1977: 1, emphasis in original)

What Hegel suggests for prefaces might also hold for introductions such as this one, in which case this introduction is now no longer necessary. It must break down into stuttering; but not as an individual stuttering as described by Deleuze but to a collective stuttering as we become naive and become child together.

REFERENCES

Ackroyd, S. and S. Fleetwood (eds) (2000) *Realist Perspectives on Management and Organisations*. London: Routledge.

Ackroyd, S. and S. Fleetwood (eds) (2004) *Critical Realist Applications in Organisation and Management Studies*. London: Routledge.

Aristotle (1984) 'Metaphysics', in J. Barnes (ed.) *Complete Works of Aristotle* (vol. 2). Princeton, NJ: Princeton University Press.

Benjamin, W. (1999) *The Arcades Project*, trans. H. Eiland and K. McLaughlin. Cambridge, MA: Harvard University Press.

Böhm, S. (2006) *Repositioning Organization Theory: Impossibilities and Strategies*. Basingstoke: Palgrave Macmillan.

Burrell, G. and G. Morgan (1979) *Sociological Paradigms and Organisational Analysis: Elements of the Sociology of Corporate Life*. London: Heinemann.

Chia, R. (ed.) (1998) *In the Realm of Organization: Essays for Robert Cooper*. London: Routledge.

Consumers International (2006) *Branding the Cure: A Consumer Perspective on Corporate Social Responsibility, Drug Promotion and the Pharmaceutical Industry in Europe*. Report published June 2006, available online at www.consumers international.org.

Deleuze, G. (1998) 'He stuttered', in *Essays Critical and Clinical*, trans. D. W. Smith and M. Greco. London: Verso.

Deleuze, G. and F. Guattari (1988) *A Thousand Plateaus*, trans. B. Massumi. London: Athlone.

Descartes, R. (1955) 'The passions of the soul', in *Philosophical Works of Descartes* (vol. 1), trans. J. Cottingham, R. Stoothoff and D. Murdoch. Cambridge: Cambridge University Press.

Elias, N. (1984) *What is Sociology?* New York: Columbia University Press.

Hancock, P. and M. Tyler (2001) *Work, Postmodernism and Organization: A Critical Introduction*. London: Sage.

Hassard, J. and M. Parker (eds) (1993) *Postmodernism and Organizations*. London: Sage.

Hegel, G. W. F. (1977) *Phenomenology of Spirit*, trans. A. V. Miller. Oxford: Oxford University Press.

Jones, C. (2007) 'Philosophy of science', in S. Clegg and J. Bailey (eds) *International Encyclopedia of Organization Studies*. London: Sage.

Jones, C. and R. Munro (eds) (2005) *Contemporary Organization Theory.* Oxford: Blackwell.

Jones, C., M. Parker and R. ten Bos (2005) *For Business Ethics.* London: Routledge.

Kirkeby, O. F. (2000) *Management Philosophy: A Radical-Normative Perspective.* Berlin: Springer-Verlag.

Kundera, M. (1985) *The Unbearable Lightness of Being.* London: Faber & Faber

Lee, D. (1982) 'Translator's introduction', in Plato, *The Republic,* trans. D. Lee. New York: Penguin.

Linstead, S. (2002) 'Organizational kitsch', *Organization,* 9(4): 657–682.

Linstead, S. (ed.) (2004) *Organization Theory and Postmodern Thought.* London: Sage.

Linstead, S. and A. Linstead (eds) (2005) *Thinking Organization.* London: Routledge.

Marx, K. (1976) *Capital: A Critique of Political Economy, Volume One,* trans. B. Fowkes. London: Penguin.

Marx, K. and F. Engels (1964) *The German Ideology.* Moscow: Progress Publishers.

Parker, M. (2002) *Against Management: Organization in the Age of Managerialism.* Cambridge: Polity

Plato (1954a) *The Republic,* in *Complete Works,* ed. J. Cooper. Indianapolis, IN: Hackett.

Plato (1954b) *The Statesman,* in *Complete Works,* ed. J. Cooper. Indianapolis, IN: Hackett.

Plato (1954c) *Theaetetus,* in *Complete Works,* ed. J. Cooper. Indianapolis, IN: Hackett.

Rancière, J. (1999) *Disagreement: Politics and Philosophy,* trans. J. Rose. Minneapolis, MN: University of Minnesota Press.

Rancière, J. (2004) *The Philosopher and his Poor,* trans. J. Drury, C. Oster and A. Parker. Durham, NC: Duke University Press.

Sheldon, O. (1923) *The Philosophy of Management.* London: Pitman & Sons.

Sørensen, B. M. (2004) *Making Events Work, or, How to Multiply your Crisis.* Copenhagen: Samfundslitteratur.

Starkey, K. and A. McKinlay (eds) (1998) *Foucault, Management and Organization Theory: From Panopticon to Technologies of Self.* London: Sage.

ten Bos, R. (2000) *Fashion and Utopia in Management Thinking.* Amsterdam: John Benjamin.

ten Bos, R. (2003) 'Business ethics, accounting, and the fear of melancholy', *Organization,* 10(2): 267–285.

van Wyck, P. (2005) *Signs of Danger: Waste, Trauma, and Nuclear Threat.* Minneapolis, MN: University of Minnesota Press

Wittgenstein, L. (1961) *Tractatus Logico-Philosophicus,* trans. D. F. Pears and B. F. McGuiness. London: Routledge.

Žižek, S. and G. Daly (2004) *Conversations with Slavoj Žižek.* Cambridge: Polity.

Part One

Images

Chapter 1

Organization

Recovering philosophy

Damian O'Doherty

What do you consider to be the main problem, the primary task of organization studies? Why do you do it? What do you want to achieve? Where are you in organization? *Who* do you think you are, you who do organization? For many students philosophy has been brought to contemporary organization studies in the form of Burrell and Morgan's (1979) *Sociological Paradigms and Organisational Analysis*. We might say that they have *covered* the philosophy which underpins our subject; but philosophy has always been there plying its trade in the background of all we do in organization, with or without Burrell and Morgan. Indulgent, and seen as a distraction from the specificity and proper curriculum of organization studies, however, philosophy is often viewed with a great deal of suspicion. Labour process analysis represents one form of organization studies that tries to steer clear of philosophy and its complex problems (Thompson, 1993). They lose philosophy, a condition from which we will seek to recover in this chapter. Take Marx, for example. Is it not correct to say that concepts and analysis lived with him in an ever-open dialogue of philosophical reflection and questioning that opened and transgressed the boundaries of what it was/is possible to think?

This chapter reviews the work of Burrell and Morgan (1979) before examining some of the critical responses that have emerged in labour process study in response to what is deemed to be an idle and speculative trend in philosophising organization studies (Thompson, 1990). We make the claim there is a systematic philosophical cover-up in organization studies. What we explore here *will not have been* an essay on philosophy and organization, but an introduction to help clear the decks of this space-time from where our text might then arise to encourage practitioners of philosophy (and) organization. This will be to *discover*. Philosophy cannot be *covered* in the way that Burrell and Morgan attempt. Consider the possibility that philosophy cannot be applied, that she cannot be broken on the altar of representation; she is precocious and effete – something that will cost us our lives. For those who are picking up this text and asking: 'What's new in philosophy and organization?', 'What are the emerging themes in philosophy and organization?', 'What is being said?', 'What is being said that is incorrect?' and 'What can I say in the interstices?', these people will be confused and disappointed. Philosophy entails a certain balance between health and

21

sickness, between body and mind. For Plato it meant the daily practice devoted to the correct guidance of the soul. If we are sick, what matter who is speaking, especially if we are, finally, *recovering* philosophy? We have always-already been philosophy and without it we could not take action in this world.

SOCIOLOGICAL PARADIGMS AND PHILOSOPHICAL FOUNDATIONS IN ORGANIZATION ANALYSIS

Burrell and Morgan (1979) provide one of the most comprehensive classificatory summaries of the field of organization studies in their *Sociological Paradigms and Organisational Analysis* where they establish that there are four broad 'paradigms' as possibilities for studying organizations. Here, organization analysis was understood, essentially, as a form of applied sociology, and sociology in its turn was seen as a development of the social sciences formed out of the resolution of underlying, fundamental philosophical (and) political questions.

In brief, there was an epistemological and ontological question, one concerning the logic of *episteme* (knowledge, thought) – or that mode of thought which is best or most suited for studying the world – and one that addressed the nature of being, or reality (*onto*) – the nature of the world itself. The basic dilemma the organization analyst faced was to decide whether they understood the world as an *objective or subjective phenomena*. In other words, did the world pre-exist my observations and application of knowledge. If it did the task of the analyst was to eliminate the prejudice of bias and subjective interference in order to allow the world to reveal its unadorned truth. The alternative understanding perceives the world as one that is emergent out of interpretation and subjectivity. This might mean that the world appears coherent and stable – and one made up of regular bits and pieces of phenomena – but more often than not, with the recognition that the reality of the world 'out there' is a product of subjective agency, comes an awareness that the world is more fluid and contingent than can be catered for in the objective paradigm. This opens up a world that is seen to be composed of jostling difference and competing interpretative claims. Unlike a mountain that appears to have an objective form to which it is easier to agree exists beyond and outside all different perspectives – to maintain a 'truth' independent of its multiple observations – the social, or society, waxes and wanes in shape and form according to the different subjective wills and world-making activities of its social agents (Giddens, 1976). We make the social world collectively. Phenomena we know as customs and habits, routines, institutions, and norms, are historically emergent from the 'ground up' but then rapidly disappear as background furniture in our mundane, everyday world: no longer seen, but that which we see with, the 'media' of our pragmatic concerns and social activity.

The world does then assume the form of a stable, predictable entity. One could only go on perceiving at all, at one extreme, because of this repressed and forgotten discrimination and division that in some way makes stable the flux of a primordial being-in-the-world. The most basic perceptual organization carves out orientation by separating out foreground and background, inside from outside, text/context, stability and change, all of which form a basic repertoire of spatial and temporal positioning that allows us to look-out at and act-in the world. Out of all the competing and subjective interpretations, collective norms establish agreement and consensus to form a collective social reality, but the important point to grasp in coming to terms with 'subjective' epistemology, is the recognition that the social world does not exist autonomously but has to be made and remade, maintained through the ongoing repetitions and reproductions of its members. The world is made out of interpretation and bias; and because it is impossible to completely rid yourself of all historically embedded enculturation and training in an effort to attain a neutral point of value-free observation, it follows that 'there is' only a world at all because we are inextricably intertwined with it, an interrelation that provides resources to participate and communicate with others.

In addition to the subjective–objective continuum Burrell and Morgan (1979) projected an axis delineating the relative influence of conservative and 'radical' sociology. Practitioners of *conservative sociology* assume that when they look out at the world of practical human affairs there is a basic consensus that underpins and informs the activities of dispersed and differentiated groups and agents in the social world. Social relations, other things being equal, tend towards order and 'agreement'. Although there may be misunderstandings and confusions, which impart temporary disruption and conflict within social relations, at the fundamental and foundational level the social world is a natural and spontaneously emergent order that maintains the principles and values of liberal democracy and meritocracy. A series of naturally recurring feedback mechanisms and regulating principles ensure that an equilibrium is maintained, an equilibrium that best serves the collective interest that inevitably wants to maintain a neutral ground of what is understood to be 'freedom', 'harmony' and 'stability', so that each can live and let live. A central and neutral arbiter of interests is sometimes required to help steer the social towards and through these integrative and binding procedures of self-regulation, a role performed by the state and democratically elected governments, but essentially the social observes a natural ecology of order and natural justice.

These assumptions combine to form what Burrell and Morgan (1979) called the sociology of regulation. The sociology of *radical change*, on the other hand, perceives the social world to be one that is constitutively crisis ridden. For the sociologist of radical change the world is riven by contradiction and incompatible differences, evident, for example, in the diametrically opposed economic interests of the class of capital owners and that 'class' of the social who have nothing to sell but their own labour-power. This class is what sociologists used to call, without causing too much controversy, the 'working class'. Roughly divided into epistemology and ontology, Burrell and Morgan then excavate the basic philosophical underpinnings that allow us

23

to make sense of the diversity of organization analyses that has developed and prolifer-ated in the twentieth century – from Weberian-style studies of bureaucracy, through to Marxist inspired research of the labour process in work organization (Braverman, 1974; Thompson, 1983). More specifically, the two axes allow Burrell and Morgan to categorize organization analyses within the four quadrants of their much cited 2 × 2 matrix where the degree or extremity of commitment to one or the other side of the respective epistemological and ontological divisions determines the relative position of analyses within the quadrants.

FORMS OF ORGANIZATIONAL ANALYSIS

'Radical humanism' and 'interpretive sociology' occupy the subjective end of the ontological divide, which tend to see the world of work organization as one that is continually created and recreated by the activity and thoughts of its members. Radical humanist forms of organization analysis were greatly influenced and informed by a number of sources, including the early Marx; anarchist theory; existential theory and its literature published by writers like Sartre and Camus in the 1950s and 1960s; and by forms of radical or alternative psychoanalytical and psychological studies of sub-jectivity and identity developed by people such as Ronald Laing and David Cooper. The 'Frankfurt School' of Marxist theory also formed an important intellectual influ-ence on radical humanism, particularly the work of Habermas, Marcuse and Erich Fromm. To gloss the most important basic philosophical assumptions that tie together these diverse strands of intellectual legacy and to which radical humanists subscribe would identify ideas that illuminate how society and its inequalities get reproduced as much through the consciousness and ideas of subjects as through formal and 'object-ive' phenomena such as economic status or structural roles. Society and its contradic-tions get produced and reproduced through the active, conscious, wilful practices of its members, which means that subjects bear the scars and traces of the struggles that form around the ontological imperative that fosters radical change. All manner of accommodations, defences, neuroses and psychoses at the level of subjectivity and identity help siphon off and mediate wider political and social conflict and contradic-tion. In sum, subjects are divided within themselves, at war and 'internally' incoher-ent. Within the realm of organization analysis, research is trained to track the complex and diffuse forms of micro-struggle, conflict and agitation that form through and around subjects in their individual and collective world-making activities. Social relations are riddled with pools of flux and disturbance that form complex lines of conflict and disorder out of which only a partial and contingent social order can emerge.

Interpretive sociology is less persuaded that subjects are denied emancipation or that they remain frustrated and alienated by an oppressive ontological reality that perpetuates suffering and inequality. Social relations are less animated by radical change and are mobilized to a far greater extent by forces of conservation and stability. While society is still understood to remain a concertive accomplishment of the ongoing thoughts and activities of its members, like a house or a building that needs to be built and rebuilt each day as its agents return to work (see Giddens, 1986), people in general don't want radical change. Their demands and desires are far more mundane and limited, and one commits a gross error in assuming that this somehow reflects a 'false' consciousness that disguises or sublimates their 'real' interests. For many organization analysts working in this quadrant there can be no empirical basis for testing such an assumption and so studies informed by interpretive sociology tend to be far more modest in their ontological assumptions. Whether this means they lack an ethical or political stance on that which they are studying – they may claim to be able to 'bracket' this question or problem and deem it irrelevant to the task of social science – remains a moot point. Phenomenology, phenomenological sociology, and hermeneutics are located within this quadrant of the 2 × 2 matrix and provide resources for forms of organization analysis that are concerned with how collective order is secured through language and meaning as it is 'negotiated' through the everyday routine interaction of social agents. For both radical humanism and interpretive sociology the term 'structure' imposes too much stability, order and reification on the forces and dynamics that shape and pattern 'the social' over time through the complex and always precarious disaggregated minutia that is the 'raw material' of society.

Writing in the late 1970s organization analysis was predominantly conducted through the application and extension of that form of 'functionalist sociology' developed by Talcott Parsons and guided by assumptions that understand the world to be composed of pre-existing, objective, entity like structures, categories and dynamics. For structural functionalism the social world is essentially objective and predictable and its social relations tend towards natural order and meritocracy with agents the product of a social conditioning and socialization that recruits and mobilizes its 'workers' in order to position them in roles and relations that reproduce the status quo. This objectivity of phenomena means that organization analysis can basically employ the methods of the natural sciences to measure, test and define societies components and their interactions in producing what comes to be perceived at the abstract and aggregate as 'the social'.

PHILOSOPHY AND ITS DISCONTENTS

Sociological Paradigms and Organisational Analysis has become one of the most widely cited publications in organization studies, at least in the United Kingdom, and it has been the source of inspiration and influence for a considerable amount of contemporary research. Provoking extensive debate, commentary and controversy, Burrell and Morgan (1979) were probably more important for the influence they had in carving

25

open a space for alternative modes of organization analysis. Their encyclopedic review of the philosophical archaeology underpinning social theory and sociology helped students of organization analysis see – particularly those coming to organization studies from within the expanding business school and its curricula – how the text-book orthodoxy in organization analysis could be placed in one quadrant of an expanded field of inquiry and possibility.

The mainstream suddenly seemed a minority interest, a hegemony built upon very slim foundations. Normal science and the routinized procedures of natural science methodology was not the only way to conduct organization analysis. Students could read Burrell and Morgan's philosophical sensitivity and discover a catalogue of possibilities from Marxist and existential forms of alienation – citing the literature of Beckett, Camus, Kafka and Sartre – to radical ecology, cybernetic epistemology, 'systemic wisdom', and ethnomethodology which opened up the possibility that there were multiple coexisting realities. This paved the way for a series of publications and collections that worked in a similar vein, pushing the possibilities of this new 'radical humanist paradigm', on the one hand, while exploring and extending the repertoire of philosophical rethinking in organization analysis on the other (Hassard and Parker, 1993; Hassard and Pym, 1990; Reed and Hughes, 1992). Here we began to read about Lyotard, Foucault, Baudrillard, Derrida, and Deleuze and Guattari, readings that seemed to take organization studies into another 'realm' (see Chia, 1998; Cooper and Burrell, 1988). The talk was of postmodernism, desire, the panopticon, bodies without organs, simulacra, hyper-reality, undecidability, and *différance*; for a whole generation of students coming to organization analysis in the 1990s these leitmotifs seemed to resonate with a relevance that could not be equalled by the discourse of structure, system, function and role.

To understand organization analysis as a derivative of philosophical speculation, an application, or an empirical under-labourer to the more serious, high-minded and scholarly endeavour of philosophy, was a sobering prospect. Organization studies was often conducted with little attention to the philosophical rigour of its categories, concepts and methods. Passed on by generation to generation, the latent philosophical controversies out of which founding concepts have been abstracted and resolved, at least for all practical purposes, were soon forgotten. Moreover, the world of organization could be accessed and studied without too much philosophical anxiety about epistemology and ontology. A counter reaction to the return to philosophical groundwork and the redirection of organization analysis is clearly evident in the writings of Paul Thompson (see Thompson, 1993; Thompson and Smith, 2000; Thompson et al., 2001).

Thompson writes with a certain degree of impatience about the endless philosophical speculation that has followed in the wake of Burrell and Morgan (1979). His preference is for a mode of labour process analysis that might be approximately categorized as a form of 'radical structuralism' within the Burrell and Morgan matrix. Thompson would rather forgo the philosophical 'niceties' of conceptual definition and rigour for the 'real' world social science responsibilities: action, intervention, and ameliorative change for those who most suffer most from the exploitation and degradation extant within existing political and economic arrangements (see Thompson, 1993). He is not so much interested in establishing beyond all reasonable doubt the nature of organizational reality, nor in the fine-tuning of epistemological categories that would allow him to engage with organization in a philosophically satisfactory way – whether this be through the complexities of rigorously established theoretical and methodological media or by way of a more limited and circumscribed set of ideas and concepts. His highly influential 'core theory' proposal for labour process analysis, for example, seems to amount to little more than a rough and ready template for organization studies, at best a sensitizing device to orientate empirical research, but at worst – or, at least, worst for Thompson given his 'philosophical' temper – a set of metaphors within a language game that can be used to narrate or build narrative of organization.

Of course, Thompson, like many others in organization studies, whether consciously or by virtue of an unproblematized, taken-for-granted inheritance, assumes the authorial responsibility for representing organization and the underlying reality of its workings that variously position, put-to-work, and ensnare employees of capitalist organization (see Ackroyd and Fleetwood, 2004). Working within an intellectual legacy that combines elements of Marx and Weber, with more recent work in critical realism (see Thompson et al., 2001), Thompson assembles a series of concepts and sense-making devices that allow him to enter organizations (or even to believe he is 'entering'/(an)/'organization') in ways that enable him to locate and categorize what he sees and hears from the experience of interviews and case studies and what he gathers from other forms of empirical 'evidence' of organization and its activities. Core theory might be seen as an attempt to formalize and proceduralize the study of organizations through a form of labour process analysis that establishes a basis for 'normal science', a mode of procedure that prepares, therefore, the ground for the accumulation of empirical 'findings'.

LABOUR PROCESS THEORY: A RETURN TO NORMAL SCIENCE?

If we take just one of the four components that constitute core theory we might begin to see some of the problems associated with this attempt to sidestep philosophical problematics in organization studies. Thompson (1990: 99) begins with the observation that what is most important about capitalist employment relations is the 'central indeterminacy of labour potential'. This serves to identify the central preoccupation of core theory. What marks out the distinctiveness of a specifically *capitalist* labour process is the commodity status of labour, Thompson writes, which can be defined as a situation that emerges historically and prevails 'when the capacity to work is utilised as a means of producing value' (Thompson, 1990: 99). While labour might be treated as a commodity it possesses, however, a set of unique characteristics that are not shared by other factors of production. Capital can buy only the *potential* to labour; what actually gets produced is indeterminate and open-ended – dependent on the skills of supervisory or managerial persuasion, inducement, discipline and control.

It is these 'unique characteristics' that introduce and explain many of the features and dilemmas, the complexities and dynamism associated with that domain in organization identified as the labour process. The first element in core theory follows from this contextualization and states that there is a relatively autonomous realm in organization where the 'role of labour and the capital–labour relation is privileged'. It is these moves that open up this delimited enclave in organization and which help provide the basis and justification for the claim that the labour process demands a distinctive form of inquiry with its own specialist discursive and conceptual tools and resources.

This 'privileging' of the capital–labour relation abstracts and carves out from the multiplicity and complexity of phenomena in organization one possible strand of analytical focus which is brought into focus and relief by analysis because things that happen in this space and time of organization are deemed to have a significant impact in other parts of the organization. The capital–labour relation also delineates that point in production where exploitation occurs and therefore signals one moment of profound vulnerability in organization and its capacity for ongoing reproduction. The basis of this vulnerability is 'the appropriation of surplus labour by capital' (Thompson, 1990: 99), a process that provokes all manner of reaction and symptom formation including expressions of recalcitrance, resistance and contestation. Essentially, labour is expended for which it is not paid its full contribution to capital, and because of this there is always likely to be a sense of injustice, which at times muted or otherwise deflected always remains an ever-present latent threat to the smooth functioning of capital valorization. Thompson maps out a tracery or trellis of nodes and categories connected by causative chains of influence and association. One node in this network is 'labour'; yet, as a category it remains peculiarly 'black-boxed', an ahistoric and essentialist designation that is derived from a limited and reductive attention to conceptual or theoretical clarification. As soon as any effort is invested to analyse what the category 'labour' might include or exclude its usefulness as a handle on what is happening 'out-there' in the world of organization becomes somewhat more doubtful.

Is labour in the public sector, for example, the same as labour in the private sector? Is female labour the same as male labour, Muslim labour the same as Christian, or gay labour the same as heterosexual labour? To what extent can we conflate 'white-collar' labour with labour expended in car production factories? What about management? If management does not own capital or land and is forced to sell its own labour-power in order to earn income, does it also become included as part of the category labour? We might usefully extend our thinking by asking the question whether it is necessary to be formally employed with a contract of employment to count as labour? Is the young

28

son of a shopkeeper working in the evening and weekends a member of the labour force? To what extent are professional footballers labour? A soldier? A prostitute, or pimp? What about self-employed cleaners working for and running their own cleaning contract company? Once we remove all these forms of work from the classificatory category of 'labour', what percentage of the working population would be left? In other words, of all those people working, how many are employed full time in factories on production lines with their blue-collar overalls covered in oil and grease – which is the imagery and associations that accompany the deployment of the category 'labour' in labour process study?

RECALLING MARX: BEGINNING PHILOSOPHY IN ORGANIZATION

Once we begin to ask these questions we are beginning to sound a little like a protagonist in a Socratic dialogue and it may well be thought that this dialectic reflects the exercise of a more philosophical style of organization analysis. There is clearly such diversity and contingency of phenomena which may be subsumed under the label of 'labour' that abstracting and generalizing to build neat theoretical architectures courts the danger of distortion. Now this distortion is not necessarily the problem, although for Thompson (1990), with his commitment to realism and representation, this may well be the cause of some paradox and confusion. One of the reasons why scholarship abstracts and generalizes to build models and generate theory is so that explanations can be developed and proposed in order to postpone endless questioning and to replace the confusion that inevitably accompanies the more contemplative appreciation of complexity and diversity. Theory and explanation extended on the basis of generalization and abstraction distils out of the flux of phenomena to isolate patterns, patterning that can be discerned once the discipline of a certain focus and atunement to scale can be achieved. Various categories and concepts, indeed language itself, helps organize and classify phenomena, putting things into some sort of scale and relief.

The question then becomes how much explanatory weight can we attach to the abstracted model; in other words how much 'reality' can it satisfactorily explain and, therefore, to what extent does this explanation improve understanding and promote modes of intervention and change that might alleviate unnecessary suffering in organization, or, in terms of labour process analysis and critical management studies, enrich and enliven, or even emancipate, the lives of those employed in capitalist organizations? In many ways these justifications conform to the assumptions that have informed modern social science since its foundation in the modern European liberal 'enlightenment' with its ideals of reason, progress, freedom and emancipation. However, how many people will recognize organization through the category and terms of labour process analysis and its privileging of the capital–labour relation?

What justification might there be in training people, through education and the dissemination of labour process analysis, to relabel their status as 'labour' and to see the world in terms of core labour process theory?

Within labour process analysis the term 'labour' is part of a complex architectural whole that has been partly inherited and partly evolved over time, an understanding of which is necessary in order to be able to see more precisely what is meant by the deployment of the term labour and what this signifies in terms of wider organizational claims. Philosophically it follows the materialism of Marx, of whom it was said in the Preface to *Capital* that he turns Hegel's idealism on its head. Marx was interested in the dialectical evolution of history as it is experienced and shaped by people in the world of practical affairs, those people who worked in manufacturing or spinning cotton, in the detail of production lines, machinery and industry. Marx invented categories and conceptual resources; he put history and time into the abstract categories of orthodox economic theory, and showed how theoretical labour was intimately related to the 'material' tensions and contradictions of history experienced by members of society. Theory was in constant need of revision and demanded perpetual reinvention and the ever-ready willingness to abandon old worn-out concepts (Blum, 1973; Ryan, 1982); here we can see that theory is less divorced or abstract from the 'material' struggle of historical actors employed in production and manufacturing and forms part of a dialectic of refinement, abstraction, deployment and popularization distributed through contemporary 'media' channels such as the *feuilleton* and manifestos, pamphleteering, trade union meetings and other, more clandestine, publications.

The problem with the contemporary use of 'labour' as a category in labour process analysis is that it has failed to evolve, it has become something of a conservative deadweight and a retardation conjuring up images of smokestack industries, masculine brawn and physical effort. Divorced from the creative philosophical work exercised by Marx, a philosophy that embraced an historical and ontological vision that was not afraid to conjecture utopian dreams and even fantasies, to invent language to inspire and capture this vision and to trace its antecedents through an imaginative representation of the material exigencies of members of society, labour process analysis becomes dull and benign. Blum (1973) shows how Marx was driven by an ethical and ontological commitment to something that resembled Plato's 'good life'. The corpus of his theoretical effort was not directed at a rigorous or scientific exposition of capitalism. This was what he talked about, to be sure, but it was a 'strategic' means or 'vehicle' through which to raise bigger questions, so that when he speaks about capitalism he is really *saying* something far deeper (see Levinas, 1998). The categories within which we can understand (which in part constitute and therefore reproduce) the 'objects' of capital are transitory and historical but they become divorced from this constitutive reflexivity and history, and as a consequence they begin to take on, unfortunately, the appearance of alien, ahistoric things.

Marx's problem is how to *use* these categories and objects without becoming completely trapped and ensnared by their overarching logic; he must speak about something which is ghost-like (cf. Derrida, 1994), with concepts and categories that are equally spectral and unreal. So, to speak of capitalism as if it were something real and incorrigible is to fall victim to a reification that seduces and oppresses. This would be to speak like a 'nothing' (see Blum, 1973). In a sense, we can understand our society, and communicate this understanding, only within the terms and categories, on the 'inside' (so to speak) of its contemporaneous recognition. In other words, the paradoxical task is how to escape from a history, a being here-and-now, of this time and place, that allows us to understand and communicate but at the cost of a certain loss, the loss of a possible understanding (but would it be *under*-standing?) of an alternative logic, another form of Reason. So, Marx is also thinking and drawing sustenance from an 'outside', from that which hasn't yet been thought, or cannot be fully thought or articulated. This aporia is both condition of possibility and impossibility; the 'impossibility' resolved strategically by Marx through the rendering of a concrete state of affairs into metaphor (Blum, 1973). As Blum tells us, Marx's Ideal is 'that for the sake of which he speaks and not that which he speaks *about*' (Blum, 1973: 27).

BECOMING HISTORIOLOGICAL: THE INFINITE MYSTERIES OF ORGANIZATION

Labour process analysis has become procedural and mechanistic and has settled down into the routines of normal science. As one commentator argued, it no longer puts 'bums on seats' (Burrell, 1990). We can see this through the summary inquiry we have made into the use it makes of the category 'labour'. It has, in other words, lost a certain sense and practice of philosophy. Fewer and fewer students of organization can relate their incipient and inchoate sense of struggle to the objects and categories that furnish the world of the 'labour process'; it has become, quite simply, irrelevant to the material exigencies of the contemporary socius. To understand our situation today we may need to acknowledge a far more complex and subtle conception of the 'material'. It is, no doubt, the embryonic intuition of this materiality that sends our students to the texts of Foucault, Derrida, Baudrillard, Irigaray, Deleuze, Guattari, Hardt and Negri, etc., who think of materiality in the form of a new ontology – in terms of 'the virtual' and the simulacra, the 'hauntological', fluidity and multiplicity.

The discourse of deskilling and control, wage-effort bargains, capital, labour, class and technology, seems to hearken back to the experience of modern western economies in the 1970s, but it is a discourse that has become crude and imprecise, superseded by events. Students struggle to relate to its doom-laden language of degradation, control and oppression. With its incarceral logic and categories of discipline and control, labour process analysis, in its curricula and methodology, its teachings and research, has become very much akin to that which is putatively criticizing.

We know how the prisoner soon learns to love the prison guard, how the hunter becomes the hunted, and so it may be of little surprise to learn that we often begin to take on the guise of that which we are studying. Perhaps it this which explains the reluctance of labour process analysts to recognize the 'phantasmagoria' (see Benjamin, 1999) of contemporary capitalism, where everything seems colourful and light, a dazzling exhibition of virtual reality in which everything flows and transmutes seamlessly through the fibre optic cables of digital media. In this phantasmagoria, all that is solid and object like becomes plastic and surreal, an unbearable lightness of being, no less, and instantly available on download for consumers to become stars of their own private movies. This is not to claim that there is no poverty, suffering and incarceration; only that the forms and media within which this needs to be understood have changed so profoundly that it now lies beyond the purview of shopfloor industrial sociology. We need to return to something like the beginnings of philosophy: which is the beginnings of organization. Students of contemporary capital are always already 'philosophers' but our universities today prefer to control and channel its students through the routines and bullet points of 'banking' knowledge (Freire, 1972), rather than open up and cultivate the critical faculties latent within the nascent philosophy of their everyday praxis.

While labour process analysis and industrial sociology have become disconnected from its philosophical roots, Burrell and Morgan (1979) lose philosophy in another sense. The philosophy of organization as it is presented in *Sociological Paradigms* forms an a priori or primordial set of assumptions that operate in the background of the text. These latent assumptions might be called 'commitments', which appear to provide both a basic orientation in the analysis of organization and help organize and make sense of the diverse field of organization studies. Philosophy, in other words, provides some kind of foundation or underpinning to the study of organization. Once we can settle the question as to whether the world of the social is basically objective or subjective in nature, and discover whether the society tends towards cohesion and integration, or fragmentation, contradiction and struggle, we can then return to organization studies and proceed with its analysis. The claim seems to be that we need to make an initial survey of philosophical possibility, and to delve deep into the dilemmas of epistemology and ontology to get the basic issues of philosophy sorted out before returning to the surface of organizational analysis as a routine practice of academic research.

Burrell and Morgan also write as if from some neutral position of survey and observation and so their depiction of paradigms remains a transcendental conceit. From where, within the matrix of possibilities for organization analysis, for example, do they write? This is a philosophy of ideal speculation, of high sovereignty and neutrality. The reader is left with the impression that the time and place of the composition and discovery of the conceptual structure of the text is irrelevant. We are not offered any insight into the possible material struggle of its authors, the *Sturm und Drang* on the streets of 1970s Britain, the race riots, the campaign for nuclear disarmament, the clash of police baton on striking print workers and so on, nor do we understand the process of thinking and reasoning that has gone into the production of *Sociological Paradigms*. We are offered an encyclopedia of ideas and organization, a summary set of revision notes from which we might plunder a quote or two to pepper our texts with the appearance of learning and scholarship, but only in a *simulation* of philosophy and its struggle.

How did they form the understandings they did; how have they read the texts of Marx, Weber and Sartre? What did they do when they first read Heidegger's *Being and Time*, for example, who writes in his introduction that 'The ownmost meaning of Being which belongs to the inquiry into Being as an historical inquiry, gives us the assignment [*Anweisung*] of inquiring into the history of that inquiry itself, that is, of becoming historiological' (Heidegger, 1962: 42)? This cannot have been easy to read. Moreover, this is the Macquarrie and Robinson translation. It is, strictly speaking, not even Heidegger. To compare the meticulous and obsessive treatment of text by, say, Derrida, is to read and participate in the philosophical mind, to witness the evolution of thought in process with the demonstration of its, more often than not, *tentative* arrival at conjecture, thought and statement. To have Marx or Heidegger summarized in a couple of sentences for the purposes of grounding forms of organization analysis in the respectable pantheon of philosophical thought does little more than invite the normalization of an orthodoxy. Who is in a position to judge the accuracy or felicity of their readings of Marx or Heidegger, particularly if their text is presented as an introduction, or they are breaking new ground by importing new texts and sources into the field of organization analysis?

One can truly think only by engaging with the words of others, to struggle and translate, to breathe the text-inside-out through the outside-in of one's being-in-the-world. The irony is that Section 6 of *Being and Time* read carefully and treated meditatively, particularly through its gesture towards the possibility of a 'twisting out', a gesture that becomes possible as we tarry with(in) the hermeneutic circle, introduces and opens up what Heidegger will slowly exposit to be the extremely *insecure* and *enigmatic* 'foundations' of thought that provides more of a shock, a *foundering* of being and thought, rather than its *foundation*. Despite what is said about his work, Heidegger is not at all abstract. It is, if anything, an obsessive excavation and amplification of the minutia and grain of our very thought and being in the world. It is forensic and instructive and like a guide in a gallery it slowly takes you by the hand and leads you out of your house and down the road from where you currently live and patiently allows you to see and hear, to sense things you've never attended to before, or never seen in the way that Heidegger invites you to see them. You may return to your street after months of being away to find your house is there, but it looks completely different, and your family a set of strangers, speaking a foreign language.

To become historiological is to risk the loss of self in an ecstatic opening to being (here-and-now) in which our *Dasein* discovers its limits through an awareness of the mutual imbrication and mutually supporting interconnectivity of all phenomena through which so much of our very being and understanding is maintained by a web of taken-for-granted convenience, illusion and fiction. The very last thing that is possible on this return is to write a conventional descriptive and expository account cataloguing the ideas that are of use and have informed the development of organization analysis. Rather, organization begins to appear both more complex and vast but also incredible in its fragility; difficult to articulate, it appears both inescapable and illusory, both inside and outside, the body of organization isomorphic with the flesh and blood of its thinking matter – the human subject who can study 'it' only because of participation in the socius and by virtue of the struggles this necessarily entails. Out of this excursus organization and its challenge might even be translated as a question of philosophy; those working and studying organization are engaged in the problems of philosophy – 'Who am I?', 'What is there to know?', 'What is to be done?' and 'What can I become?'

In the process of this philosophical excursion you have been emptied out and turned inside-out so that philosophy – as the love (*philo*) of knowledge, or knowing (*sophia*) – becomes tempered with a horror of its absurdity and aporia; its sublimating and soporific attractions might offer some containment and withdrawal, but philosophy as an end-in-itself only confirms a series of denials, displacements and ongoing frustration. To keep open the *quest*-ion, while still believing in the value of 'quest', demands that one forget this way of posing the problem, and it therefore follows that philosophy must become other, as too must organization. Here our language begins to sound strange. This is the task and responsibility of thinking-in-(dis)organization, to discover the archaeological and genealogical exhaustion that will yield the possibility of creativity from where one can assume the onus of invention and discovery that also (perhaps paradoxically) leads out of the human.

Burrell and Morgan (1979) seem to write free of these questions in some kind of bad faith, in ways that only gesture towards the outside and the beginnings of philosophical practice – but which actually remains on the inside of conventional organization analysis. It does not, therefore, serve or revitalize the study of organization. Moreover, philosophy can offer no guarantees, foundations or reassurance. As a 'way of life' (Hadot, 1995; see also Case, Chapter 5 in this volume) philosophy leads to an inevitable estrangement from one-self and others, a rendering incompetent that often leaves one stuttering and babbling in tongues, on the cusp of articulacy and sanity. *Sociological Paradigms* does not provide the entrance or resources for the navigation of this philosophical question. To be readily accessible and understood, to be welcomed and celebrated, is fine proof that one is not exercising philosophy nor taking seriously its challenge as practised by the ancient Stoics or by the Epicureans, by Socrates who never wrote a word, and by Zarathustra dancing on the side of ice-covered mountains speaking only to his animals where he lived alone for ten years.

What kind of philosophy is it that Burrell and Morgan (1979) serve in *Sociological Paradigms*, what values, and what ethics? For whom do they write, and what is it for which they speak? What are they/is their *saying*? Which muse do they serve in their 'say', a word which it will be recalled derives etymologically from 'sage' and 'saga', from which also yields up the word 'saw'. To see, or to have 'seen', is to be a seer, and to invite people to their own possibilities of seeing it is necessary to enter into dialogue, to *give* into dialogue, to help people discover/invent their own story by way of what Rimbaud called the 'careful disarrangement of the senses': to *see-saw* is to tell one person it is necessary to 'go left' to find organization, while for another the correct tutorial advice is to 'go right' (Rimbaud, 1999). Burrell and Morgan provide a highly competent dictionary of concepts and terms. It doesn't speak to its readers, it doesn't beguile and provoke, it doesn't invite a careful return to its words or its telling, nor does it open a space in which one can dwell on the infinite mysteries of organization.

CONCLUSION: TODAY IN THE DEAD LETTER OFFICE

Today we verge on the solipsistic, the decadent, and nihilistic. Not only do we appear to have no common language and no ears to hear one another, but also we do not really care very much about speaking, listening and thinking. And this 'we'? Which 'we' can this be? The 'I', the 'I' who thinks? The 'I' who many still think and believe is only there and only exists because of thought: I think therefore I am? What's happening to this 'I'? From where does thought come if 'the subject' – conscious, ego-bound, identity, individuality and agency – is a metaphysical delusion retained for the purposes of discipline and control, a false unity that is increasingly being recognized to be more 'distributed', fragmented, schizophrenic and multiple in late modern or postmodern organization? Do we have thoughts, or do they have us? What's happening to 'the subject' today when technology intrudes and reprogrammes its 'malfunctioning' components and supplements what are deemed to be its deficiencies: regulating mood, prolonging life, improving basic cognitive processing speeds, and replacing the slow contingency of human thinking with automated and simulated, even artificial, intelligence? Moreover, given these conditions, what is this thing called 'thinking'?

These are basic questions, but they are vital to organization. We have been attempting here to evoke philosophy *and* organization, but in this evocation and provocation we may not have been particularly philosophical. We have discovered that philosophy is everywhere in organization analysis; sometimes it is an explicit feature of its practice, but mainly philosophy remains implicit and unproblematized in organization studies, providing a background set of assumptions about the nature of reality and the nature of knowledge that allows organization studies to proceed with its social scientific claims to be accumulating knowledge and 'improving' the practical exercise of organizing. Burrell and Morgan (1979) are central to contemporary organization studies. *Sociological Paradigms and Organisational Analysis* unearths the hidden philosophical assumptions and commitments that inform organization studies and in

35

bringing this background to our attention opens up the space for a more reflexive and critical interrogation of the commitments we all might unwittingly serve as we proceed with our claims about organization. Burrell and Morgan take us beyond the technical kind of 'reflexivity' championed recently by North American journals, such as *Organization Science* and the *Administrative Science Quarterly*, in which theoretical development in organization analysis is understood to be largely a matter concerning representational accuracy and the rigorous specification of social scientific modelling and its variables. Critical questioning and reflexivity is possible only when the most basic and fundamental assumptions are brought out into the open, the exercise of which helps illuminate how so much of organization studies is hidebound by restrictive and conservative commitments that serve disciplinary and normalizing ends. However, we have also discovered that Burrell and Morgan *lost* philosophy.

If Burrell and Morgan lose philosophy because they provide a primer or dictionary that summarizes the ideas of the most prominent modern philosophers, subsequent developments in areas of organization studies lose philosophy in other ways. The popular school of labour process analysis for example might be seen as a counter-reaction to what may appear to be an over-indulgent preoccupation with philosophical issues in organization studies. Core-theory (Thompson, 1990) returns the subject to a form of normal science that is motivated to provide clear and systematic empirical mappings of work organization that helps reveal the exploitation and degradation of capitalist work relations. At times there is a philosophical cleanliness to this work, at least in so far as there is an acknowledgement that labour process study is explicitly political and serves an a priori set of commitments, namely the collective 'interests' of 'labour' and its emancipation. In other words, it is bias and tells its story through selectivity and a partial rendering of the ontological and epistemological complexity of organization. Problems emerge once we begin thinking more carefully about what collective labour interests might be, of course, or what the analytical category 'labour' references or represents in the world(s) of organization. Moreover, the play of bias without the philosophical labour of reflexivity and self-examination is dangerous, abandoning bias in the circulation of discourse to a whole series of effects and repercussions, not least of which is the self-effacement and denial that occurs in the exercise of choice, selectivity and bias.

Writing is never simply representational or abstract. It forms part of a realm of discourse-practice that circulates through social relations in ways that help constitute the 'reality' of social relations – as it helps constitute our subjectivity and identity. In this sense philosophy *is* political, as the political is always-already philosophical and personal. Here we begin to recover philosophy *at the moment* we begin to lose it, where absurdity wavers and flickers, in what we have called, towards the end of this chapter, the see-saw of organization. The world tilts, but only for a second. The challenge is to endure these moments where consciousness begins to disintegrate, to extend the second into a third, and the third into a fourth . . . a pregnant pause . . . and to learn to dwell in its reverie of imagination and flight. We may have taken leave of our self in this chapter. Philosophy without a subject might leave us free to diagnose organization and (re)invent organizational futures to come without recovery.

REFERENCES

Ackroyd, S. and S. Fleetwood (eds) (2004) *Critical Realist Applications in Organisation and Management Studies*. London: Routledge.

Benjamin, W. (1999) *The Arcades Project*, trans. H. Eiland and K. McLaughlin. Cambridge, MA: Harvard University Press.

Blum, A. (1973) 'Reading Marx', *Sociological Inquiry*, 43(S): 23–34.

Braverman, H. (1974) *Labor and Monopoly Capital*. New York: Monthly Review Press.

Burrell, G. (1990) 'Fragmented Labours', in D. Knights and H. Willmott (eds) *Labour Process Theory*. London: Macmillan.

Burrell, G. and G. Morgan (1979) *Sociological Paradigms and Organisational Analysis: Elements of the Sociology of Corporate Life*. London: Heinemann.

Chia, R. (ed.) (1998) *In the Realm of Organization: Essays for Robert Cooper*. London: Routledge.

Cooper, R. and G. Burrell (1988) 'Modernism, postmodernism and organizational analysis 1: An introduction', *Organization Studies*, 9(1): 91–112.

Derrida, J. (1978) 'Cogito and the history of madness', in *Writing and Difference*, trans. A. Bass. London: Routledge

Derrida, J. (1994) *Specters of Marx: The State of the Debt, the Work of Mourning, and the New International*, trans. P. Kamuf. New York: Routledge.

Freire, P. (1972) *Pedagogy of the Oppressed*. London: Penguin.

Giddens, A. (1976) *New Rules of Sociological Method*. London: Hutchinson.

Giddens, A. (1986) *Sociology: A Brief But Critical Introduction*. Basingstoke: Palgrave.

Hadot, P. (1995) *Philosophy as a Way of Life*, ed. A. Davidson. Oxford: Blackwell.

Hassard, J. and M. Parker (eds) (1993) *Postmodernism and Organizations*. London: Sage.

Hassard, J. and D. Pym (eds) (1990) *The Theory and Philosophy of Organizations*. London: Routledge.

Heidegger, M. (1962) *Being and Time*, trans. J. Macquarrie and E. Robinson. Oxford: Blackwell.

Levinas, E. (1998) *Otherwise Than Being, or, Beyond Essence*, trans. A. Lingis. Pittsburgh, PA: Duquesne University Press.

Reed, M. and M. Hughes (eds) (1992) *Rethinking Organization: New Directions in Organization Theory and Analysis*. London: Sage.

Rimbaud, A. (1999) *Poésies: une saison en enfer – Illuminations*. Paris: Gallimard.

Ryan, M. (1982) *Marxism and Deconstruction: A Critical Articulation*. Baltimore, MD: Johns Hopkins University Press.

Thompson, P. (1983) *The Nature of Work*. London: Macmillan.

Thompson, P. (1990) 'Crawling from the wreckage: The labour process and the politics of production', in D. Knights and H. Willmott (eds) *Labour Process Theory*. London: Macmillan.

Thompson, P. (1993) 'Postmodernism: Fatal distraction', in J. Hassard and M. Parker (eds) *Postmodernism and Organisations*. London: Sage.

Thompson, P. and C. Smith (2000) 'Follow the redbrick road: Reflections on pathways in and out of the labour process debate', *International Studies of Management and Organization,* 30(4): 40–67.

Thompson, P., C. Smith and S. Ackroyd (2001) 'If ethics is the answer, you are asking the wrong questions: A reply to Martin Parker', *Organization Studies,* 21(6): 1149–1158.

Chapter 2

The uselessness of philosophy

Ruud Kaulingfreks

PHILOSOPHERS AND MANAGERS

Organizations have a growing interest in philosophy. Managers profess philosophical affinities and seek inspiration in the work of great philosophers. There is a growing idea that great leaders are also philosophers with deep insight in the world and a clear vision of what is best. One could say that this interest is natural. Managers have always been interested in other fields besides organization theory. Doing the unexpected and extraordinary attains competitive advantage. Philosophy appeals to the intellectual excellence managers are supposed to have. Philosophers are considered to be very bright and wise. They are capable of seeing through reality and saying things nobody dares to say. They seek the truth and demystify common beliefs. They unsettle the existing order and are therefore creative and dangerous for the masses. But they are right in doing so because they really have thought about it and have the erudition to search further. Philosophy gives us new insights in our world. These are the same qualities a great leader of a corporation needs if their organization is to excel and gain competitive advantage. Managers are also supposed to have the same intellectual excellence. If not they would never become managers. Taylor's famous distinction between workers and planners has located thinking and intellectual power in the top floor offices, while workers use their muscles and not their brains. Corporate leaders are then of course the brightest and have visions normal workers can't have. Philosophy comes naturally to them and helps them to sharpen their minds and develop tools in order to excel.

But on the other hand, philosophy is considered to take too much time and effort. Managers seek practical value in the insights of philosophy. They don't have the time or patience for reading difficult texts, so they approach these things as they always do: they hire a philosopher to teach them quickly the highlights of the history of philosophy or seek fast textbooks. Philosophers are keen to be of help since it appeals to a deep philosophical frustration of having little or no influence in the world and very often not even being wanted. A career as a consultant is therefore an attractive perspective. So philosophers make their knowledge practical and available and offer their expertise on needed fields like ethics for instance. They research a question and conclude that something is ethically sound. That according to philosophical traditions a certain conduct is morally acceptable. They even develop ways to demonstrate the morality of something. Quantitatively.

But a more serious matter is the interest of philosophers in organizations. Philosophy is reflection on the world. In this age organizations are an important part of life of people. So philosophy should think about organizations. But its concern with organizations should come from the discipline itself. Philosophy studies reality and organizations from its own perspective and own methods. Its primary concern is not to aid managers in their work. Philosophy endangers itself into being a management tool by presenting itself as a practical instrument in the pursuit of competitive advantage or moral excellence. The question is if philosophy makes itself practical in order to meet the demands of managers or does it keep a critical distance? I am not implying that there should be a fundamental incompatibility between philosophy and management. But I do think that the relation between the two should be examined carefully and critically.

In this chapter I want to explore the usefulness of philosophy for organizations. This I want to do from a philosophical perspective. Even if the practice is there it is in no way certain that organizations have any use for philosophy or that they should listen to it. If philosophers should have organizational ambitions and pursue appointments as consultant or philosophical employees, then this should matter. These questions also should matter for business studies. As management schools preparing future leaders it is in no way certain they should approach philosophy. The common opinion that philosophy helps to think and helps to understand reality may be better achieved by a scientific approach. If organization studies on the other hand is interested in organizations beyond the mere practicalities of running an organization, the story is different. Philosophy should then be involved as a specific form of philosophy of culture. Still the question stands if philosophy can be of any help.

USEFULNESS AND USELESSNESS

Much of what follows has to do with the usefulness or uselessness of philosophy. I will argue that philosophy is of no use for managers and that it should be considered as a useless activity. By use I mean a means to an end. As I will explain later, usefulness points towards an economy of means: something is useful when it helps to reach a certain goal that lies outside the thing itself, and in this case usefulness is synonymous with efficiency. The goal is given and the means help us to realize it. Only matters that help to the realization of the given goal are considered useful, and all others are useless. The difference between usefulness and efficiency is economical. Some useful matters help us attain the goal with less effort, are better in being a mean than others.

When stating that philosophy may be useless I mean that philosophy is not a means to an end outside the philosophical activity itself. Management may not have any use for philosophy because it remains to be seen that philosophy is of any assistance to the managerial logic. On the contrary, philosophical doubt could weaken management in the sense that it postpones decision making. It may inject doubt in the managing process and therefore lead to indecision. As I will argue later on, uselessness is not related to senselessness. On the contrary.

It follows from my definition of usefulness that art for instance is a very good example of something useless. Although Marcel Duchamp, ironically, once proposed to use the *Mona Lisa* as an ironing table, there is no use for art. Art is just there to be enjoyed or better, to be seen. There is no other goal in art than showing. It is exactly this evasion of being a means that makes art so pregnant with sense. As spectators we are confronted with something we cannot put to use in any of our goals, cannot integrate in our pre-existing world as Heidegger (1978c: 170) clearly explained. Art confront us with uncanniness and opens our eyes to the world we live in. Because we cannot put it to use we are forced to create a new world around the work. This world is meaningful, it is new. Or to put it otherwise it makes us see the world with new eyes. It gives meaning to it and to us.

This is not the place to go deeper into art and aesthetics. What I want to show here is that uselessness, not being a means, is related to meaningfulness (whether the correlation effectivity–meaninglessness applies I leave open). It is in this sense that I want to advocate the uselessness of philosophy. By not being a means to an external goal, philosophy is able to show us meaning, to show us the world and help us to see meaning, to discover it. Philosophy is useless in the sense that it does not help existing practices – they are better off without philosophy – but it creates its own practice. This makes philosophy more related to art than to science. But now I might be getting ahead of my argument.

PHILOSOPHY: WHAT IS THAT?

So we start with the old and often examined question: 'Philosophy: What is that?' Posing the question in this way, I am making explicit reference to Heidegger's (1958) text *Was ist das: Die Philosophie?* Much of what follows is inspired by Heidegger. However, the question is too ambitious and probably not answerable. Philosophy is by definition always plural. The point being that in order to answer it one must do philosophy. In other words one can only answer the question of what philosophy is afterwards. Therefore it is dependent on the decisions, predilections, interpretations and knowledge, of the thinker himself. To pose the question is to place oneself in an ongoing discussion about different ways of doing philosophy.

In the sixth century BC the followers of Pythagoras asked him about the secret of his wisdom, and he answered that he was in no way a wise man, and further, that to think of oneself in such a way was hubris. 'Only the gods are wise, man can only long for it, can only be a *philosophos*'. The philosopher is somebody who loves and desires

41

wisdom. Ever since, we call the discipline philosophy. The name itself thus gives an indication of what it is about. As desire, longing, passion, it is about love for falling short, for a failure. One desires what one does not have, what one misses. Philosophy is being painfully conscious of a lack, of a failure. It is a true desire: it will never fulfil itself.

As the Surrealists already said, to fulfil a desire is violence, it destroys it. Desire is in this way to stay on the threshold, to wait, as it was put by Blanchot (1992: 174). Remaining at a certain distance but engaged with the object of desire. Desire never possesses the object and makes sure that there is no appropriation. Desire speaks then of respect and attention, of an in-between where one doesn't take a step towards grabbing the object but doesn't turn away either. When we are longing we are under the spell, fascinated by the object and really wanting to have it, to fall together. But as long as we desire, we don't have it. And we want it because it is not us. Because it is different from us. It is the Other. We never desire what we already have or are. We desire what we want but are not.

Desire, as we said, emphasizes a difference with us. It makes us conscious of a lack or an absence. But Desire never fulfils its goal. Fulfilment is the destruction of the desire. Once achieved there is no desire anymore but appropriation and the violence of incorporation. Therefore there is no object of desire either. It loses its independence. It becomes an object of utility. Fulfilling a desire brings us into a spiral of appropriation and destruction, because we always need to find new objects. Hence a subjugation to possession. There is no subjugation in desire while we keep a distance. There is only a longing relation by being under the spell of the object, being seduced by it. Engaging in a play of seduction, of attraction and dismissal. Or, as Barthes (1975) said, the erotic play of postponement. Being in the in-between:

> it is intermittence . . . which is erotic: the intermittence of skin flashing between two articles of clothing (trousers and sweater) between two edges (the open-necked shirt, the glove and the sleeve) it is the flash itself which seduces, or rather: the staging of an appearance-as-disappearance.
>
> (Barthes, 1975: 9)

Desire is then all about maintaining a difference, staying in the in-between. Longing for it but keeping a distance, not coming near. Desire is never about attaining the longed object.

DOCTA IGNORANTIA

Philosophy is indeed all of this. As a love for wisdom, as a desire for it, it is an erotic play of search and distance. The goal of philosophy is not to remove the lack or to become wise but, as Pythagoras said, the goal is to become a philosopher! That is to know that one is not wise. Philosophy can then be regarded as a failure. Being very conscious that one does not attain the goal and that one is missing something essential. Because desire still means one wants to achieve the goal. It wants to achieve without achieving it.

Philosophy is in this sense opposed to science. It is a discipline of failure and is directed to not knowing. Philosophy is the discipline that knows that it does not know. Nicholas of Cusanas explained this paradoxical situation as *docta ignorantia*. Nicholas of Cusanus (1400–1464) was bishop of Brixen after holding various diplomatic positions for the Vatican. According to him, knowledge leads to the realization of not knowing. The more we learn, the more we know we don't know. All knowledge is a reasonable movement from something we know already to a conclusion that is (still) uncertain. If the distance is infinite then we will never reach the goal. The infinite is the absolute; hence we never know the infinite. We can never comprehend God and thus truth. We can have only conjecture, a rapprochement but never reach the goal. So the more we know the more we are aware we do not reach our goal, or that we don't know. Hence *docta ignorantia*. Cusanus turns the common idea of knowledge development around. We normally think we start in ignorance and by hard work and proper use of reasoning we acquire knowledge. In Cusanus' eyes we start thinking we know all and by study and reasoning we gradually discover we know too little. Wisdom is to see the borders of our knowledge. This leads directly to a respect for the object of knowledge or truth (or God); since we can never know it, we can't grasp it, it always evades us. It always remains unknowable or bigger than us, and hence we have to respect it as something beyond our faculties.

Cusanus can offer a powerful critique of our present condition of erudition. Our culture, dominated by science and technology, has made vast amounts of knowledge available so that we can manage our world. We have unravelled the secrets of the universe; at least that is what popular belief tells us. The question is if we have attained truth, or if it is more a matter of control and believing we know it all. Is it more, as Heidegger says, a matter of being *right* instead of knowing the truth? A matter of counting instead of thinking. And don't we look surprisingly akin to those two friends who had access to all the knowledge of the books of the world, wonderfully described by Flaubert in his book *Bouvard and Pécuchet* (1976). In this book, these two clerks decide, after winning a vast sum of money, to retire to the province and dedicate themselves to knowledge. Therefore they read vast amounts of books and put what they learned into practice. Of course this incredibly funny book is an account of disaster after disaster. Still the two heroes are delighted with all the available knowledge. Flaubert shows a specific form of stupidity that I call 'learned stupidity' and that epitomizes our culture (ten Bos and Kaulingfreks, 2001). Thinking we know everything because science and technology have made such a wonderful progress. Exactly as Cusanus describes the not-learned as someone who think they know. Stupidity becomes thinking and being certain one knows it all and not being prepared to accept our lack of knowledge and certainly not his *docta ignorantia*.

43

SOPHIA

Philosophy is not science. Science is directed towards *logos*, towards the recollection of the knowledge of a certain area. Science collects and adds knowledge to the existing corpus, and by so doing it manages knowledge. It selects knowledge claims and assimilates them into the ever expanding body of knowledge. Other claims are rejected. This way of doing ensures that science grows and develops. The achievement it attains brings prosperity to the world. Science is a progress; it brings new light to the area it shines upon. There is more and more knowledge available and new discoveries reinforce and broaden knowledge.

Philosophy is not a *logos* but a *sophia*, a love-for. Philosophy is a passion, and it is therefore a sentimental activity. It knows no development. As being in love does not know development, the same applies to philosophy. Philosophy starts over and over again as something new. It is there or it is not. It has to start anew every time, like Sisyphus, who was punished by having to push a rock up a hill and each time he nearly reached the top the rock rolled down so he had to start again. Philosophy tries to go beyond what is known, it puts existing knowledge between brackets in order to arrive at the abyss of not knowing. Every time it realizes that we lack knowledge and that we don't know, and therefore after a lot of effort it inevitably arrives at a failure.

In philosophy we are still dealing with the same problems Pythagoras had and none of them has been solved and none of them will be solved. This is not to say that there is no body of knowledge in philosophy. The writings of the great names have to be approached with respect. But this respect is based on the great power of their thoughts and on our predilections. In philosophy, we like a certain philosopher or we do not. We respect the thorough fullness of some thinkers and are impressed by their clarity or deepness. But still, none of them tells us the truth. None of the philosophical questions that have been posed since the ancient Greeks have been solved. It is even impossible to solve them because they are questions about questioning.

Surprisingly enough, it is this failure to reach a goal that is philosophy's main strength. Starting over and over again, philosophy underlines the fragility of thought. It makes us careful and therefore accurate. There is no precedent, and each philosopher has to start all over again and approach the questions from the beginning. Of course philosophy will make thankful use of the writings of others but that is a philosophical choice based on respect for the grandeur of it. Philosophy has in this respect a strongly aesthetic quality. A philosophy appeals to us or not, it touches us and opens a new perspective or not. It gives us pleasure or joy, as Barthes explained about texts:

> Text of pleasure: the text that contents, fills, grants euphoria, the text that comes from culture and does not break with it, is linked to a *comfortable* practice of reading. Text of bliss: the text that imposes a state of loss, the text that discomforts (perhaps to the point of a certain boredom), unsettles the reader's historical,

cultural, psychological assumptions, the consistency of his tastes, values, memories, brings to a crisis his relation with language.

(Barthes, 1975: 14, emphasis in original)

In both cases the relation is sensual, based on sensitivities toward the world. Some theory endorses the way I am in the world, some shatters my beliefs and leaves me shaking in bewilderment, changing the way I look on things.

The aesthetic quality of philosophy works not only for the reader but also for the writer. Each philosopher is in a certain sense a dilettante, an amateur, driven by passion and pleasure, by the love of it: *sophia*. A philosopher is also a dilettante because – strictly speaking – the philosopher never overcomes the stage of absolute beginner. Thoughts always have the brittleness of an attempt. Philosophical texts are therefore always essays. They are literally so 'tryouts' or 'trials', in the sense that the French word *essayer* means to attempt to do something. Likewise, in philosophy each statement has no authority of its own. Philosophical statements are hypothetical, are questions even if they are not put in the form of the question as Heidegger (1978d) once said.

As a longing for truth, philosophy is always confronted with Cusanus' infinite distance and therefore can never say that this or that is true. All statements are then temporary as well. Each statement has the authority of the moment. They work for the time being, even if they are meant for all posterity. Philosophical statements are not opinions of the moment, but are efforts to discover a truth, something that stands in time. And philosophical texts have a kind of timeless topicality. We can still read ancient Greek texts and find them remarkably contemporary. They are written in search of a truth and not as responses to opinions. What the Greeks called *episteme* instead of *doxa*, true knowledge rather than common opinion.

Still, philosophical statements never finally establish certain truth. Rather, they attempt to seek truth. As attempts they necessarily have a temporal character. It is possible that one has to change them. For the time being they articulate the attempt and enunciate the question. They are never definitive and therefore are prone to discussion and interpretation. Of course, some statements are so strong that we accept them as authority. But again the authority of a great philosopher is based on admiration and awe. I wish I could have thought that but I'm incapable of such a great achievement. They appeal to me, open up a new area, give me new insights. Philosophical statements arouse enthusiasm, clarity, upsetting, recognition, and so on, but never 'rightness'. They show not the hardness of facts but the inevitability of the argumentation.

TRUTH AND CONCEALMENT

Philosophy searches for truth and knows it will never find it. At least not the absolute truth Cusanus is talking about. Still, there is truth, and philosophy opens up a space wherein truth is at work. By unsettling or reinforcing our worldview the philosophical text gives us insight. This is according to Heidegger (1978b: 130) the working of truth as *aletheia*, truth as 'unconcealing'. Classical philosophy has looked at truth as the perfect crystal ball of Parmenides, pristine and without any flaw. Unchangeable and transparent. From there on it has searched for ways to determine whether a statement is true or not. The correspondence and coherence theories of truth have long been accepted as the two main theories of truth. The former states that a statement is true if it corresponds with what is found in reality, while the latter states that a statement is true if it is coherent with another statement that is already accepted as true. Both theories presuppose truth already and don't say anything about truth itself. They are rules for the determination of truth. Or better, they are not about truth but about 'rightness' (Heidegger, 1978b: 118). In order to attain truth we have to open up to the truth. Therefore, according to Heidegger, truth presupposes freedom. But it is not a matter of decision here. It is the truth itself that opens a space for us to step in. In other words freedom is opening ourselves to the event of truth. And this is the essence of Heidegger's idea of the essence of truth. Truth is an event!

The Greek concept of *aletheia* denotes truth as the opening up of a world. It denotes the event of the opening, the moment when a light shines upon us and we discover something. We see something. Truth as *aletheia* is the event of unveiling Being. It manifests itself to us. This is what happens when we read a philosophical text. The text opens up something for us. By so doing it disturbs and provokes anxiety or reinforces a tacit way of being in the world, a hunch sometimes, or just the recognition that I'm not the only one to see things in this or that way. But by opening up, everything else closes down. By unveiling Being it also conceals itself. Each unveiling is always a concealment of the world. By opening up it closes the rest. So *aletheia* carries also concealment with it. In other words truth always has untruth with it. This Heidegger (2002) calls the mystery of truth. It is a mystery because the concealment is the first to conceal itself in the unveiling. Because we forget this concealment we think we unveil the world and we are able to grasp truth. We forget the double movement of *aletheia:* unveiling and concealment. This is what Heidegger (1978b: 133) calls errancy: 'Man's flight from the mystery towards what is readily available, onwards from one current thing to the next, passing the mystery by – this is *erring*' (emphasis in original). Errancy is the counter-essence of truth. It is the essence of error. It makes us go astray and forget all about the mystery of truth, thinking that what is 'at-hand' is the standard for beings. But philosophy is just the opposite – it is the thinking of Being. Philosophy is the ably conserved articulation of truth.

But because the full essence of truth contains the non-essence and above all holds sway as concealing, philosophy as a questioning into this truth is intrinsically discordant. Philosophical thinking is gentle releasement that does not renounce the concealment of being as a whole.

(Heidegger, 1978b: 135)

So philosophy is not the keeper of truth, it is not a movement to truth itself, as it would be if it were a method. Philosophy is the asking of questions around truth. It knows that by posing truth, by trying to disclose it, it also conceals. In other words, philosophy does not bring truth into the openness or make it ready at hand, but releases or cares for its withdrawal. Being is always Otherness or, in Cusanus' language, truth is endlessly a long way away from us.

AESTHETICS

As a longing or a desire it is not surprising that philosophy has an affinity with aesthetics. Much of philosophy appeals to sensibilities. It is driven by emotion. A desire, although it points to a lack, is an emotional engagement. It cares for the lack. As I said above, desire exists only as long as it is not realized, as long as it is conscious of the lack. Realization of desire is in this sense a destruction of the desire. Defining philosophy as a desire means it remains in postponement. Philosophy is living in postponement, endlessly not attaining goals, in a sense caring for failure. A journey without end and taking care of not attaining the end but putting the steps in between in brackets, doubting them constantly. Living in the postponement is living in the doubt: 'yes but . . .'. It is exactly in this aspect that lies the great fascination for philosophy.

It was Socrates who made popular the idea of postponing knowledge, in the idea of 'knowing that I don't know'. To never going beyond the essay is an erotic attitude, the attitude of provocation, flirting and fascination of leaving all possibilities open. As long as I don't know, everything is possible. Each knowing restricts the field of possibilities, pins us down in a certain direction. At the same time postponement is a respect for everything that is not-me. As long as my statements are tentative I have to be respectful towards the matter I am considering. It could all be a mistake. Philosophy forces us into cautiousness and therefore into a reflective attitude. Nietzsche always kept reminding us of this in his quest against *hubris*, and was always fulminating against the arrogance of knowing. Hubris is to believe in one's own statement. It is to challenge the gods and be disrespectful of the world and others by thinking one sees through them, understands them and dominates them. Philosophy is a good antidote against having too high an idea of ourselves and the belief that we can control the world.

By explicitly relating philosophy to aesthetics, I am placing aesthetics at the core of the philosophical activity. Aesthetics is the youngest philosophical discipline. It started in the eighteenth century with the work of Alexander Baumgarten (1714–1762) but it was Kant who was the first to make aesthetic theory an integral part of his system (for a detailed discussion on aesthetics see Warren and Rehn, Chapter 10 in this volume). Here I just want to point out to the importance of aesthetics for contemporary philosophical inquiry. In his third critique Kant tries to link the realms of freedom and nature or between the theoretical and the practical reason that were the subjects of his previous two Critiques. The *Critique of the Power of Judgement* (1790) studies taste judgements and shows how taste links abstract principles to empirical experience, how it links general concepts to singular sensitive experiences. The judgement of taste is led by sensibility or imagination. This becomes a third faculty besides intelligence and reason.

Judgements of taste have four characteristics. First, disinterested satisfaction, the judgement has no other purpose than the enjoyment of beauty. Second, the judgements of taste are of a subjective universality; taste is subjective but we claim universality. Our taste is related to reason without being part of it. We say that something is beautiful while we know that it is our feeling for the thing. Third, the judgement of taste has purposiveness without purpose; everything in the object of beauty points to the beauty but the beauty itself has no other purpose than to please. The object is purposive in its form but has no function. Finally, the judgement has a necessity without concept. Beauty is known as an act of necessary beauty. Everyone should be moved in the same way we are moved, or the aesthetic object is exemplary. Beauty lies in a *sensus comunis*. From here Kant shows that in aesthetic judgements imagination and reason are in a balance, our knowledge faculty is in a free play. Aesthetics then is related to Enlightenment but at the same time criticizes it as being one sided. It shows that reason needs something to balance it and searches for a free play of reason and sensibility. Aesthetics is not an advocacy of sheer sensorium but the balance of both.

It is precisely this critical perspective that has come to the fore in the twentieth century. From the moment our culture starts to realize intellectual reason is not the faculty that rules the world and that it has brought us to a position of planetary dominance of technique, as Heidegger calls it, then aesthetics emerge as a way to counterbalance the dominance without falling into anti-intellectualism and unreason. Presenting philosophy as an aesthetic activity emphasizes this critical role and forms an invitation for a detached diagnosis of our culture. It is no wonder then that especially contemporary French philosophy embraces aesthetics for critical analysis of our culture. This is a path delineated by Heidegger and his critique of intellectual rationality even if philosophers as Badiou, Nancy and Levinas to name a few explicitly turn against Heidegger. The same applies to Deleuze and Guattari, who state in *What is Philosophy?* (1994) that philosophy is the creation of concepts and not the articulation of a wonder. Although Deleuze and Guattari clearly distinguish philosophy from art, their approach to philosophy is comprehensible from an aesthetic perspective. Concepts are created by a play of imagination and reason. There are however no aesthetic objects; the creation of concepts is an aesthetic activity.

PHILOSOPHERS AND MANAGERS

In describing philosophy in this way it becomes clear that there is rather a large gap between philosophy and management. Managers are appointed in order for the firm to survive in competitive markets. We expect them to act energetically, to make decisions without hesitation and to have strategic vision based on facts and not on conjectures. Managers have knowledge of reality, while philosophers doubt knowledge of reality. Organizations need to take a firm stand and not to postpone, they seek certainty and not mild thinking. It is then perhaps no wonder that all attempts to have philosophers as kings have failed miserably. From the first megalomaniac idea of Plato to put the philosopher as ruler of the Republic it always has ended in disaster and loss of freedom. Whenever philosophers start to believe in their own ideas, then totalitarianism and dictatorship are very near. Happily for humankind this does not happen very often but remains a theoretical exercise. Still, when philosophers start to believe in themselves and want their theories put into practice, freedom is in danger. Consider for instance Heidegger's pathetic attempt to change German universities in the 1930s. But perhaps Thomas More is a good example of the horrors of practical philosophy. Utopia is an unbearable state wherein happiness as defined by More (2003) is compulsory and no deviation is allowed. From thereon the whole utopic genre bears this unbearability with it. Philosophy and management or bosses are two different worlds and let's hope they stay apart.

In this sense Marx's wish that philosophers should not interpret the world but change it is the end of philosophy or, even worse, will result in the apocalyptic end of the world. Of course philosophers can change the world, or set to change it, but they do this not as philosophers but as human beings. The same applies to managers who are not certain of their decisions and have fundamental doubts about the firm standing of their grounds. What I'm talking about here is the logic of management and the passion for philosophy, not the personal attitude one can take. Still, being two different logics does not mean they should not be interested in each other. It just says that they are two different worlds and managers should not be philosophers and philosophers should not be managers. We still have to think about what makes these things of interest to each other.

WONDER

Philosophy deals with thinking. But everyone thinks. Philosophers just think in a specific way. Since Aristotle, philosophical thinking is seen as a specific competence that allows us to see beings as what they are (see Heidegger, 1958: 27). In other words philosophy is a competence that allows us to see that something is what it is. Philosophy deals with Parmenides' famous question: 'Why is there something and not nothing?' Philosophy accounts for the fact that something is, it sees that something is as it is. Philosophy is thus putting into words an amazement or sense of wonder. It may sound strange but we seldom see things as they are. They are almost always already imbedded in a schema of thought that categorizes them beforehand. We normally see more of this schema than the thing itself. Things fit into a pre-existent world. We deal then more with the world than with the thing itself. Wonder shows us that there is more between heaven and earth than we think. There are not just things or matter. Wonder means a listening attitude as explained by Dutch philosopher Cornelis Verhoeven:

> To wonder implies that an active life suddenly is broken and comes to a stand still . . . To stand still is to stop talking, and in silence the otherness of the things come to the fore. One has to listen in order to perceive it. There is thus the possibility not to perceive it by drowning it out.
>
> (Verhoeven, 1967: 42)

The task is then silence in order not to drown out the things, to make an inner space in order to perceive in amazement that the world is like it is. Especially not to drown out is important. Philosophy does not build up knowledge but does the opposite. Schopenhauer said it clearly: 'Philosophy as science of concepts is odd and unworthy' (1977: 11§1). Philosophy is directed towards silence:

> The fundaments where upon all our knowledge rest is the inexplicable. Each explanation brings us through one or more steps to that point just like a lead line sometimes deep other times shallow, but always reaches the bottom of the sea.
>
> (Schopenhauer, 1977: 11§1)

In wonder we come face to face with the inexplicable. We are turned over to things in the sense that they appear to us without their use. They are things and not mere 'equipment' as Heidegger (1978b: 154) explained. Equipment is a thing determined by its use and its adjustment to our world. We don't see the hammer itself but only the hammering, but a thing is a thing beyond its use and adjustment. In wonder there is an equal relation between us and the world.

> In wonder things present themselves as meaningful . . . In wonder the things are not for man, but man is for things . . . Man cannot exhaust the meaning of things by putting them in the realm of his interest or by using them.
>
> (Verhoeven, 1967: 34)

Wonder as a basic philosophical attitude makes us go in a direction to that normal in research. It is not about knowing or about speaking, but about silence and listening. Thoughts depart from silence and point back to it. They try to evoke silence. Silence has a need of speaking in order to be silent as was demonstrated on several occasions by John Cage. The stake is to speak in such a manner that silence is evoked and not drowned out. This is possible in the philosophical essay, by putting the statement in between brackets. As Bergson (1959: 1347) pointed out: 'The philosopher does not start from existing ideas, on the contrary one can say that he arrives at them'.

CRITIQUE

In this sense, philosophy does exactly the opposite of what science does. Philosophy is directed towards questions and is very pleased when the result of its work is a dilemma, a way of not knowing. By doing this it does not achieve very much. Philosophy does not do much more than literally reflect upon the world. And it never has enough. Is this a negative image? Not at all. The failure of philosophy is its value. We need a lot of effort to see that the world escapes us and that life goes beyond our understanding. That there is more between heaven and earth than philosophy ever dreamt about. To understand that we are humans and are not able to see the feast of gods at the top of Olympus is not a given. We will never be wise.

I have given quite a simplified image of a strange activity. I have done this in order to underline the difference between our normal thinking and philosophy. The above makes clear, I hope, that philosophy is a critical activity. It embodies a radical critique of our thinking and self-image. It questions our customs. The customary beliefs that tells us that we know the world, that we control it and that we progressively know more about ourselves. It questions the complacency with everything we have achieved and our ability to act in the world, our ability to change the world according to our own goals.

A fundamentally critical position means that philosophy will always be marginal. Wonder happens in silence and in emptiness, not in an active life. Culture is built upon activity. We change the world, and culture can do without philosophy. Philosophers are known obstructionists, they are the ones who postpone decisions and start the discussion anew. In a world where decision-making is highly valued there is no place for philosophy. Perhaps it is useful as an extra check-up or as a challenge, but not as a fundamental aid for decisions. All in all I hope to have shown that philosophy is an utterly useless discipline. Arguments to integrate philosophy into our industriousness will meet with practical failure or shallow philosophy. As Heidegger warned us:

> Philosophy is in the constant predicament of having to justify its existence before the sciences. It believes it can do that most effectively by elevating itself to the rank of science. But such an effort is the abandonment of the essence of thinking.
>
> (Heidegger, 1978a: 218)

CONCLUSIONS, IF POSSIBLE

So should philosophy be abolished? Not at all. Its uselessness is its necessity. As Nietzsche (1974: 163) said about art: 'If we didn't have art then reason would lead to nausea and suicide'. A utilitarian and efficient world is perhaps the worst thinkable world, and that is the trouble with utopias. They are all so efficient, so well thought out, so useful. We need superfluity, uselessness and futility. Meaning always resides outside use, outside practicalities, outside applications and efficiency. It is because of the uselessness that a horizon of possibilities accompanies our deeds. There is always more than necessity. That is why Gods feast at Olympus: because they don't know necessity.

Uselessness and futility have negative connotations these days. We see them as empty, shallow and superficial, not leading anywhere and thus senseless. But uselessness is something that has no other goal than the matter itself. Uselessness is analogous to play, that which we do because of the doing itself. It has no other goal than the activity itself (Gadamer, 1986: 22). It has no external goal. While we normally act in order to attain goals, in futility the activity is sufficient. It has a meaning of its own, in itself. This can exist only in freedom. Doing something for the sheer pleasure of it means there is overabundance and we have freed ourselves from the chains of necessity. It is this point that utilitarianism never has understood. For utilitarians action always needs to be directed to external goals. By doing this they degrade activities for means to an end. Use and efficiency transform the world into means and therefore make it invisible. We are preoccupied only with the efficiency. The world becomes equipment for our supremacy. Nothing then has value of its own but only value for our use and disposition of it. In the end the world becomes meaningless and as Baudrillard (1990: 36) said: 'because nothing any longer has meaning, everything should work perfectly'.

Philosophy's apology for uselessness reminds us that the world is what it is. It brings wonder to the fore, the amazement that we are who we are, that there always is more than we can apprehend and that meaning is right in front of us. A lightness of being as an affirmation of life: Why is there something and not nothing? Because the world exists by itself, beyond our supremacy and transformation. It exists beyond our organizing principles. Philosophy is a good antidote against complacency with us as rulers of the world, as efficient managers of everything. As the American novelist Tom Robbins wrote:

> In time of widespread chaos and confusion, it has been the duty of more advanced human beings – artist scientists, clowns and philosophers – to create order. In times such as ours, however, when there is too much order, too much management, too much programming and control, it becomes the duty of superior men and women to fling their favourite monkey wrenches into the machinery. To relieve the repression of the human spirit, they must sow doubt and disruption.
>
> (Robbins, 1990: 201)

Philosophy is a separate and antithetical domain from management and organization. One produces order, the other doubts it. I have tried to advocate the uselessness of philosophy in an aesthetic manner. This I believe is especially needed in a world that overemphasizes intellectual rationality and the consequent utilitarian practicality of a technical approach where everything is seen in terms of a purpose of domination and transformation. The world is at-hand as Heidegger explains. Nothing is in itself of value but exists only in order to be transformed by us into our goals. This domination leads paradoxical to the subjugation of humans to their own domination. We cannot do otherwise than to dominate and manage and are not free any more. Freedom can be attained by a respectful position wherein we understand that we are a being among beings and have no preferred position. We then understand that the world exists independently of our will. This understanding starts by realizing that our knowledge is not almighty and that we move into a *docta ignorantia* as posed by Cusanus. Philosophy helps us to counterbalance the efficiency of decision making by amazing us about the world. It doesn't help to achieve much except futility and play, but it keeps a passion alive that shows us there always is more than we can organize or manage.

REFERENCES

Barthes, R. (1975) *The Pleasure of the Text*, trans. R. Miller. New York: Harper & Row.

Baudrillard, J. (1990) *Fatal Strategies*, trans. P. Beitchman and W. G. J. Niesluchowski. New York: Semiotext(e).

Bergson, H. (1959) *Oeuvres*. Paris: Presses Universitaires de France.

Bergson, H. (2002) *Key Writings*, trans. M. McMahon. London: Continuum.

Blanchot, M. (1992) *The Infinite Conversation*, trans. S. Hanson. Minneapolis, MN: University of Minnesota Press.

Deleuze, G. and F. Guattari (1994) *What is Philosophy?*, trans. H. Tomlinson and G. Burchell. New York: Columbia University Press.

Flaubert, G. (1976) *Bouvard and Pécuchet, with the Dictionary of Received Ideas*, trans. A. J. Krailsheimer. London: Penguin.

Gadamer, H. G. (1986) *The Relevance of the Beautiful and Other Essays*, trans. N. Walker. Cambridge: Cambridge University Press

Heidegger, M. (1958) *What is Philosophy?*, trans. W. Kluback and J. T. Widle. London: Vision Books.

Heidegger, M. (1978a) 'Letter on humanism', in D. F. Krell (ed.) *Basic Writings*. London: Routledge.

Heidegger, M. (1978b) 'On the essence of truth', in D. F. Krell (ed.) *Basic Writings*. London: Routledge.

Heidegger, M. (1978c) 'The origin of the work of art', in D. F. Krell (ed.) *Basic Writings*. London: Routledge.

Heidegger, M. (1978d) 'The question concerning technology', in D. F. Krell (ed.) *Basic Writings*. London: Routledge.

Heidegger, M. (2002) *The Essence of Truth*, trans. T. Sadler. London: Continuum.

Kant, I. (1790/2000) *Critique of the Power of Judgement*, trans. P. Guyer and E. Matthews. Cambridge: Cambridge University Press.

More, T. (2003) *Utopia*. Harmondsworth: Penguin.

Nietzsche, F. (1974) *The Gay Science*, trans. W. Kaufman. New York: Vintage.

Robbins, T. (1990) *Even Cowgirls Get the Blues*. New York: Bantam.

Schopenhauer, A. (1977) *Werke*. Zurich: Diogenes.

ten Bos, R. and R. Kaulingfreks (2001) *De Hygiënemachine*. Kampen, Netherlands: Kok Agora.

Verhoeven, C. (1967) *Inleiding tot de verwondering*. Bilthoven, Netherlands: Ambo.

Chapter 3

What is philosophy of organization?

Sverre Spoelstra

The philosopher takes the side of the idiot as though of a man without presuppositions.

(Deleuze, 1994: 130)

INTRODUCTION

Throughout the centuries philosophers have made statements that do not seem to make any sense, at least not according to the established language that we use. Examples include Spinoza's idea that a belief in miracles 'would lead to atheism' (2002: 448), Bergson's insistence that we laugh at a 'particular mechanical arrangement' (1911: 86), and Heidegger's claim that 'we are not yet capable of thinking' (1993: 369). Or take the following (rather confusing) sentence by Deleuze: 'a clear idea is in itself confused; it is confused in so far as it is clear' (1994: 213). Some philosophers have even maintained that they are not philosophers at all (e.g. Arendt, Foucault), which doesn't seem to make much sense either. Why is it that philosophers make these kinds of paradoxical statements? Are these merely unrepresentative examples? Do we need sociological, psychological, or even psychopathological theories in order to explain them? Or has this apparent nonsense something to do with the 'essence' of philosophy itself?

Different concepts of philosophy produce different effects; they also shed different kinds of light on what a 'philosophy of organization' could mean. In this chapter I emphasize the role of common sense and paradox in philosophy through a reading of Deleuze and Guattari's concept of philosophy. When philosophy is understood as being engaged with 'para-sense' (Deleuze, 1994), rather than common sense, it no longer provides any ground upon which the social sciences can stand. Instead, we might distinguish between two concepts of a radically different nature: philosophical concepts and social scientific concepts. They cannot be translated into one another, yet they affiliate. Such a concept of philosophy is by no means common sense in organization studies. As I will argue, organization studies tends to understand philosophy as the under-labourer for the social sciences. Philosophy, thus conceived,

55

becomes something located *outside* of organization studies rather than a positive force *within* organization studies.

COMMON SENSE

We live, literally, in common sense: a sense we have in common (from the Latin, *sensus communis*). There is no human life without common or shared sense. Yet common sense, in so far as it can be understood as constituting social reality, is never natural. That is to say, it is never natural *itself*; social reality cannot be explained by natural laws. While fictions as such might not be against the laws of nature, their contents cannot be explained through laws of nature. Common sense nonetheless *appears* as natural; it takes the form of the natural: 'Everybody knows . . .', 'We all know it is true that . . .', 'Of course you must . . .', 'It is only natural to . . .'. Common sense appears under the guise of nature; it is the creation of the natural within social reality. Common sense is operative without regards to its effects; it is operative without regards to logic or reasoning and it does not need a cause. Common sense is abstracted from social reality. This is the paradox of common sense: common sense is abstracted from the social reality it creates.

The abstractions of common sense, through which we live our lives, are indispensable. They are needed to communicate, to give meaning and purpose to our lives, to form an identity, to recognize and to predict. Nowadays we tend to understand common sense as an inner voice of reason; much like Jiminy Cricket as the 'official conscience' of Pinocchio in Disney's adaptations of Carlo Collodi's famous children's book. When we are about to do something stupid there is common sense correcting us. As the novelist José Saramago (2004: 145) says, common sense is always there to 'throw a brutal bucket of cold water' over dangerous ideas we form in our heads. Common sense, however, can also be harmful. The abstractions which we inhabit, and which protect us from chaos, tend to impose severe restrictions upon us: thoughts become dogmatic and our bodies behave in programmatic ways; they can stabilize or 'naturalize' oppression. Common sense can also cause war and misery. To quote Saramago one more time: 'Common sense has often been mistaken about consequences, badly so when it invented the wheel, disastrously so when it invented the atomic bomb' (2004: 47).

Common sense is indifferent to representational truth: it does not matter whether the contents of common sense statements are truths or fictions (in the instances where this question can be resolved). What matters is that common sense itself constitutes truth: it produces truth in social reality. Thus common sense itself, as the producer of the truth in social reality, is the object of the social sciences. For example, when Durkheim (1982) calls for knowledge of the 'collective mind', he is essentially indicating the role of common sense in human interaction: the common sense that is formed on a supra-individual level or the common sense of a given society.

Common sense needs affirmation, in what we say and how we act. New common sense pushes aside old common sense: we take part in the recreation of the natural in social reality on a daily basis. Social reality is haunted by a continuous battle over common sense; the changing nature of common sense partly makes up the changes in social reality. We might think of organizations as the systems in which common sense is stabilized. Organizations give us rules and prescriptions; they place us in an organizational culture; they define the natural in working life. Here we could make a distinction between 'organization', understood as the ordering of common sense (or structuring that is aimed at the continuous regeneration of common sense) and 'an organization', which is a structured place in which the battle for common sense takes place; *organizations* as places of structure-struggling and organization as structuring.

Common sense can appear spontaneously, without conscious intention, but common sense can also be taught or manipulated: through the education of 'social facts' ('Africa is the poorest continent in the world'), state propaganda ('Of course you vote'), marketing ('Naturally you buy a Honda'), and so on. Social science can also participate in the conscious creation of or intervention in common sense. So-called 'critical' social science in particular can be understood as consciously working upon common sense: it takes a stand in the production of common sense in order to emancipate an oppressed group, in order to change public opinion about social dangers, and so on. Thus critical social science does not coincidentally produce 'shock-effects'; rather, it deliberately aims to disrupt social reality itself by drawing attention to the role played by common sense in social problems, a role that would otherwise go unnoticed or be taken for granted.

Philosophy, too, can be conceptualized in relation to common sense. In fact, ever since Socrates, this is a common way of conceptualizing philosophy within the philosophical tradition. Most philosophers, with the notable exception of the eighteenth-century Scottish 'philosophy of common sense' (Thomas Reid, Dugald Stewart and others), agree that philosophy is against common sense. There is, however, little agreement regarding the nature of this 'against'. In the sections that follow I will discuss two contrasting conceptions: first, the under-labourer conception of philosophy as we find it in Locke and others, in which philosophy is conceptualized as that which effaces contradictions in common sense, and second, the conception of philosophy as the creation of concepts as we find it in Deleuze and Guattari, in which philosophy becomes the autonomous creator of paradoxical sense, or 'para-sense', a sense that opposes common sense rather than that which corrects it. The first conception will lead us to *philosophy for organization studies*; the second to *philosophy of organization*.

THE UNDER-LABOURER CONCEPTION OF PHILOSOPHY

In relation to philosophy, the term 'under-labourer' is first found in Locke. In *An Essay Concerning Human Understanding*, he writes:

> The commonwealth of learning is not at this time without master-builders, whose mighty designs, in advancing the sciences, will leave lasting monuments to the admiration of posterity; but every one must not hope to be a Boyle or a Sydenham; and in an age that produces such masters as the great Huygenius and the incomparable Mr. Newton, with some others of that strain; it is ambition enough to be employed as an under-labourer in clearing ground a little, and removing some of the rubbish that lies in the way to knowledge.
>
> (Locke, 1976: xlii–xliii)

Locke was perhaps too humble here; it is unlikely that he actually saw such a minor role for himself in the development of knowledge – especially when one considers the grand theories he develops in the same book. The idea of philosophy as under-labourer, as Locke here defined it for the first time, has nonetheless become a popular conception of philosophy. The central idea is that common sense is not always based upon logic or reasoning. Thus within the common sense language that we use we are often inconsistent, we use ambiguous or ill-defined concepts. As scientists are part of social reality, confused concepts will also enter the works of science. The under-labourer conception of philosophy understands the role of philosophy as 'clearing up' this confusion in order to create a tidy environment for the scientist. The philosopher, as it were, becomes the assistant of the scientist. Philosophizing clears the path of scientific progress by removing some of the obstacles, rectifying linguistic confusion or resolving logical contradictions. One also finds traces of this conception of philosophy in Kant's concept of critique. Kant says that, 'a critique of pure reason' serves 'not for the amplification but only for the purification of our reason, and for keeping it free of errors, by which a great deal is already won' (Kant, 1998: 149). In more recent times one finds defenders of the under-labourer conception of philosophy in the analytical philosophy of A. J. Ayer and Gilbert Ryle (Winch, 1990) and in the critical realism of Bhaskar (for example, Bhaskar, 1989).

Central to the idea of philosophy as the under-labourer is a particular concept of science, in which science is understood to steadily progress through the application of scientific methods. However, in the 1960s and 1970s, philosophers of science have put this conception of science into question. Science, Thomas Kuhn famously argues in *The Structure of Scientific Revolutions* (1970), is practised within the context of a 'paradigm', which can be understood as the common sense in a particular research community. Every so many years the shared sense embedded in the paradigm gets confronted with results that do not fit within the presuppositions of the paradigm. The old paradigm falls apart after which, in a period of 'extraordinary science', a new paradigm will be established. What is important in the context of this chapter is that science cannot advance without common sense; paradigms are necessary for scientific research. Only an environment of shared presuppositions enables 'normal science' (Kuhn, 1970).

In a peculiar move, Kuhn's attack on positivist concepts of science, on which the under-labourer conception of philosophy is traditionally built, has not harmed the popularity of the under-labourer conception in social science. In fact, we might say that it has strengthened it. After the publication of Kuhn's book social scientists began searching for their 'philosophical' presuppositions, which resulted in the identification of different paradigms (for example, Benton, 1977; Johnson et al., 1984). Within organization studies, the search for philosophical foundations has become popular especially through Burrell and Morgan's highly influential *Sociological Paradigms and Organisational Analysis* (1979) (see also O'Doherty, Chapter 1 in this volume). Loosely based on Kuhn (1970), Burrell and Morgan identify four 'mutually exclusive' paradigms in the social sciences, each based on different assumptions about the nature of social science and the nature of society. Central to their book was the idea that all theories of organization are based upon a philosophy of science and a theory of society. Different sets of assumptions result in different paradigms in which organization theorists conduct their research. For example, one of the assumptions Burrell and Morgan discuss is the voluntarism–determinism axis: does nature, or 'the environment', determine what it means to be human or do we have a free will? The presumption of voluntarism in social science, Burrell and Morgan argue, results in a type of social research that is different from the presumption of determinism. The link to philosophy seems clear enough: after all, it is simply common sense that philosophers have created 'determinist philosophies' and 'voluntarist philosophies' which are mutually exclusive, thus incommensurable.

The book sparked immense debate throughout the 1980s and early 1990s, with the idea of paradigm incommensurability in particular being heavily criticized (see Hassard and Pym, 1990). What interests me here, however, is not so much the idea of the incommensurability between paradigms. What leads me to conclude that the under-labourer conception of philosophy has risen in popularity is that with the identification of paradigms, philosophy is thought to prove its usefulness for organization studies. Philosophy, in a sense, 'uncovers' the ontological and epistemological presuppositions of science. Philosophy, thus conceived, makes us see how different sets of presuppositions 'bias' social research. Due to the critique of Kuhn and others on positivist concepts of science the idea of philosophy as mere 'fault-finding' has lost ground but it did not harm the under-labourer conception of philosophy in organization studies in any radical way. What lay in the way of knowledge was a poor understanding of the presuppositions articulated in philosophy, and the paradigms make clear what these were. Indeed, some saw in the combinative strength of different paradigms the possibility of more complete knowledge through 'multi-paradigm' research (for example Hassard, 1993; Lewis and Kelemen, 2002; Schultz and Hatch, 1996).

59

With regards to philosophy, however, something strange has happened. If it is the merit of philosophy to 'understand' the presuppositions of social science, what, exactly, is the difference between a philosopher and a social scientist? There is indeed no fundamental distinction at all as both the philosopher and the social scientist study common sense. The philosopher has effectively been turned into a social scientist; a sociologist, anthropologist or ethnographer of common sense as it exists within the social sciences.

Through Burrell and Morgan's book many scholars came to realize that there are a number of assumptions at work in sociological research: one cannot simply 'do' empirical analysis, as one always begins from ontological and epistemological assumptions. As I will argue in this chapter, however, these assumptions are not themselves philosophical, even though they loosely refer to philosophical problems in the history of philosophy. In this sense there are few 'philosophical moments' in the paradigm debate of the 1980s and 1990s, even though this debate did create a greater awareness of the kind of problems that philosophers (particularly the philosophers of science) are working with. The paradigm debate, in short, was predominantly a sociological debate about common sense within social theory.

THE POSITIVE NATURE OF PHILOSOPHY

We might say that according to the under-labourer conception of philosophy, the philosopher occupies a staff-function in the organization of knowledge: the philosopher is, so to speak, a quality controller, the one who ensures nothing goes wrong. Philosophy does not have its own nature, it does not create anything; philosophy is there to help science. How could it have a positive function, if knowledge is the exclusive domain of the sciences?

Knowledge of actual reality is the domain of science: through propositions, functions and variables, scientists seek to acquire an understanding of actual reality. The social sciences create social scientific concepts; concepts that map common sense formations. For Deleuze and other philosophers (like Bergson, Derrida and Serres), however, reality is not exhausted by the actual: reality is made up of the actual, 'the given', and the virtual, 'that by which the given is given' (Deleuze, 1994: 140). The actualizations are always doubled by the virtual from which orders and forms that we seek to capture in stable knowledge emerge and disappear. This is how Deleuze manages to conceptualize philosophy against the sciences: that by which the given is given is the unique 'object' of philosophy.

This object of philosophy, however, must not be confused with the search for universal truths. In *Difference and Repetition* (1994), Deleuze fiercely turns against the tradition in philosophy that seeks to establish universal truths. What happens when a philosopher claims to have found a universal? The common criticism (for example Fish, 2003) is that the clear skies of the philosopher are in fact abstracted from the contingency of the real world. They are abstracted from worldly affairs to the point where they are fully disconnected from everyday life and common sense. Deleuze, however, makes the opposite argument: the universal of the philosopher is not based upon the abstraction *from* everyday life, but on the abstractions *of* everyday life. Hence when philosophy formulates universals, it seeks refugee in the *pre-philosophical* or in common sense. Deleuze gives the example of Descartes:

> [W]hen the philosopher says 'I think therefore I am,' he can assume that the universality of his premises — namely, what it means to be and to think . . . — will be implicitly understood, and that no one can deny that to doubt is to think and to think is to be . . . *Everybody knows, no one can deny* is the form of representation and the discourse of the representative.
>
> (Deleuze, 1994: 130, emphasis in original)

The universals of the philosopher, Deleuze says, are abstract, but they are in this regard not different from the 'concrete' language we use or the common sense we establish among ourselves. For Deleuze, any representation of the actual world in which we live that understands this world as *complete* is an abstraction. What we experience as 'natural givens', for example the 'fact' that we are individuals or the 'fact' that we live in societies, miss not only what it means to be an individual or what it means to live in a society, but also that this meaning is continuously changing. The earth upon which we live continually invents itself in new ways. To define or to understand what it means to be human is always only a partial and static picture: nature redefines what it means to be human continuously. The static orders we form in our representations are in reality always open.

What, however, is 'that by which the given is given'? It is, Deleuze says, difference itself; a pure field of indeterminate flux. As difference is not something actualized, it cannot be captured in knowledge. It cannot be discovered as it is not covered: it is a pure beyond which is constantly at play. The method of philosophy is therefore not discovery but experimentation. Philosophy is not concerned with finding actual problems or finding solutions to actual problems. Philosophy itself creates problems; as such it is entirely positive. Philosophy is a self-positing system: the problems it creates are not looking for 'real-life' answers, as the 'solution' of a philosophical problem corresponds with itself. Philosophical problems take the side of 'non-being' (Deleuze, 1994) or 'extra-being' (Deleuze, 1990) rather than 'being'. The creation of philosophical problems means entering unknown territories. Philosophy thus allows us to formulate problems in different ways; ways that are not already solved by actual experience. It allows us to think about the world through concepts that are not forced upon us, or pre-structured, by the actualized. In this context, Deleuze likes to compare philosophy to swimming or learning a foreign language:

> Learning to swim or learning a foreign language means composing the singular

points of one's own body or one's own language with those of another shape or element, which tears us apart but also propels us into a hitherto unknown and unheard-of world of problems.

(Deleuze, 1994: 192)

Philosophical concepts are for Deleuze and Guattari (1994) precisely the way by which the philosopher articulates the incomplete or indeterminate nature of our world. Philosophical concepts 'tear open the firmament and plunge into the chaos' (Deleuze and Guattari, 1994: 202).

THE PARA-SENSE OF PHILOSOPHICAL CONCEPTS

For Deleuze, too, common sense is the target of philosophy. Contrary to the under-labourer conception of philosophy, however, common sense is not corrected by dis-covering contradiction or confusion, but doubled by creation of paradox. Paradox (from the Greek *paradoxon*) should be taken literally here: *beyond* (*para-*) opinion or common sense (*doxa*); beyond the sense that is the co-producer of social reality. Philosophy is revealed by the paradox captured in philosophical concepts. It is in this context that Deleuze creates the concept of para-sense (Deleuze, 1994): philosophy does not engage with common sense, it counters common sense with para-sense.

Philosophy as para-sense divides things up in surprising ways: 'it groups under one concept things which you would have thought were very different, or it separates things you would have thought belonged together' (Deleuze, 2006: 214). Philosophy offers a breath of fresh air that allows us to think or see things differently: a philo-sophical concept of organization makes us think and see organization in ways we hadn't before. These divisions and unifications do not simply turn the virtual into the actual; they do not directly invent new forms of living, or new forms of being human. They create the conditions from which new forms can emerge without spelling out exactly what form the new could take. The virtual remains the virtual and not a possible: the formulation of 'an alternative'. Philosophy, Deleuze (1990) says, 'counter-actualizes'. Philosophy happens in confrontation with the actual.

Philosophical concepts, despite their practicality, cannot be put to practise in turn; they hang on to a chaotic element and are as such always 'out of tune', 'out of order' or 'out of step'. Philosophy 'plunges into chaos', but philosophy cannot stay in chaos, as it would then lose its power to counter-actualize. Philosophy must remain a (non-) relation to common sense in order to counter-actualize. Thus, while it is true that, as Peter Winch (1990: 2) says, 'the day when philosophy becomes a popular subject is the day for the philosopher to consider where he took the wrong turning', it is equally true that philosophy ceases to be philosophy when it loses its (non-)relation with common sense; when it ceases to act on 'the flows of everyday thought' (Deleuze, 1995: 32). In other words, when philosophy moves too far into chaos it loses its ethics and politics as it fails to attack its prime target. It would therefore be unfair to say that philosophy is not interested in the actual. The contrary is true: its engagement with the abstractions of the actual are expressed by its disengagement. Philosophical concepts move, as Deleuze and Guattari (1994: 199) say, between two 'extreme dangers': chaos and common sense.

How do concepts survive between chaos and common sense? What prevents them, on the one hand, from dissolving into chaos and, on the other, from lapsing into common sense? Deleuze and Guattari answer that they form a plane with other concepts. Every concept has other concepts as its components and is itself a component in other concepts. Philosophical concepts are therefore both absolute and relative (Deleuze and Guattari, 1994). They are absolute in so far as they move independently from the actual, in so far as they do not refer to an actual state of affairs. But they are also relative to other concepts: only through its connections with other concepts do philosophical concepts attain a relative stability that allows them to exist. Philosophers never create one concept; they always create a plane of concepts. Thus philosophical concepts do not fight common sense alone: their strength is always a collective strength. Philosophical concepts exist as multiplicities and can never be isolated. This is the reason why it is difficult, if not impossible, to establish straightforward links between philosophers operating on different planes. This is what Deleuze and Guattari mean when they say, 'Cartesian concepts can only be assessed as a function of their problems and their plane' (Deleuze and Guattari, 1994: 27). They do not argue that in order to understand the Cartesian concept of the *Cogito*, one would need to leave this world and trade it for the metaphysical world of Descartes. What they mean is that one cannot pick just one concept and leave all the others, on the same plane, behind.

Philosophical concepts, in short, can be considered a success only when they prove their 'usefulness' (in the specific sense of *using* them to think and see in ways that common sense does not allow us to think and see, cf. Kaulingfreks, Chapter 2 in this volume). But this usefulness never consists of isolating a concept and putting it back in a commonsensical context. In the preface to *Nietzsche and Philosophy* (1983), Deleuze puts it very clearly:

Like Spinoza, Nietzsche always maintained that there is the deepest relationship between concept and affect. Conceptual analyses are indispensable and Nietzsche takes them further than anyone else. But they will always be ineffective if the reader grasps them in an atmosphere which is not that of Nietzsche. As long as the reader persists in: 1) seeing the Nietzschean 'slave' as someone who finds himself dominated by a master, and deserves to be; 2) understanding the will to power as a will which wants and seeks power; 3) conceiving the eternal return as the tedious return of the same; 4) imagining the Overman as a given master race – no possible relation between Nietzsche and his reader will be possible.

(Deleuze, 1983: xii)

63

PHILOSOPHY AND SOCIAL SCIENCE

Following Deleuze and Guattari's (1994) concept of philosophy, social science is not based upon philosophical concepts. Philosophy and social science do not rest on each other: philosophy is not the condition for social science, nor is social science the condition for philosophy. This idea entails a direct break with the commonsensical idea of philosophy in organization studies as the under-labourer. Philosophy, as Deleuze and Guattari conceptualize it, is not the foundation for social science. Its activity radically differs from the activity of social science, which attempts to grasp and intervene in social determinations. Contrary to social science, philosophical (and therefore para-sensical) concepts touch upon the indeterminate or virtual and, for this reason, only attain relative stability on a plane with other concepts. Social science, in contrast, maintains a direct relation with actuality by asking questions such as 'How do people actually relate to each other?', 'How do people actually organize themselves in organizations and institutions?' and 'What collective beliefs do people actually have?' Concepts in social science attempt to grasp the determined (even when the undetermined nature of the world is acknowledged); they maintain a direct link with everyday abstractions or common sense.

Philosophical concepts do not need to be 'translated' into the concepts of social science. Translation (from para-sense to common sense) is precisely what neutralizes philosophy's positive power. It is exactly this positive power of philosophy which is forgotten in the under-labourer conception of philosophy. Philosophical concepts cannot be lifted from their plane without losing their positive power. This, I think, is what Jones (2003) touches upon when he discusses the different ways in which Jean-François Lyotard's *The Postmodern Condition* (1979) has been 'translated' within organization studies. Jones (2003: 514) says, 'When enlisted simply to make an argument for pluralism, one might wonder if Lyotard has not been effectively disarmed, in a way that makes him say old things in a reassuring way.' The verb 'to disarm' captures precisely what is at stake: when a philosophical concept is read as if it were isolated, as if it were a social scientific concept, it loses its armament against common sense, with the consequence of falling back into common sense.

The strict division between social scientific concepts and philosophical concepts does not divide the practice of philosophy and social science. The contrary is true: it rather points at the interconnectedness of philosophy and social science. In the preface to the English translation of *Difference and Repetition*, Deleuze writes that science and philosophy are 'caught up in mobile relations in which each is obliged to respond to each other, but by its own means' (1994: xvi). Philosophy and social science can battle the same opponent, strive to have similar effects, but they do so through different means: by creating para-sense and by intervening in common sense respectively. The affiliation of philosophy and social science can go further than each responding to the other from their own faculties and disciplinary traditions. The responses can happen within one single text, as many 'social philosophers' or 'social theorists' (such as

64

Simmel, Goffman, Baudrillard, Bauman, Hardt and Negri) demonstrate in their writings.

Traditionally, organization studies has not shown much interest in becoming a meeting place for philosophy and social science. As Böhm (Chapter 6 in this volume) argues in relation to Alvesson and Willmott's work on critical theory, organization studies has been good at placing heterogeneous writers, who themselves write heterogeneous works, under one homogeneous signifier. I understand these partial readings of philosophy as symptomatic of the desire 'to establish clear theoretical grounds for critical-radical studies in organization' (Parker, 1995: 554). In the wake of the paradigm debates, philosophy has often been conceived as an outsider that is welcomed for bringing a post-positivistic or critical method to organization studies. If there is such a method I do not know. Perhaps we have found it, perhaps not. If we have, philosophy as the creation of concepts will not lose its importance for organization studies; if we haven't, maybe it's because a positive engagement with philosophy should be part of this 'method'.

CONCLUSION

What, then, is 'philosophy of organization' understood through Deleuze and Guattari's (1994) philosophy of philosophy? The answer is almost becoming common sense by now: philosophy of organization is the creation of philosophical concepts of organization. Yet what is the relation between philosophy and organization studies?

If the object of organization studies is to be defined as 'actual organization' or the behaviour of 'actual organizations', there is no need for philosophy in organization studies. Organization studies can then safely be regarded to fall entirely under the umbrella of the social sciences. Not everybody agrees with this definition, however. Gibson Burrell has said that 'sooner or later organization studies must enter an area where only the foolhardy dare to tread – the place where philosophy and social science meet' (1994: 15). Drawing on Deleuze and Guattari's distinction between philosophy and science, I have tried to show that organization studies can exactly be such a place. This is a place where philosophy of organization is welcomed as part of organization studies, rather than something that must prove its usefulness for organization studies. It is a place where presuppositions do not count.

A meeting between philosophy and social science is never common sense. The paradigm debate of the 1980s and 1990s has made clear that the social sciences are themselves embedded in common sense from which there is no straightforward liberation, but the subsequent popularity of the under-labourer conception of philosophy has hardly resulted in 'a turn toward philosophy' in organization studies. The neat organization of singular planes of philosophy in paradigms or sets of presuppositions only results in the denial of the positive power of philosophy: the singular para-sense of planes of philosophy is done away with as particular forms of common sense.

65

Philosophy, as understood through Deleuze and Guattari, enters organization studies only when one installs oneself on a plane of philosophical concepts. From this instalment it is only a small step to 'doing philosophy' by inscribing the plane with conceptual changes and the establishment of new conceptual links. Philosophy, however, remains a fragile undertaking, in organization studies and elsewhere. It is constantly in danger to be overtaken by a common sense – a common sense that sometimes even disguises itself as 'philosophy'.

One can engage with philosophy only by leaving behind the 'ontological commitments' and 'presumptions' of critical theory, postmodernism, post-structuralism, critical realism, and all these other 'schools' sometimes identified in organization studies. These short-cuts might assist in trying to identify a post-positivistic method for doing organizational research, but they also come at a price. This price is the creative nature of philosophy itself. There is, however, an increasing interest within organization studies for philosophy in its own right, to which the book you are now reading bears testimony. Is the under-labourer conception of philosophy losing ground?

ACKNOWLEDGEMENTS

I am very grateful to Nick Butler, Stephen Dunne, Ruud Kaulingfreks, Martin Parker, Michael Pedersen, and the editors of this volume for their helpful comments on earlier versions of this chapter.

REFERENCES

Benton, T. (1977) *Philosophical Foundations of the Three Sociologies*. London: Routledge.

Bergson, H. (1911) *Laughter: An Essay on the Meaning of the Comic*, trans. C. Brereton and F. Rothwell. London: Macmillan.

Bhaskar, R. (1989) *Reclaiming Reality: A Critical Introduction to Contemporary Philosophy*. London: Verso.

Burrell, G. (1994) 'Modernism, postmodernism and organizational analysis 4: The contribution of Jürgen Habermas', *Organization Studies*, 15(1): 1–45.

Burrell, G. and G. Morgan (1979) *Sociological Paradigms and Organisational Analysis: Elements of the Sociology of Corporate Life*. London: Heinemann.

Deleuze, G. (1983) *Nietzsche and Philosophy*, trans. H. Tomlinson. New York: Columbia University Press.

Deleuze, G. (1990) *The Logic of Sense*, trans. M. Lester. London: Continuum.

Deleuze, G. (1994) *Difference and Repetition*, trans. P. Patton. New York: Continuum.

Deleuze, G. (1995) 'On *A Thousand Plateaus*', in *Negotiations: 1972–1990*, trans. M. Joughin. New York: Columbia University Press.

Deleuze, G. (2006) 'Portrait of the philosopher as a moviegoer', in *Two Regimes of*

Madness: Texts and Interviews 1975–1995, trans. A. Hodges and M. Taormina. New York: Semiotext(e).

Deleuze, G. and F. Guattari (1994) *What is Philosophy?*, trans. H. Tomlinson and G. Burchill. London: Verso.

Durkheim, E. (1982) *The Rules of Sociological Method and Selected Texts on Sociology and its Method*, trans. W. D. Halls. London: Macmillan.

Fish, S. (2003) 'Truth but no consequences: Why philosophy doesn't matter', *Critical Inquiry*, 29: 389–406.

Hassard, J. (1993) *Sociology and Organization Theory: Positivism, Paradigms and Postmodernity*. Cambridge: Cambridge University Press.

Hassard, J. and D. Pym (1990) *The Theory and Philosophy of Organizations: Critical Issues and New Perspectives*. London: Routledge.

Heidegger, M. (1993) 'What calls for thinking?', in D. F. Krell (ed.) *Basic Writings: Martin Heidegger*. London: Routledge.

Johnson, T., C. Dandeker and C. Ashworth (1984) *The Structure of Social Theory*. London: Macmillan.

Jones, C. (2003) 'Theory after the postmodern condition', *Organization*, 10(3): 503–525.

Kant, I. (1998) *Critique of Pure Reason*, trans. P. Guyer and A. W. Wood. Cambridge: Cambridge University Press.

Kuhn, T. (1970) *The Structure of Scientific Revolutions* (second edition). Chicago, IL: University of Chicago Press.

Lewis, M. W. and M. L. Kelemen (2002) 'Multiparadigm inquiry: Exploring organizational pluralism and paradox', *Human Relations*, 55(2): 251–275.

Locke, J. (1976) *An Essay Concerning Human Understanding*, ed. J. W. Yolton. London: Dent.

Lyotard, J.-F. (1979) *The Postmodern Condition: A Report on Knowledge*. Minneapolis, MN: University of Minnesota Press.

Parker, M. (1995) 'Critique in the name of what? Postmodernism and critical approaches to organization', *Organization Studies*, 16(4): 553–564.

Saramago, J. (2004) *The Double*, trans. M. J. Costa. London: Vintage.

Schultz, M. and M. J. Hatch (1996) 'Living with multiple paradigms: The case of paradigm interplay in organizational culture studies', *Academy of Management Review*, 21(2): 529–557.

Spinoza, B. de (2002) *Complete Works*, trans. S. Shirley. Indianapolis, IN: Hackett.

Winch, P. (1990) *The Idea of a Social Philosophy and its Relation to Philosophy* (second edition). Atlantic Highlands, NJ: Humanities Press.

Chapter 4

Critique and resistance

On the necessity of organizational philosophy

Martin Fuglsang

In effect, capital acts as the point of subjectification that constitutes all human beings as subjects . . . The wage regime can therefore take the subjection of human beings to an unprecedented point, and exhibit a singular cruelty, yet still be justified in its humanist cry: No, human beings are not machines, we don't treat them like machines, we certainly don't confuse variable capital and constant capital.

(Deleuze and Guattari, 1987: 457)

THE QUESTION

In this chapter, we will concern ourselves with what might be conceived as a tedious and to some extent problematic concept, one which has been the self-circulated presupposition and proclaimed legality throughout the social sciences and the humanities for a very long time. Due to the loss of any transcendence and due to the impossibility of the grand narratives of truth, this concept has been declared outdated and even dead. Yet, at the same time it experiences a growing attention inside an expanding and diversified field of management and organization studies which has, somewhat exorbitantly, labelled itself as 'critical'. Not only has this left scholars in the field in a state of bewilderment and disorientation, but much more importantly and probably as a consequence of this, it has led these scholars to challenge the sensible logic constituted by the concept of 'critique' and its productive functionality inside a field that labels itself critical.

This chapter will engage in this challenge, by trying to sketch out the machinery that constitutes the conceptual multiplicity known as 'critique'. We will investigate its capability to create resistance inside the infinite speed and circulation of late capitalism, composing an assemblage we will identify as 'organizational philosophy'. It is exclusively in this sense that we are to understand the notion of necessity stipulated in the subtitle of this chapter, since it is only through the concept of 'critique' that we are able to talk of organizational philosophy, as an autonomous field that has become external to the terms defining its relation. It is as Deleuze states in his early writings on Hume:

> Whether as relation of ideas or as relation of objects, relations are always external to their terms. What Hume means is this: principles of human nature produce in the mind relations of ideas as they act 'on their own' on ideas.
>
> (Deleuze, 1991: 66)

From such a position, organizational philosophy is, we submit, able to unfold an inquisitive parallelism, not so much as to portray or reveal the phenomena in which management and organization studies purport to be interested, but to map out their generative and transformative components that facilitate their statements and their collective plane of enunciation. In this sense, organizational philosophy becomes a symptomatology rather then a phenomenological contemplation or a hermeneutical investigation, tracing the symptoms of late capitalism and its biopolitical technologies embedded in organizations and their managerial practices.

But in order to pick up speed, let us be absolutely frank, straightforward and to some extent simplistic and crude in stating that this conceptual outline is very far removed from what in general terms seems to characterize the notion of 'critique' in the growing and to some extent important field of critical management studies. In stipulating this, it is significant to explain that we do not propose to argue from a position outside this field of collective enunciation. On the contrary, we find ourselves deeply engaged in the social-analytical endeavour of critical management studies, that is, its attempt to diagnose and thereby intervene in the social order produced and composed by the principles and practices of management and organization. In this sense we do not oppose anyone, but instead we engage in this milieu by inquiring into the conceptual conjunction that brings these heterogeneous analytical components together constituting a collective plane of enunciation that we will recognize as critical management studies (CMS).

There are, so to speak, no villains or heroes to criticize or celebrate, but a transversal commonality that expresses itself through the conceptual logic that is silently embedded in the concept of 'critique' while simultaneously dominating the functionality and expressivity in CMS. This inquiry is therefore an attempt to high-light and stage the concept of 'critique' up front and not, as it is customary at present, as a resonating background, as a common silent signifier which operates as an unspoken axiomatic bringing cohesion in the field. Putting critique up front forces us at once to clarify in what world the concept of 'critique' is supposed to function as well as what kind of practices it enables and constitutes. This is not just a question of classical academic rigour, understood as the traditional good manners of justification and rationalization, but rather as a part of critical practice itself. We have to bear to mind that every critique is always at risk of becoming the necessary other of whatever it seeks to problematize, especially when we are dealing with the ever

69

increasing speed and circulation of late capitalism and its principles of organization. It is exactly this danger that permeates an unreflected use of the concept of 'critique' which is, we maintain, not alien to CMS (Böhm and Spoelstra, 2004: 97–100).

In CMS, we experience an overwhelming tendency to stratify the idea of critique inside a purely intellectual corpus which can be recognized by its dominating tendency to overcode each and every existence by an ethos seeking unification, hierarchization and totalization. By and large this corpus is traversed by what Nietzsche diagnosed as a 'slave morality' in the sense that it operates by negating anything that does not fit in with a humanistic ideal of emancipation that is simply presupposed and that leads to the binary logic implicated in the dictum 'you are evil, therefore I am good'. This of course is in all its simplicity a pure *ressentiment*, governed by a moral righteousness blessed by political correctness and good academic manners. But it also lacks any productive force, offering only an indignant and offended faciality. It reduces the power of critique by becoming a *reactive* will embedded in the common *doxa* of values, a horizon of good taste and knowledge. Furthermore, it reduces any affirmation of an ethical differentiation to a judgemental transcendental morality, that is, evil is not within us but elsewhere and more importantly, whatever is constituted as good is derived from an external cause posed by a negative judgemental act established by the propositions of evil. In this sense, 'critique' is always derived from the 'higher' human quest for an authoritarian knowledge, the individual we today recognize, not as the priest, but the 'expert' and the symbolically imitative manager. It is as Deleuze formulates in a commentary on Nietzsche:

> [T]he will to power has two tonalities: affirmation and negation; and forces have two qualities: action and reaction. What the higher man presents as affirmation is no doubt the most profound being of man, but it is only the extreme combination of negation with reaction, of negative will with reactive force, of nihilism with bad conscience and *ressentiment* . . . The higher man claims knowledge as authority: he claims to explore the labyrinth or the forest of knowledge. But knowledge is only a disguise for morality; the thread in the labyrinth is the moral thread . . . In the end man replaces God with humanism; the ascetic ideal with the moral ideal and the ideal of knowledge. Man burdens himself, he puts on his own harness – all in the name of heroic values, in the name of man's values.
>
> (Deleuze, 1997a: 100–101)

This is the real menace connected to the negative and oppositional logic of critique grounding itself on the moral foundation of a humanistic ideology and its unity of values such as autonomy, transformation, self-determination and emancipation. These values are, of course, fostered by late capitalism, especially through its sophisticated social-technologies such as value-based management, appraisal interviews, lifelong education schemes, therapeutic self-improvement courses and spiritual enlightenment programmes. These are biopolitical technologies producing, organizing and controlling the worlds in which our subjectivities are given sense, significance, and not least value (Rose, 1990: 95–103).

Unfortunately, philosophy in its classical form, indulging in its own historical grandeur and magnificence as a superior form of knowledge, does not pose any solution either. Organizational philosophy can therefore not be an application of the history of philosophy, as if it could enlighten the alleged 'stupidity' of management and organization studies, even though this often seems to be the case when a philosophical 'thought' encounters the materiality of institutions, organizations, agents and actors. To be more precise and to some extent harsher, this 'sublime' and 'enlightened' form for critique only collects its territorial judgements from a history that believes in a pure and secluded 'outside', which is both a naive and a dangerous gesture because such a critique supports the negative will with reactive force. In doing so, it supports the continued and persistent expansion of late capitalism, by becoming the necessary opposition through which it evolves and changes. In this sense, it is merely an imagined outside that is easily folded inside the logic of capitalism, because this critique always stands as the necessary and recognized otherness of capitalism folded inside itself, but staged as 'something' always other. It is in relation to this internal apparatus of capture in capitalism that we are to stage an organizational philosophy which is capable of creating resistance. As such, we should realize that capitalism, as Deleuze and Guattari make clear:

> is not at all territorial, even in its beginnings: its power of deterritorialization consists in taking as its object, not the earth, but 'materialized labour' the commodity. And private property is no longer ownership of the land or the soil, nor even the means of production as such, but of convertible abstract rights. That is why capitalism marks a mutation in worldwide or ecumenical organizations, which now take on a consistency of their own: the worldwide axiomatic, instead of resulting from heterogeneous social formations and their relations, for the most part distributes these formations, determines their relations, while organizing an international division of labour.
>
> (Deleuze and Guattari, 1987: 454)

Capitalism is in and by itself driven by transmutation, disorder, unrest and oppositional mutation. It is an ongoing deterritorialization of its own structural fixations. It is by its own means a revolutionary continuum controlling its oppositional critique by expanding through these 'critical' propositions, so stunningly exemplified by the idealistic components of humanism mentioned above that have led to the creation of the contemporary co-worker, a specific and localized subject of self-discipline, self-regulation and self-determination recognized in content by the managerial concepts of self-management, self-development and self-valorization. This creates an all-embracing and immanent fraternity between Capitalism and Academia. The result is an ongoing consensus-driven conversational debate about lofty questions such as

'What is the most efficient and humane organization?', 'What is a happy workforce?' or 'How to reconcile profit with good conscience?' This pseudo-debate, of course, creates a vast landscape of mere opinion, a stratum of relational oppositions which produce nothing else than a reactive will that can best be understood as a combat against anything that is deemed to be wrong, as a will to destruction based on a judgement of God that turns destruction into something 'just' (Deleuze, 1988: 133). This debate is in fact an organization of critique, that is nothing else than an intellectual abstraction, substituting one abstract notion for another. Its conceptual components are 'negation', 'opposition' and the like and are set in motion by the institution of an exterior transcendence, a self-righteous telos, driven by a dialectic and synthetic kind of contemplation.

This may all seem extremely superficial, not taking into consideration the many nuances and sophistications in this polite and well-mannered conversation inside the triangle capitalism/politics/academia where the gesture of having an opinion, even a critical one, is the name of the game (Grey and Willmott, 2005). Well, this might very well be the case, but this is not the place to seek nuance and sophistication. We are rather interested in the transversal diagrammatic traits that constitute how critique is conducted inside the rapid circulation of people, opinions, senses, styles, taste and values constituted, formed and chiselled by late capitalism. We are, so to speak, interested in the production of a certain kind of scholarly subjectivity, perhaps even in the way our existence as academics is becoming actualized. It is exactly from within the midst of this ever expanding circulation that we are to constitute a concept of 'critique' and what it means to be critical. This is probably what organizational philosophy should be all about, provided that we take for granted that this peculiar way of philosophizing is about the power of transferability rather than about application, intervention rather than about explanation, and about the flow of organizational and managerial practices rather than about the theory and the history of philosophy. Organizational philosophy, as we see it, should help us to engage in the creation of a concept, which does not just pose yet another opinion, another relational opposition, or another dialectical play, but instead tries to reconfigure the stratum of the sensible by posing variations, relays and differentiations in the very same machinery that produces our subjectivity, that is, our identity and, more importantly, the self-relation to our identity. In this sense, the composition of 'critique' is still bound to its classical vow, which is intimately related to some understanding of liberation. However, the crucial question becomes how we will be able to keep the temptations of a moral transcendence and universality at bay, when we no longer can 'theorize' from an unaffected outside but have to compose any critique and its components in the midst of our own production and actualization.

ITS WORLD

To be produced is to be assembled, to be assembled is to be organized and to be organized is to be sedimented and segmented inside a specific and localized logic of sense. Whatever is produced is, in other words, marked by signs and composed as a body. How do these signs and bodies speak to us? What has been their function since, let us say, the Second World War? Factories, meanwhile transformed into corporations and enterprises, are no longer primarily producing goods and services to meet pre-existing demands. Through the exponential growth in advertising, they are now producing consumers, more particularly, the worlds in which goods, demands and desires become interconnected and thereby sensible on the white canvas of subjectivity (Gorz, 1980; Klein, 2001). Roughly at the same time, management is no longer primarily about regulation and protocol or about order and command but rather about the technologies of social-psychology, about motivation-techniques and about self-related decision-making procedures. As such it has become a machinery of incorporeal transformation: the worker is replaced by a co-worker, the workforce is now conceived of as human resources, in other words, by an immaterial and affective multiplicity of self-regulated individualities striving for their own emancipation. This is, of course, a raw and undigested picture, but one just has to follow the literature in organization and management studies and their theoretical conceptualization to see how this machinery of incorporeal transformation has picked up speed. The bewildering variety of idealistic and liberating imperatives relating to efficiency, self-regulation, autonomy, self-development and self-management goes hand in hand with a wholesale transformation of worker, workforce, control, knowledge, discipline, power and forms of subjectification (see for example Brody, 2005).

In a kind of commentary remark, or if one prefers, a diagnosis of our present state of affairs, Deleuze shows how we have entered a new area of endless organizational and segmented variation. The body is being dismantled in an ongoing incorporeal differentiation which takes place everywhere all the time. It is a 'society of control' where

> you never finish anything – business, training, military services being coexisting metastable states of a single modulation, a sort of universal transmutation . . . the key thing is no longer a signature or number but a code: codes are passwords, whereas disciplinary societies are ruled (when it comes to integration or resistance) by order-words. The digital language of control is made up of codes indicating whether access to some information should be allowed or denied. We're no longer dealing with a duality of mass and individual. Individuals become 'dividuals' and masses become samples, data, markets and banks.
>
> (Deleuze, 1995a: 179–180)

We are no longer just free-flowing wills moving from one closed space to the other,

73

finding our secluded existential sanctuary between the different modes of discipline. On the contrary, today we are assembled into different spaces at all times. The binary segmentation that traditionally provided us with content and boundaries has given way to zones and passages of imperceptibility. It is in this sense that we have to continually reinvent ourselves, to actualize ourselves, or to 'take care of ourselves' (Foucault, 1986, 1988, 2005).

From this conception of continuous incorporeal transformations attributed to bodily actions and passions, Maurizio Lazzarato has reworked and reconceptualized our understanding of 'immaterial labour'. This concept designates not just the growth of an intellectual workforce, but also the transformation of the manual workforce into areas of intellectual modalities and procedures, that have radically transformed the concept of work since the early 1970s. It is not just a question of the modality we know as the knowledge-worker, so often portrayed in management studies (see, for example, Drucker, 1993, 1999), but a more fundamental transformation of the 'mode of production', both as a transcendental principle of regulation and as its basic functionality. It is a transformation of labour into something that is no longer confined to the production of a given commodity in any stratified space, but a new concept of labour and control which extends into all areas of the Socius. We are talking here about a

> transition from formal subsumption to real subsumption. Marx, as is clear at various points in his work, foresaw this transition and described it as the achievement of the subjection by the capitalist mode of production, of the whole society.
>
> (Negri, 1989: 72, emphasis in original)

It is a mode of production in which subjectivity becomes both the cause and effect of production and thus becomes directly productive as a machinery of knowledge, power, desire and signs, and not just as an apparatus for reproduction. It is, as Lazzarato maybe teasingly suggests, no longer a question of understanding the mode of production but of understanding its incorporeal transformation into the production of modes (2004a: 202), preconditioned by the machinic processes defining the social formations, which in their expansion becomes a production of lives. The concept of 'immaterial labour', itself a multiplicity of heterogeneous intensities, establishes a very different conception of contemporary life, not just in relation to work, but to the conjunction of work-life-existence. This conjunction is a relational modality in which

> [t]he activities of this kind of immaterial labour oblige us to question the classic definitions of 'work' and of 'workforce', because they are the result of a synthesis of varying types of *savoir-faire* (those of intellectual activities, as regards the cultural-informational content, those of manual activities for the ability to put together creativity, imagination and technical and manual labour; and that of

entrepreneurial activities for that capacity of management of their social relations and of structuration of the social cooperation of which they are a part). This immaterial labour constitutes itself in forms that are immediately collective, and, so to speak, exists only in the form of network and flow. The organisation of its cycle of production, because this is precisely what we are dealing with, once we abandon our factoryist prejudgements, is not immediately visible because it is not confined by the walls of a factory.

(Lazzarato, 2004b: 3)

As we have just mentioned, this involves a real subsumption in open space, not understood or portrayed by the classical and common binary segmentation that has been employed by sociology or social-psychology, so dominant in the analytical structures of organization and management studies. Rather, this involves an autonomous and self-sufficient conjunction composing the traits and qualities that produce and constitute the mixed body we call work-life-existence. The open space is, according to Deleuze and Guattari (1987: 351–424), the space that inhabits the nomads and their flow of intensities, the nomads being a tribe, a pack or even an incorporeal idea with the capability to transform into a war-machine. But also, it now seems that the smooth space of nomadism and its flow of creative and experimental intensities have been brought inside the capitalist organization of production. There, it is expanding its vigorous transmutations though continuous processes of de- and re-territorialization. Indeed, capitalism has taken on a kind of nomadic intensity. It seems as if nomadology has become its most forceful machinery in the struggle for world-wide expansion. Late capitalism and nomadology are therefore not in any opposition. On the contrary, the latter is becoming the necessary precondition in the production of the receptive and affective universe – we have become beautiful souls of self-valorization and self-actualization – that fosters capitalism.

ITS AFFIRMATION

This powerful conjunction makes up for the transformation of the matter-flow of work and the workforce into the receptive and affective world so elegantly identified by Michael Hardt and Antonio Negri (2000) as a hallmark of 'Empire'. Hardt and Negri have elaborated on concepts such as 'societies of control' and 'immaterial labour' so as to compose a cartography of the connective syntheses between late capitalism, open space and the biopolitical production of subjectivity. In the world of Empire, just as in the societies of control, there is no need to ask 'whether the old or new system is harsher or more bearable, because there's a conflict in each between the ways they free and enslave us' (Deleuze, 1995a: 178). This therefore poses the difficult task for any form of critique and the resistance implicated in it, that it has to be composed and constructed within the given. This coincides, so it seems, with the

75

ambience we find in the political thought of 'immanent criticism' (see, for example, Jones, 2005; see also Böhm, Chapter 6 in this volume).

The task is all the more difficult since it places any critical conceptualization in the midst of our own becoming, which is transversely produced, assembled and organized by the micro-political technologies of late capitalism staged by an unquestionable and all-embracing order-word to become a subject. Essential to these technologies are understandings of ourselves as self-sufficient, self-regulated and self-disciplined reflective subjects. The managerial practice of self-management is exactly this self-imposed control established through our own repeated self-valorization. In this sense we have to engage ourselves with an ongoing transformative and moral code to become 'free' through the demands for a flexible production into which the notion of self-management and self-development actualizes a double-bind of control by its inherent notion of freedom. Self-management, flexible management and other micro-political technologies of contemporary management require exactly this kind of ideological freedom and it is in this way that we understand their contribution to the drama of contemporary work-life-existence.

This is orchestrated by what Paolo Virno so strikingly formulates as the 'communism of capitalism' (2004: 110). In a post-Fordist world, it is not first and foremost the body with its actions and passions that is confined and disciplined. This would be highly unproductive with regard to the demand for a rapid circulation of desire and a highly flexible production of values, tests, commodities and consumption. Nowadays, incorporeal transformations manifest themselves in bodies and are controlled by the horizon of sense in which values, tests, commodities and consumption have become essences by the consistency and content of significance given by the ongoing mutation of late capitalism. It is in the midst of this world that we have to reinvent the concept of 'critique', not by enrolling an antithetical and oppositional logic as the driving force of critique, but by an idea of counter-actualization through composing organizational philosophy as a symptomatology unfolding a different and more sensible mode of judgement. We propose an affirmative rather than a negative diagnostics (see also Spoelstra, Chapter 3 in this volume).

This may sound like a medical practice. Indeed, to some extent it parallels the kind of praxis and judgement unfolded by the physician. Part of the reinvention of the concept of 'critique' is a diagnostics of sorts. Or, if we are more confident with the literary influence picking up speed in field of organization and management studies, we could say that the enterprise of organizational philosophy becomes a 'literary' endeavour where 'the writer as such is not a patient but rather physician of himself and of the world. The world is a set of symptoms whose illness merges with man' (Deleuze, 1997b: 3). It becomes a pursuit to map out symptoms inside the modulation of control as it unfolds through the self-conception of freedom, but not just in order to make a diagnosis of the state of affairs, its configurations and actualizations, but also to find its point of crisis, its rupture, its abysses. 'There is no diagram', Deleuze writes, 'that does not also include, beside the points which it connects up, certain relatively free or unbound points, points of creativity, change and resistance' (Deleuze, 1988: 44).[1]

But why symptoms and not the presupposition of underlying causes themselves? This, after all, seems to be the classical quest in the enterprise of conducting social analysis, a quest to which organization and management studies would no doubt subscribe. The answer is quite simple, even though the social-analytics that needs to be composed to map them out are quite difficult. It is because symptoms are first and foremost recognized by their effects. They are so to speak directly productive due to their transformative qualities on the corporeal body and they are also often in conjunction with one another, functioning by their mixed semiotics and connective composition. Rather then being linear, symptoms are lateral traits effectuating one another and can as such not be reduced to nor represented by pre-given concepts with an underlying axiomatic. It is this axiomatic that needs to be created to pose the diagnosis, as every diagnosis is always a concrete and localized problematics (and not a logic!) combining symptoms as components into a concept. It is what Deleuze, in relation to Nietzsche, designates as the 'method' of dramatisation, seeking the presupposed forces inhabiting every proposition, because

> any proposition is itself a set of symptoms expressing a way of being or a mode of existence of the speaker, that is to say the state of forces that he maintains or tries to maintain with himself and others (consider the role of conjunction in this connection). In this sense a proposition always reflects a mode of existence, a 'type'. What is the mode of existence of the person who utters any given proposition, what mode of existence is needed in order to be able to utter it? The mode of existence is the state of forces insofar as it forms a type which can be expressed by signs or symptoms.
>
> (Deleuze, 1986: x)

This is a highly creative act which combines, connects and merges symptoms into a concept, always activating the experience with modes of existence so as to make possible a diagnosis as well as an affirmative judgement of what is given. It is the creative and affirmative action of the doctor that becomes the diagnostic purpose of organizational philosophy in relation to late capitalism and its omnipresent organization and management theories and its practices. To get a flavour of what we are thinking of, see here what Smith (2005) points out:

> One might think that doctors make 'determinate' judgements: they have learned the concepts of illnesses, and simply need to apply them to their patients. But in fact medical diagnoses are examples of reflective judgements, since in relation to an individual case the concept itself is not given, but is entirely 'problematic'. What a doctor confronts in an individual case is a symptom or group of symptoms and his diagnostic task is to discover the corresponding concept (the concept of the

77

disease). No doctor would treat a fever or headache as a definite symptom of a specific illness; they are rather indeterminate symptoms common to a number of diseases, and the doctor must interpret and decipher the symptoms in order to arrive at the correct diagnosis.

(Smith, 2005: 183)

Analogous to this description of diagnostic practices in medicine, organizational philosophy should become crucial in exposing and understanding the life modulated in the organizational and managerial assemblages of late capitalism. Rather than proceeding by the continuous display of determinate judgement, founded by the predefined distinction of 'good/evil' unfolding on a moral plane, we suggest a symptomatology focusing on the generic, transformative, diagrammatic and machinic components constituting and composing these assemblages and their continuous variations.[2]

The question of symptomatology, as it unfolds as a specific kind of social-analytics, mapping out these four components, does therefore not first and foremost focus on the subject or the object, but on the juxtaposition and the production of expression and content as meta-stable assemblages which constitute us as subjects of enunciation in relational to the sensible objects. In this sense the present state of affairs undergoes a complete destruction by the act of mapping out these social assemblages by its analytical movement towards the diagrammatic and the machinic components affirming that which is not yet actualized, that is, the active state of forces, as modes of existence not yet constituted on the transcendental plane of the subject–object relation (Deleuze, 2001).

By this analytical modulation, it should be clear that the concept of 'critique', as discussed in the opening section of this chapter, is still bound by its traditional pledge to liberate and to effectuate itself by as a specific kind of judgement, but now this is not through a constraining moral code judging actions, but by the creational act of an actual practice of diagnostics. Critique then judges by its composition of symptoms, that is, it creates a concept, exactly in the way we suggested is possible with respect to the concept of immaterial labour. This concept is not recognized by its intention or extension, it is not a bibliographical or lexical container, but a consistency holding together heterogeneous elements, pointing towards modes of existence and their transformation. It does not pose an axiomatic posture, but a dynamism, which submerges itself into the question: 'How is the subject constituted in the given?' (Deleuze, 1991: 107).

To be critical is therefore not a question of unfolding a morality and its attributes, that is, to be against, to oppose, to speak for someone or something, which are, according to Deleuze, the reactive actions of war and not the passionate forces of combat. Rather, it is to compose a consistency of the heterogeneous elements constituting the worlds in which we become; it becomes an affirmation of the optional rules that are capable of evaluating what we think and do in light of a life not yet actualized, but real. Or to put it differently:

It's no longer a matter of determinate forms, as with knowledge, or of constraining rules, as with power: it's a matter of optional rules that make existence a work of art, rules at once ethical and aesthetic that constitutes ways of existence or styles of life (including even suicide). It's what Nietzsche discovered as the will to power operating artistically, inventing new 'possibilities of life'.

(Deleuze, 1995b: 98)

It is here that critique reaches its highest degree of intensity. Here, it affirms existence through an ongoing differentiation of what a life can be, negating the present and its territoriality by a pure destruction, but only as a derived effect by the utterance that confirms a life in its becoming. This is by no means an abstract or traditional theoretical enterprise, but a new empiricism beckoning to organizational philosophy and as such, this philosophy

must constitute itself as the theory of what we are doing, not as a theory of what there is. What we do has its principles; and being can only be grasped as the object of a synthetic relation with the very principles of what we do.

(Deleuze, 1991: 133)

Organizational philosophy as a critical diagnostics is much more than a discipline inside the turmoil of Academia. It is an ethics of symptomatology, including one of Academia itself. It is so to speak, an ethical inquiry into the moral codes and their functionality on the surface of the sensible body, not in relation to what they mean, but to what they do in the composition of the social bios, this world which enables us to speak, feel and act.

NOTES

1 In a more scholastic fashion than the style adopted in this chapter, one might say that it becomes significant to understand that in order to move the concept of critique from the immediate *modus agendi* of judgement, which needs a pre-established transcendence and a double negation, does not imply the renunciation of judgement as such. Rather, judgement now only appears as a derived effect of a pure affirmation (the will to power). The concept of critique is thereby removed from its contemporary sense to its etymological origin, to the Greek *krenein*, which at once designates a *poesis* and its effectuated judgement, to scrutinize, to distinguish and to judge. It is thereby decisive to note, that *krenein* also is the main constituent in the notion of *krisis* and *krinomenon*, the scene of rupture and that of doubt, for which reason it obviously becomes crucial to constitute the concept of critique as an intermezzo in the passage where rupture and doubt reigns, which is to say, in the autonomic zones inside any regimes of sign, because in these zones and passages of indetermination and imperceptibility there is always an excess of forces and signs with is not yet sedimented or segmented in common sense, giving way for something new to arise. It is of course essential to note

that these notions would be the components that should be extended in the reinvention of the concept of 'critique'. What remains to be done and what exceeds the scope of this chapter is to show their specific conjunction and interrelatedness when they function diagnostically as a practice of counter-actualization.

2 Readers familiar with the writing of Deleuze and Guattari will recognize these components as the main elements in what they call 'schizoanalysis' (Deleuze and Guattari, 1983, especially Part 4). Schizoanalysis is a pragmatics, a specific kind of social-analytics that has an ontological configuration rather than an epistemological perspective which is so common in most of our contemporary social-analyses. For a short description of these components see Deleuze and Guattari (1987: 145–147), or for a more comprehensive understanding, Chapters 3 and 4. See also Fuglsang and Sørensen (2006).

REFERENCES

Böhm, S. and S. Spoelstra (2004) 'No critique', *ephemera: theory & politics in organization*, 4(2): 94–100.

Brody, R. (2005) *Effectively Managing Human Service Organizations*. Thousand Oaks, CA: Sage.

Deleuze, G. (1986) *Nietzsche and Philosophy*, trans. H. Tomlinson. New York: Continuum.

Deleuze, G. (1988) *Foucault*, trans. S. Hand. Minneapolis, MN: University of Minnesota Press.

Deleuze, G. (1991) *Empiricism and Subjectivity: An Essay on Hume's Theory of Human Nature*, trans. C. V. Boundas. New York: Columbia University Press.

Deleuze, G. (1992) *Expressionism in Philosophy: Spinoza*, trans. M. Joughin. New York: Zone Books.

Deleuze, G. (1995a) 'Postscript on control societies', in *Negotiations*, trans. M. Joughin. New York: Columbia University Press.

Deleuze, G. (1995b) 'Life as a work of art', in *Negotiations*, trans. M. Joughin. New York: Columbia University Press.

Deleuze, G. (1997a) 'The mystery of Ariadne according to Nietzsche', in *Essays Critical and Clinical*, trans. D. W. Smith and M. A. Greco. Minneapolis, MN: University of Minnesota Press.

Deleuze, G. (1997b) 'Literature and life', in *Essays Critical and Clinical*, trans. D. W. Smith and M. A. Greco. Minneapolis, MN: University of Minnesota Press.

Deleuze, G. (2001) 'Immanence: A life', in *Pure Immanence: Essays on A Life*, trans. A Boyman. New York: Zone Books.

Deleuze, G. and F. Guattari (1983) *Anti-Oedipus: Capitalism and Schizophrenia*, trans. R. Hurley, M. Seem and H. R. Lane. Minneapolis, MN: University of Minnesota Press.

Deleuze, G. and F. Guattari (1987) *A Thousand Plateaus: Capitalism and Schizophrenia*, trans. B. Massumi. Minneapolis, MN: University of Minnesota Press.

Drucker, P. F. (1993) *Post-Capitalist Society*. Oxford: Butterworth-Heinemann.

Drucker, P. F. (1999) *Management Challenges for the 21st Century*. Oxford: Butterworth-Heinemann.

Foucault, M. (1983) 'Preface', in G. Deleuze and F. Guattari, *Anti-Oedipus: Capitalism and Schizophrenia*, trans. R. Hurley, M. Seem and H. R. Lane. Minneapolis, MN: University of Minnesota Press.

Foucault, M. (1986) *History of Sexuality, Volume Three: The Care of the Self*, trans. R. Hurley. London: Penguin.

Foucault, M. (1988) *Technologies of the Self: A Seminar with Michel Foucault*. Amherst, MA: University of Massachusetts Press.

Foucault, M. (2005) *The Hermeneutics of the Subject: Lectures at the Collège de France, 1981–1982*, ed. and trans. F. Gros and F. Ewald. Basingstoke: Palgrave Macmillan.

Fuglsang, M. and B. M. Sørensen (eds) (2006) *Gilles Deleuze and the Social*. Edinburgh: Edinburgh University Press.

Gorz, A. (1980) *Paths to Paradise: On the Liberation from Work*. Boston, MA: South End Press.

Grey, C. and H. Willmott (eds) (2005) *Critical Management Studies: A Reader*. Oxford: Oxford University Press.

Hardt, M. and Negri, A. (2000) *Empire*. Cambridge, MA: Harvard University Press.

Jones, C. (2005) 'Practical deconstructivist feminist Marxist organization theory: Gayatri Chakravorty Spivak', in C. Jones and R. Munro (eds) *Contemporary Organization Theory*. Oxford: Blackwell.

Klein, N. (2001) *No Logo*. London: Flamingo.

Lazzarato, M. (2004a): 'From capital–labour to capital-life', *ephemera: theory and politics in organization*, 4(3): 187–208.

Lazzarato, M. (2004b) 'General intellect: Towards an inquiry into immaterial labour', trans. E. Emery, *Multitudes*. Online at http://multitudes.samizdat.net/article.php3?id_article=1498. Accessed 17 January 2006

Negri, A. (1989) *The Politics of Subversion: A Manifesto for the Twenty-First Century*, trans. J. Newell. Cambridge: Polity.

Rose, N. (1990) *Governing the Soul*. London: Free Association Books.

Smith, D. W. (2005) 'Critical, clinical', in C. J. Stivale (ed.) *Gilles Deleuze: Key Concepts*. Chesham: Acumen.

Virno, P. (2004) *A Grammar of the Multitude*, trans. I. Bertoletti, J. Cascaito and A. Casson. New York: Semiotext(e).

Part Two

Engagements

Chapter 5

Ask not what philosophy can do for critical management studies

Peter Case

> Philosophy is a conversion, a transformation of one's way of being and living, and a quest for wisdom. This is not an easy matter.
>
> (Hadot, 1995: 275)

INTRODUCTION

Embedded within the chapter title is a thinly veiled allusion to Austin's (1976) seminal book on language philosophy, *How to Do Things with Words*, my explicit intention being to examine the *performative* nature of organization theory and philosophy. I seek to challenge the presumption that philosophy of organization is some form of adjunct to 'real' philosophical endeavour that, by this implied division of labour, must be being expedited by others in a different time and space. Those of us engaged in the philosophy of organization are likely to suffer from a form of guilt or envy deriving from an uneasy sense that, 'Real Philosophers don't read Mintzberg' (see also Jones and ten Bos's introduction to this volume concerning the problem of marrying 'philosophy' with 'organization'). To remedy this dis-ease, a performatively reconstructed philosophy would strive not simply to position itself as a legitimate *intellectual* endeavour for critical management studies (CMS) scholars but to find ways of making philosophy *co-nascent with* or *immanent to* acts of organizing. Marxists have, of course, long insisted that everyday action should ideally be a form of praxis: a healthy commingling of theoretical reflection and practice based on dialectical principles.

My purpose, however, is to probe the meaning of praxis and explore alternative possibilities for philosophy-as-practice through a questioning of the assumptions that have, historically, facilitated a facile and harmful theory–practice duality.

In seeking to re-evaluate praxis and contribute to the current CMS debate, this chapter pursues a number of interrelated strands of scholarship. It begins by examining the nature of the 'things' we ostensibly do with words and invokes A. S. Byatt's (2000) novel, *The Biographer's Tale*, as a vehicle for exploring academic disaffection

85

with exclusively wordy pursuits. This leads into a discussion of the political quietism characteristic of contemporary academic life and a questioning of how this state of affairs has arisen. Political inaction is one consequence of the rejection of philosophy as a way of life in favour of philosophical discourse. Using the work of the French classicist Pierre Hadot (1995), I trace a genealogy that reveals how modern 'philosophy' has been systematically emptied of both the 'love' and the 'wisdom' that lie at its semantic core. Austin's work is also pivotal to my argument in so far as it forms the basis of Derrida's deconstructive reading of *How to Do Things with Words* and thus permits me to ponder the kinds of (re)solutions of the praxis debate provided by this particular type of post-structural analysis. These alternative perspectives allow us to conceive of differing discourses of 'truth' and to construe an embodied ethics based on the reinstated virtues of 'love' and 'wisdom'.

NOW THERE'S A THING

Who among us has not, at some point in her or his career, stopped to ponder the worth of their contribution to the world? For most students and professional academics, I suspect, there occur many profound moments of self-doubt and a sense of ennui that follows from a life dedicated in large measure to abstraction and acts of representation. We find ourselves in seemingly interminable language games of various sorts: examining, interrogating, analysing, evaluating or criticizing this or that text; challenging and probing, deconstructing, engaging in ironic revelation of sub-text, unconscious or hidden motive in the works and espousals of this or that author, practitioner, 'research subject' or 'respondent'. In this respect, many of us would doubtless be able to empathise with Phineas G. Nanson, the main protagonist in A. S. Byatt's novel, *The Biographer's Tale*, who, having had an epiphany in the middle of a Lacanian seminar, decides to forsake literary theory in favour of an imagined life grounded in the certainty of facts and *things*. 'I've decided to give it all up,' he informs his intellectual mentor, Ormerod Goode, 'I've decided I don't want to be a postmodern literary theorist' (Byatt, 2000: 3). Phineas goes on:

> 'I felt an urgent need for a life full of *things*.' I was pleased with the safe, solid Anglo-Saxon word. I had avoided the trap of talking about 'reality' and 'unreality' for I knew very well that postmodernist literary theory could be described as a reality. People lived in it . . . 'I need a life full of *things*,' I said. 'Full of facts.' 'Facts,' said Ormerod Goode . . . 'The richness,' he said, 'the surprise, the shining *solidity* of a world full of facts.
>
> (Byatt, 2000: 4, emphases in original)

Byatt's novel resonates with my purposes here in two ways. First, her evocation of the Anglo-Saxon word 'thing' is germane to my interest in what philosophy and words can or cannot do and second, Phineas' discontents and aspirations testify to a broader 'problem with philosophy' that I shall be at pains to expose. Byatt employs the term 'thing' in its familiar contemporary form to connote the facticity or objective exist-ence of individual entities (see Munro, Chapter 12 in this volume, for a discussion of the language of 'things'). This is all well and good but, according to the *Oxford English Dictionary* (*OED*), the first category of definitions of this semantically rich word derives from its Nordic and Saxon origins and holds 'thing' to mean, 'A meeting, assembly, *esp.* a deliberative or judicial assembly, a court, a council' (1961,Vol. XI: 308). The earliest usage of the word dates from the seventh century and is evidently the source of later semantic accretions that denote, inter alia,

> A matter brought before a court of law, a legal process . . . an affair, business, concern, matter . . . That which is done or to be done; a doing, act, deed, transaction . . . a fact, circumstance, experience . . . That which is said; a saying, utterance, expression, statement; with various connotations, for example, a charge or accusation made against a person, a story, tale; a part or section of an argument or discourse; a witty saying, a jest (usu. *good thing*).

I conjecture that this semantic detail would not have escaped J. L. Austin's atten-tion, particularly given his professional interest in jurisprudence. If this speculation is correct, then Austin (1976) displays a remarkable degree of wit and reflexivity in choosing to entitle his ordinary language investigations, *How to Do Things with Words*. The immanent tautology of what Austin refers to as performative speech acts — whereby the saying *is* the doing — is already present in his choice of title, whereby the 'doing', the 'thing' and the 'words' are all substitutes for one another. This archly reflexive move immediately fuses word, deed and judgement in 'things.' What an odd predicament poor Phineas could have been in had someone pointed out to him the wider semantic implications of his desire to escape academia in favour of 'a world full of things.' Perhaps he fulfilled his ambition after all.

In telling us that the doing of things is immanent in the very words we utter as part of everyday discourse, however, Austin unwittingly harbours a powerful (and intel-lectually appealing) conceit. His 'ordinary language' project gives us free philo-sophical licence, as it were, to sit around in cosy armchairs, ponder the various contextual nuances of words and feel satisfied that we thereby gain a genuine philo-sophical perspective on the organizational and practical accomplishment of the human world. That this is an attractive prospect can hardly be contested, for, under the custodianship of one of his students, John Searle (see Searle, 1977), Austin's work spawned an entire school of analytic-orientated philosophy. Indeed, speech act theory has turned into an intellectual industry that Austin himself could hardly have antici-pated and of which he probably would not have approved. In the eleventh of his 'Theses on Feuerbach' Marx remarked that 'The philosophers have only *interpreted* the world in various ways; the point is to *change* it' (Marx, 1975: 423, emphases in original). With his pursuit of ever-finer gradations and logical qualifications of speech acts one would be hard pressed to find a more precise interpreter of the world than Austin. At a superficial level, at least, the very last thing one would expect to come from his project is a radical political agenda.

CMS AND POLITICAL QUIETISM

The political quietism of academic preoccupations and pursuits, of the sort epitomised by Austin's work, appears to be a cause for considerable concern for one of CMS's most vocal proponents. Martin Parker's (2002) *Against Management* sets out a series of anxieties about the CMS project in general and the potential impotence of the critique generated by those who subscribe to its manifesto (see also Böhm, Chapter 6 in this volume). He reveals, perhaps predictably, that CMS is a broad church encompassing a number of heterogeneous activities, some of which stretch credulity in terms of their espoused criticality. In arriving at a general conception of CMS, however, Parker draws on the helpful survey of the literature undertaken by Sotirin and Tyrell (1998) to characterize a body of work that is: critical of instrumentality; reflexive about the use of methods and acts of representation; suspicious of the Enlightenment project and the evolution of modernity; suspicious of globalization; questions the dominant pedagogy and management curriculum emanating from North America; and critically evaluates the appeal of much management 'guru' and populist writing. Parker also cites the tripartite scheme set out in Fournier and Grey (2000) in which CMS is seen to embody three broad qualities: first, it eschews managerialist performativity; second, it 'denaturalizes' and historicizes commonly held and taken for granted assumptions in organizations, such as the managers' prerogative to manage, the privileging of the profit motive, the 'efficiency' imperative, and so forth; and third, it is reflexive about its own epistemology and methodology and seeks to qualify claims to knowledge accordingly.

Having set out the CMS stall, Parker (2002) identifies certain key criticisms that have been levelled against the project by traditional Marxist labour process theorists. For instance, from the labour process perspective CMS academics constitute a rather motley bunch of misguided, revisionist post-structuralists and postmodernists who are blind to the true nature of the employment relation under capitalism and have so deconstructed the world of organization that they no longer think in terms of the structural realities of employer–employee, manager–managed, oppression–emancipation, and so forth. The CMS project is thus accused of having backed itself into a corner from which, 'through its sustained intellectual hypochondria', it is unable 'to articulate a political position' and has 'disqualified all the grounds for judgement' (Parker, 2002: 126). Responding to these objections from the labour process critics, Parker is careful to point out that a post-structural revision of Marxism does not necessarily entail the end of politics per se; merely the end of *representational* politics of the form that promised mass emancipation. In its place comes a commitment to *personal* politics of a more modest and local form. Although academically balanced, the sentiments Parker expresses in this regard are not entirely convincing. One infers from his argument here and elsewhere in the book that he still harbours some considerable frustration over the fact that CMS academics seem impotent in the face of those obnoxious organizational regimes and practices that is their critical target. As he graphically puts it:

> In a way that echoes the intense sectarianism of the left more generally – critical academics have been busily worrying about epistemology while Seattle was burning.
>
> (Parker, 2002: 125)

Parker explains the political quietism of CMS academics in terms of their having been, in effect, co-opted by the system. He rightly indicates that 'they are usually employees of large organizations who are paid a salary to engage in administration, the dissemination of canonical knowledge, and the production of highly specialist training for very specific audiences' (Parker, 2002: 190). In this regard, academics have no more incentive to cause trouble or effect radical change to extant systems of social relations than do managers working for commercial corporations. Like those of managers, academics' salaries depend to a large extent on the preservation of the status quo. A second important point made by Parker is that institutions of higher education worldwide are becoming increasingly corporate in the way they are constituted and run. They operate using performative managerial resource models that enable the close monitoring of expenditure in relation to teaching and research output (numbers of successful graduates, quantity and quality of publication, etc.). Where deemed expedient, cost reduction measures are introduced, such as employing part-time and contract teaching and outsourcing support services (printing, catering and so forth). These functional procedures are all carefully monitored through systems of budgetary control, financial audit and quality assurance mechanisms. Academics also have to tout for business in open markets. They are required to compete with each other in order to recruit students to courses, to place their research publications and to secure funding from various grant bodies. Held taut in these multiples cross-wires, academics are more readily positioned and manipulated by university managers, with the result that any aspiring radicalism is kept well in check. Such reasoning leads Parker to the pessimistic conclusion that the revolution is unlikely to be sparked by academics of the CMS or any other variety in the foreseeable future. Their thorough co-optation means that theory is safely insulated from the contamination of political practice. In this regard, he quotes Kierkegaard's sardonic comment on the intellectual whose 'ability, virtuosity and good sense consists in trying to reach a judgement and a decision without ever going so far as action' (Parker, 2002: 193).

PHILOSOPHIA AND THE BIFURCATION OF REASON AND PRACTICE

While acknowledging and appreciating the power of the systemic economic and social factors that Parker (2002) identifies as contributing to political quietism, I suggest that the separation of thought and action, reason and practice (which, after all, Kierkegaard is able to allude to in a time relatively removed from our own) has roots that extend far deeper than the recent marketization of academic life. Present corporatist tendencies may well further reinforce the pattern, but to uncover its origins we need to adopt nothing less than a millennial perspective on the question. One such perspective comes from the French classicist Pierre Hadot, whose collection of essays, *Philosophy as a Way of Life*, sheds a great deal of light on this central issue of praxis and the relationship between philosophy and action.

Hadot (1995) argues convincingly that modern philosophy conveys a meaning that is considerably removed from its ancient Greek origins. The word $\varphi\iota\lambda o\sigma o\varphi\acute{\iota}\alpha$ (L. *philosophia*) – a concatenation of $\varphi\iota\lambda o$ (*philo*) and $\sigma o\varphi\acute{\iota}\alpha$ (*sophia*) meaning literally 'love' and 'wisdom' respectively – originated in Greece in around the sixth or fifth century BC. It was in the writings of Plato that the term took on its strongest sense as the 'love of wisdom', that is, the passionate pursuit of self-transcending virtue and knowledge. Hadot makes much of the philosopher (*philosophos*) who, according to the Socratic dictum 'Know Thyself' is 'someone *on the way toward* wisdom' (Hadot, 1995: 90, emphases in original). What is particularly intriguing and original about Hadot's account of *philosophia*'s development is his repeated insistence that medieval Scholasticism, with its rediscovery of ancient Greek texts in the twelfth century, was responsible for a widespread *mis*-rendering of philosophy's purpose; one that systematically overlooked the practical *spiritual* dimension that, he contends, is integral to the Greek conception of philosophy and without which it reduces to mere *logos*. Of course, ancient Greek philosophies were quite diverse and sometimes contradictory. What Hadot argues by recourse to an impressive body of scholastic evidence, however, is that, despite the surface heterogeneity, each philosophical form carried at its heart a set of spiritual exercises that aimed at transforming the *practitioner* of the philosophy. This is true of Aristotelian, Platonic, Stoic, Epicurean and Neo-Platonic systems. Through the pursuit of various virtues and systematic meditations on actions of mind (conscience), word and deed, the *philosophos* was able to approach momentary self-transcendence and the apprehension of intuitive cosmic understanding. To quote Hadot at some length on this important point:

> Philosophy in antiquity was an exercise practiced at each instant. It invites us to concentrate on each instant of life, to become aware of the infinite value of each present moment, once we have replaced it within the perspective of the cosmos . . . Whereas the average person has lost touch with the world, and does not see the world qua world, but rather treats the world as a means of satisfying his desires,

the sage never ceases to have the whole constantly present to mind . . . He has the feeling of belonging to a whole which goes beyond the limits of his individuality . . . [C]osmic consciousness was the result of a spiritual exercise . . . situated not in the absolute space of exact science, but in the lived experience of the concrete, living, and perceiving subject.

(Hadot, 1995: 273)

One of the lines of investigation pursued by Hadot is an exploration of the historical currents that precipitated and reinforced the divorce between reason and practice that the modern world inherited. A pivotal factor, he maintains, is the influence of the Christian church. The advent of institutionalized Christianity in around the second century AD resulted in a conflict between it and philosophies of the ancient world. Christianity wanted to present itself as a way of life that would replace those based on the Greek practices. As Hadot has it, 'If philosophy was to live in conformity with the law of reason . . . the Christian was a philosopher, since he [sic] lived in conformity with the law of the Logos – divine reason' (1995: 269). Accordingly, authors of the Christian gospels appropriated cosmological elements of ancient Greek philosophy and, similarly, Christian monasticism adapted the Stoico-Platonic spiritual exercises associated with: attention to oneself, meditation, reflections on conscience and train-ing oneself for the moment of death (practices known collectively as *prosoche*). While *philosophia* in the monastic traditions did not lose its connotation of living practice, Hadot contends that quite a different development occurred with the advent of institutional learning and the emergence of universities in Europe during the Middle Ages:

With the advent of medieval Scholasticism . . . we find a clear distinction being drawn between *theologia* and *philosophia*. Theology became conscious of its auton-omy *qua* supreme science, while philosophy was emptied of its spiritual exercises which, from now on, were relegated to Christian mysticism and ethics. Reduced to a 'handmaid of theology', philosophy's role was henceforth to furnish theology with conceptual – and hence purely theoretical – material.

(Hadot, 1995: 107, emphases in original)

This line of analysis leads Hadot to conclude that the ascent of a modern independent philosophy in the Enlightenment period – typified in the works of inter alia Wolff, Kant, Fichte, Schelling and Hegel – was already prefigured by the medieval bifurcation of theory and practice; the 'natural' separation of thought and action. It is a legacy, moreover, that has persisted through to our own era. Writing in the mid 1970s, Hadot suggests that contemporary philosophy continues this trend. He finds exceptions to the rule only in the philosophies of Nietzsche, Bergson, Heidegger and Sartre, who each in their own way seek to reinstate the importance of *living* a philosophical life. I am tempted to suggest, in fact, that contemporary analytic philosophy represents the

91

absolute nemesis of φιλοσοφία, void as it appears to be of any semblance of either 'love' or 'wisdom' and operating in a realm that is conspicuously specialized and remote from life. This is not to deny analytic philosophy as a form of life for those engaged in it but merely to point out that it seems far removed from the ideals of ancient Greeks and philosophy as the living pursuit of the virtuous. Hadot makes much of the Stoical distinction between *discourse about philosophy* and *philosophy itself*. In other words, the acquisition of *ideas* that inform philosophy which may be categorized into differing parts – for the Stoics these would have included physics, ethics and logic – should be contrasted with the practice of philosophy that reveals, through transformational experience, the living unity and reality of these diverse ideas. His point is that modernity has become enamoured of philosophical discourse to the complete exclusion, one might say systematic marginalization, of philosophical *practice*. Philosophy is rendered purely as an exegetical exercise that focuses on texts and the representation of ideas.

In short, philosophy in antiquity was never a purely *cerebral* or ideational endeavour, as it has widely become during the intervening centuries. As Hadot asserts, 'Ancient philosophy proposed to mankind an art of living. By contrast, modern philosophy appears above all as the construction of a technical jargon reserved for specialists' (1995: 272).

READING AUSTIN

Having outlined Hadot's (1995) sweeping historical critique of philosophy's development, we are now better positioned to assess Austin's (1976) contribution and, in light of Parker's (2000) assessment, prepare the way for a re-evaluation of what philosophy might (not) do for CMS. *How to Do Things with Words* comes out of a tradition of English language philosophy whose purpose is to examine the semantics and veracity of *propositions*. As such, it exemplifies precisely Hadot's thesis concerning the spiritual denuding of modern philosophy and the abandonment of *philosophia*. Philosophy within this tradition is almost exclusively concerned with the relatively arid task of establishing the meaning of statements (in terms of their sense and reference) and the truth or falsity of their claims. That said, Austin's work can be interpreted as rebelling against language philosophy's neglect of the *social context* of language use. He attempts to recover the many functions of statements and utterances that *lie outside* the bounds of strict tests of veracity or which do not readily lend themselves to analysis through propositional logic. As Austin put it, 'In real life, as opposed to the simple situations envisaged in logical theory, one cannot always answer in a simple manner whether [a statement] is true or false' (Austin, 1976: 143). Austin's great innovation, therefore, is the recognition that 'natural language' functions within social contexts not simply to *describe* the external world but to connote and invoke attitudes and actions toward that world. To this extent, at least, he engaged in a sincere effort to reconnect philosophy with lived experience. It is a move, however, that is not without irony. What immediately strikes one while reading *How to Do Things with Words* is that, for all its espoused interest in 'ordinary language', Austin never actually examines naturally occurring utterances, preferring to stick with stylized forms of 'speech' that lend themselves to philosophical analysis (Case, 1995).

In the first half of *How to Do Things with Words*, Austin seeks to explore whether or not it is possible, in a systematic and sustainable way, to discriminate between *constative* statements – utterances which purport to describe factual (true or false) conditions in the world – and *performatives*, that is, statements which do not possess truth value as such but which accomplish something in their very utterance. Examples that Austin becomes preoccupied with are such expressions as 'I promise', 'I name this ship the Mr Stalin', 'I do' as uttered in a marriage ceremony. In the preliminary stages of the book he identifies three sets of conditions necessary for the effective accomplishment of a speech act. The first two sets of criteria relate broadly to public expression, the remaining one to private intention (although he acknowledges that even this preliminary structural distinction turns out to be rather unsteady.) For a performative to be successfully enacted, he suggests:

(A.1) There must exist an accepted conventional procedure having a certain conventional effect, that procedure to include the uttering of certain words by certain persons in certain circumstances, and further,
(A.2) the particular persons and circumstances in a given case must be appropriate for the invocation of the particular procedure invoked.
(B.1) The procedure must be executed by all participants both correctly and
(B.2) completely.
(Γ.1) Where, as often, the procedure is designed for use by persons having certain thoughts or feelings [as, for example, in a marriage ceremony], or for the inauguration of certain consequential conduct on the part of any participant, then a person participating in and so invoking the procedure must in fact have those thoughts or feelings, and the participants must intend so to conduct themselves, and further
(Γ.2) must actually so conduct themselves subsequently.

Now if we sin against any one (or more) of these six rules, our performative utterance will be (in one way or another) unhappy.

(Austin, 1976: 14–15)

Austin proceeds in the minute evaluation of a host of examples of performative utterances using these criteria, in an attempt to establish whether or not, in each selected case, the performative is 'happy' (as opposed to 'unhappy') or 'felicitous' (as opposed to 'infelicitous'). En route he finds himself running down all manner of cul-de-sac and needing further to qualify or refine his evaluative scheme. The effect this has is to draw the reader into a world of ever-finer determinations and logical precision. What appears to be a relatively innocuous expression, for example, 'I promise', turns out to invoke a plethora of social-psychological conditions of increasing subtlety. Then, to the reader's surprise, a little over halfway through the book Austin abruptly drops his initial search for binding necessary conditions that separate constative from performative. He concludes that the distinction is unsustainable and is faced with the realization that *all* utterances have a performative content. As Austin puts it:

> When we issue any utterance whatsoever, are we not 'doing something'? Certainly the ways in which we talk about 'action' are liable here, as elsewhere, to be confusing. For example, we may contrast men of words with men of action, we may say they *did* nothing, only talked or *said* things: yet again, we may contrast *only* thinking something with *actually* saying it (out loud), in which context saying it *is* doing something.
>
> (Austin, 1976: 92)

This is a seminal moment that has since reverberated throughout the contemporary philosophical world. For in this realization, Austin makes of performatives qua ethics a kind of philosophical synecdoche. It becomes impossible to speak in any context, philosophical or otherwise, without simultaneously implicating oneself or others in some form of performative (and hence ethical) nexus. An observation of this nature, made in the philosophical world of 1950s Oxford, preoccupied as it was with the traditions of English empiricism and analytic language philosophy, marked a daring departure from 'the norm'. In contrast to the Oxford traditions, here was a framework that seemed to be inclining toward the despised 'pragmatism' of North American language philosophy or even, in its implied challenge to the fundamental assumptions of propositional logic, suggestive of certain Nietzschean elements of thought. Little wonder that he chose to make his revelations in a series of lectures delivered at Harvard University.

Following his insight into the *active* nature of all utterances, Austin feels compelled to drop the constative-performative structure and develops in its place an alternative conceptual scheme for performatives that entails distinguishing between, first, *locutionary acts* which consist in utterances that have 'meaning' in a conventional language philosophic sense, that is, they possess sense and reference; second, *illocutionary acts* that have some form of immanent conventional force, such as, actions of commanding, warning, promising, apologizing, and so forth; and third, *perlocutionary acts* which classify the *effects* brought about in an audience by performative utterances – convincing, persuading, surprising, misleading, and so on. Following the introduction of this taxonomy, Austin almost immediately begins detracting from it by teasing out subtle marginal conditions where the categories overlap, seem unstable or otherwise capitulate. The entire project takes on a reasoned hesitancy and 'provisionality.' This is not to say that Austin has abandoned the notion of truth entirely; far from it. He admits himself to be driven by a 'fetish' for both the familiar truth/falsity and fact/

value distinctions of contemporary philosophy, but it is clear that the force of his own reasoning leads him to discover how even these seemingly immutable structures may be caused to wobble slightly.

Given the destabilizing direction of Austin's reasoning, it is perhaps unsurprising that his project has attracted the attention and appreciation of a number of continental European philosophers (Deleuze and Guattari, 1999: 77ff; Derrida, 1988: 321ff). Of particular relevance to the argument here is Derrida's (1982) critique of *How to Do Things with Words* and it is to his deconstructive reading of Austin that I now turn. This reading enables us to erect a temporary staging post from which to return to the question of praxis and a further consideration of how the dualities of theory-practice, philosophy-action might be reinterpreted.

READING DERRIDA READING AUSTIN

[A]ll the difficulties encountered by Austin in an analysis that is patient, open, aporetic, in constant transformation, often more fruitful in the recognition of its impasses than in its positions, seem to me to have a common root. It is this: Austin has not taken into account that which in the structure of *locution* (and therefore before any illocutory or perlocutory determination) already bears within itself the system of predicates that I call *graphematic in general*, which therefore confuse all the ulterior oppositions whose pertinence, purity, and rigor Austin sought to establish in vain.

(Derrida, 1982: 322, emphases in original)

This quotation from Derrida's essay, 'Signature, Event, Context', goes to the heart of his deconstruction of Austin's investigations in *How to Do Things with Words* (see also Munro, Chapter 12 in this volume). It is, however, a somewhat dense passage and would perhaps benefit from further exposition. In so far as the notion of the performative questions the 'unquestionable' authority of the true/false opposition, Derrida considers Austin's challenge to the orthodoxy of analytic language philosophy to be 'nothing less than Nietzschean' (Derrida, 1982: 322). It is not difficult to see how this intellectual gesture of Austin's resonates with the deconstructive enterprise and hence attracts Derrida's appreciation. As may be seen from the above quotation, however, Derrida is at pains to push the challenge further and to liberate Austin's 'performative' problematic from the bonds of locutionary sense and reference which still tie it to conventional conceptions of the 'philosophical task'. He does this in a series of moves that are concerned with *graphematic structure* and which are based essentially on arguments concerning the status and operation of 'writing' (*écriture*) first presented by Derrida in *Of Grammatology* (1976) and later elaborated and discussed through a series of interviews collected in *Positions* (1987).

In so far as writing is representative, Derrida maintains, it inexorably invokes absence. Indeed, writing is possible only because there is *implied* absence in any representative presence. Any message represented may, in principle, be read by different recipients in different contexts and hence implies both an absence of those others (who are not co-present in its writing) and an absence of the author in its reading and interpretation. Derrida refers to this immanent transferability of writing as its 'iterability' (a word deriving etymologically from the Sanskrit *itara*, meaning 'other'). The concept of iterability and its operation may be illustrated by reflecting on the process of drawing up a shopping list for 'oneself'. The act of writing the list requires one to imagine, as it were, a future self (an-other) who, by definition, is currently absent (why else would the list be necessary?) but who will nonetheless be present to read the note when doing the shopping. This example thus demonstrates how writing consists in marks – graphemes – that endure or 'remain' and which have the inherent capacity to break free of their context of origin. A necessary condition for the possibility of writing is that marks may become detached from the present and singular intention of their production. It is a structural feature of writing that all signs imply absence and all signs may be cited. Moreover, this metaphysical dimension of writing extends also to speech, whose very possibility, Derrida famously and controversially asserts, owes itself to 'writing' qua *écriture*; for when he evokes writing he means a great deal more than the conventional understanding of alphabetical marks on paper. In other words, writing – in this technical sense – precedes speech. As he states:

> This is the possibility on which I wish to insist: the possibility of extraction and of citational grafting which belongs to the structure of every mark, spoken or written, and which constitutes every mark as writing *even before and outside every horizon of semiolinguistic communication*; as writing, that is, as a possibility of functioning cut off, at a certain point, from its 'original' meaning and from its belonging to a saturable and constraining context.
>
> (Derrida, 1982: 320, emphasis added)

According to Derrida, Austin has not comprehended this fundamental quality of writing and hence is locked into pursuing an examination of speech acts that falsely require, as a condition of their felicitous or happy enactment, the existence of a bounded context and *intentional actor* (consider Austin's preoccupation with examples of the first person, singular, indicative, active grammatical forms – 'I promise,' 'I apologize,' etc.) Derrida is essentially accusing Austin of chasing a proverbial red herring, since speech acts are, in an important sense, free floating and not tied to intentionality in the way Austin imagines. For Austin, the failure of any given performative – its prospective 'unhappiness' – is an ever-present threat, whereas for Derrida it is also a condition of its possibility. So while Austin (1976: 104) seeks to *exclude* what he sees as 'parasitic' forms of speech act as they occur in poetry, fiction, theatre, jest, deception, quoting, etc., these are precisely the cases that Derrida finds interesting because they display, par excellence, the inevitable and vital operation of 'iterability'. These marginalized examples entail citation and the non-presence of the intentional speaking subject, whether on stage, screen or in a poem. For Derrida, the marginal parasitic cases that Austin excludes are indicative of how all performatives work, that is, by invoking ritualized social contexts in which sheer citation will operate to bring about its effect. There is no need to invoke the existence of a spontaneous intentional subject under this analysis. Moreover, the *graphematic structure* of signs entails that the very notion of *locution* that prefigures illocution and perlocution in Austin's scheme, is itself questionable and, along with it, all the premises of true/false, fact/value, happy/unhappy, felicitous/infelicitous oppositions that form the axes of his philosophical problematic and which, as it were, authorize his inquiry.

Derrida's critique of Austin provides an entrée into a wider consideration of the deconstructive project and the implications that it carries for the re-evaluation of praxis. His 'Signature, Event, Context' essay concludes with a generic statement of deconstruction as a radicalizing philosophy which

> [C]annot limit itself or proceed immediately to a neutralization: it must, by means of a double gesture, a double science, a double writing, practice an *overturning* of the classical opposition *and* a general *displacement* of the system. It is only on this condition that deconstruction will provide itself the means with which to *intervene* in the field of oppositions that it criticizes, which is also a field of nondiscursive forces.
>
> (Derrida, 1982: 329, emphases in original)

This is Derrida expressing clearly the *political* intent informing deconstruction. It is a recognition that the various systemic inequities and other moral absurdities that result from human acts of organizing stem from what become, in their 'writing', unchallengeable logocentric hierarchies. The non-conceptual, or 'nondiscursive' as he has it, is inextricably bound up in the conceptual and hence 'overturning' oppositional structures through deconstruction by necessity entails the 'displacement' of the naturalized order and the realization of new forms of life. For Derrida, therefore, the very framing of the question concerning praxis is misplaced. To persist in opposing 'theory and practice' or 'philosophy and action' is to be trapped by an historically contingent set of oppositional delusions. Deconstruction demands that we break free from all such delusion by engaging critically in the staking out of middle territories that have, hitherto, been logically excluded by millennia of dualistic misconception. Preoccupation by those excluded middles, moreover, necessitates the dissolution of oppositional polarities that were responsible for their marginalization in the first place. In this sense, deconstruction *qua* philosophy *is* politics, *is* praxis.

97

CONCLUSION: ASK NOT WHAT PHILOSOPHY CAN DO FOR CMS

So where does this leave the investigation of praxis? Can we enter into a performative philosophical life that re-engages *philosophia* and avoids indulging the seductive philosophical conceits that would have us merely 'do things with words' or believe in the autonomy of 'things' and 'words'? One resolution may be through deconstruction, whose critical purpose equates challenges to logocentrism with politics and which denies the meaningful opposition of philosophy and practice, thought and action. This approach could also be augmented, I suggest, by lessons drawn from premodern and non-modern forms of philosophical life. My point – following Hadot (1995), McGhee (2000) and MacIntyre (1985) – is that greater emphasis should be placed on the importance of leading a virtuous life based on reasoned moral principles. In order for this to be possible, however, we have to reinstate or accept the meaningful operation of conventional terms. We would need to speak (albeit approximately and provisionally) in terms of 'individuals' who possess 'intention' and who are able to 'act' in pursuit of the virtuous.

These assumptions are explicit in Hadot's work, for example, when he concludes that, 'Ancient philosophical traditions can provide guidance in our relationship to ourselves, to the cosmos, and to other human beings' (1995: 274). He refutes readings of ancient philosophies that accuse them of tending toward solipsism and self-indulgence. On the contrary, the philosophies of antiquity were group practices (he cites Pythagorean communities, Platonic love, Epicurean friendship and Stoic spiritual direction as examples) that in each case established clear duties for practitioners in relation to maintaining the welfare of the community; an ethical stance that resonates with Borgerson's discussion of *relational* feminist ethics (in this volume). In particular, Hadot singles out Stoicism as a potential model for the pursuit of virtue within contemporary western society, its three ethical prescriptions being to maintain moment-to-moment vigilance and restraint with respect to one's thoughts, to consent to events imposed by destiny, and to act in the service of the human community in accordance with justice. Hadot offers the following pragmatic advice and reflection for those seeking to reconcile the tensions caused by trying to develop personal wisdom while living and acting in a world of suffering and injustice:

[T]he philosophical life normally entails a communitary engagement. This last is probably the hardest part to carry out. The trick is to maintain oneself on the level of reason, and not allow oneself to be blinded by political passions, anger, resentments, or prejudices. To be sure, there is an equilibrium . . . between the inner peace brought about by wisdom, and the passions to which the sight of the injustices, sufferings, and misery of mankind cannot help but give rise. Wisdom, however, consists in precisely such an equilibrium, and inner peace is indispensable for efficacious action.

(Hadot, 1995: 274)

If one accepts his arguments concerning the pursuit of the virtuous (and I recognize, of course, that this will be a big conditional 'if' for many readers) then certain ethical implications follow for those pursuing a critical management studies agenda. To illustrate the nature of these implications I draw on an email circular from the CMS Interest Group (dated 5/6/03) that attempts to identify some of the parameters of the CMS project. Part of the email reads:

> Our premise is that structural features of contemporary society, such as the profit imperative, patriarchy, racial inequality, and ecological irresponsibility often turn organizations into instruments of domination and exploitation. Driven by a shared desire to change this situation, we aim in our research, teaching, and practice to develop critical interpretations of management and society and to generate radical alternatives.

It is plain that this mini manifesto is exclusively outer-directed. It locates the evils of the world wholly in reifications 'out there' or in the actions of irresponsible 'others'. But what if we challenge this 'premise' and consider whether we, ourselves, are sufficiently blameless to be casting such moral aspersions on others? Is this critique free from the taint of hypocrisy? Such reflection might lead us to conclude that the *first* imperative is not to look outward to the amorphous world of capitalist exploitation, social inequity and inauthenticity, but to ask searching questions of ourselves: 'Am I completely free of prejudice, do I dominate and exploit others, are my actions ecologically responsible, am I *attached* to commodities and acts of consumption?' and so forth. Moreover, 'What am I doing about it?' To engage seriously in a philosophical life that seeks consistently to pose these questions and address them through the cultivation of personal virtues would, I suggest, constitute a genuinely radical alternative to the mainstream. It is a life that would have us striving to be virtuously impeccable; to value friendliness and compassion; to exercise judicious restraint of thought, word and deed; and to aspire to be harmless and free from attachment. This is not to foster political quietism or proscribe speaking out against suffering and injustice, but it is to challenge the facile assumption that the source of every problem is always already elsewhere.

The point, of course, is that we should seek to live by philosophies that *transform* our way of being in the world (see also Brown's discussion of Artaud, Chapter 13 in this volume); that attenuate selfish impulses and enhance compassion. If this can be done collectively then all well and good for the kinds of organizations and communities that we inhabit. I think it imperative that those on the political left pursue ideals of this nature: an imagined perfect meeting of ethics and politics, as it were. In this chapter, however, I suggest that the analytical pendulum within CMS may have swung too far toward a privileging of *external* politics at the cost of neglecting personal ethics. It seems to me that personal virtue 'makes a difference' wherever, whenever and in whatever measure it is pursued, irrespective of supporting political conditions.

ACKNOWLEDGEMENTS

A version of this chapter was presented at the 'How to Do Things with Philosophy' stream, Third Critical Management Studies conference, 7–6 July 2003, Lancaster, UK. I would like to thank Damian O'Doherty and Garry Phillipson for their helpful and insightful comments on an earlier version of this work. My thanks also to the editors of this volume for their meticulous reading of my draft chapter and for their assistance in developing the published version.

REFERENCES

Austin, J. L. (1976) *How to Do Things with Words*. Oxford: Oxford University Press.

Byatt, A. S. (2000) *The Biographer's Tale*. London: Quality Paperbacks Direct.

Case, P. (1995) 'Representations of talk at work: Performatives and performability', *Management Learning*, 26(2): 423–443.

Deleuze, G. and F. Guattari (1999) *A Thousand Plateaus*, trans. B. Massumi. London: Athlone.

Derrida, J. (1976) *Of Grammatology*, trans. G. C. Spivak. London: Johns Hopkins University Press.

Derrida, J. (1982) *Margins of Philosophy*, trans. A. Bass. Brighton: Harvester.

Derrida, J. (1987) *Positions*, trans. A. Bass. London: Athlone.

Derrida, J. (1988) *Limited Inc.*, trans. S. Weber. Evanston, IL: Johns Hopkins University Press.

Fournier, V. and C. Grey (2000) 'At the critical moment: Conditions and prospects for critical management studies', *Human Relations*, 53(1): 7–32.

Hadot, P. (1995) *Philosophy as a Way of Life*, ed. A. Davidson. Oxford: Blackwell.

McGhee, M. (2000) *Transformations of Mind: Philosophy as Spiritual Practice*. Cambridge: Cambridge University Press

MacIntyre, A. (1985) *After Virtue: A Study in Moral Theory*. London: Duckworth.

Marx, K. (1975) *Early Writings*, ed. T. Bottomore. Harmondsworth: Penguin

Parker, M. (2000) *Against Management: Organization in the Age of Managerialism*. Cambridge: Polity.

Searle, J. (1977) *Speech Acts: An Essay in the Philosophy of Language*. Cambridge: Cambridge University Press.

Sotirin, P. and M. Tyrell (1998) 'Wondering about critical management studies', *Management Communication Quarterly*, 12(2): 303–336.

Chapter 6

Reading critical theory

Steffen Böhm

'Read what has never been written', says Hofmannsthal. The reader, who one should think of here, is the true historian.

(Walter Benjamin, 1974: 1238, my translation)

INTRODUCTION

In times of the increasing popularity of critical approaches to organization theory, critique seems to be everywhere. Critical organization theory textbooks, critical management studies conferences and conference streams, critical organization journals – these are all examples of the recent rise of the discourse of critique in the wider realms of organization theory. But what is critique? Critical organization scholars work with a wide variety of conceptions of critique, and critique is indeed often seen to encompass 'a broad range of positions' (Fournier and Grey, 2000: 16).

While, for example, some critical scholars see themselves working within the specific historical tradition of critical theory, as it has been practised by the so-called Frankfurt School, many see critique as something quite loose, simply regarding it as something that defamiliarizes us with our taken-for-granted world (Fournier and Grey, 2000). Despite these differences – or perhaps because of them – it seems as if critique has become an academic fashion, a logo, an obligatory passage point that one has to pass through as a contemporary organization theorist (Böhm and Spoelstra, 2004; Thompson, 2004); today we seem to have come to the point where almost anything can be called critical.

Rather than seeing critique as a 'broad church' (Ackroyd, 2004: 165; Alvesson and Willmott, 2003: 15; see also Grey and Willmott, 2005) or loose questioning of the world, my point of departure is the understanding that critique is a historically and theoretically specific practice. While for some, critical organization theory can be literally anything, for me the discourse of critical theory, which occupies a significant part of contemporary philosophy, is inherently linked to the work of Frankfurt School scholars. However, if one looks at the way critique is often deployed today, one notices that the Frankfurt School has been almost written out of critical organization theory. Why is this? To answer this question, my aim with this chapter is to study the way the Frankfurt School tradition of critical theory has been read within the realms of organization theory and evaluate the implications of this reading. My hope is that such a reading may shed some light on recent conceptions and misconceptions of critique within organization theory.

One way into this analysis, this reading, of the way critical theory has been treated in organization theory is to engage with the works of Alvesson and Willmott, who have arguably been two of the most influential commentators on the Frankfurt School in organization theory (see also O'Doherty's, 2005, review and critique of their work). My aim is thus to read Alvesson and Willmott as well as read critical theory with and against them. When I say reading, I do not simply refer to the mundane task of perceiving strings of words and constructing them into sentences. I am also not reading for the instrumental purpose of collecting reference material. Instead, the reading I am interested in here is the one that stands for engaging, tracing, contextualizing, rereading and translating. As Walter Benjamin – who was associated with the Frankfurt School in the 1920s and 1930s, but never a formal member of it – tells us in his essay 'The Task of the Translator' (1999a: 70ff), an exact translation of a text is impossible. For Benjamin, the possibility of a text does not simply lie in its words; instead it can be found between words, in the silence of the white space that surround letters, words, lines of text. Reading is a theoretical practice that aims to become worthy of the silent impossibility of a text. Reading is not strictly about reading words themselves, but the sub-text of language; to read between the lines: 'all great texts contain their virtual translation between the lines' (Benjamin, 1999a: 82). This is also to say that there is no pre-composed meaning in a text. Instead, every text has to, according to Benjamin, always be treated as a foreign language that has yet to be translated. In this sense, one does not simply read or write *about* critical theory or Alvesson and Willmott. Reading is a *doing* – a translating of, and an immanent engagement with, critical theory. Reading is an immanent critique of texts such as the ones produced by Alvesson and Willmott. If there is anything organization theory can learn from critical theory, then it is how to engage in an immanent practice of reading.

CRITICAL THEORY IN ORGANIZATION

When speaking of critical theory, most researchers have something theoretically and historically quite specific in mind. What comes to mind is the critical theoretical tradition practised by Adorno, Benjamin, Horkheimer, Marcuse, Fromm, Habermas and others associated with the Institute for Social Research in Frankfurt/Main, commonly known as the Frankfurt School. The Frankfurt School's approach is often represented as 'Critical Theory' (note the capitalization), as if we can speak of a theoretically and politically homogeneous programme developed and carried out by 'the' Frankfurt School. For me, the Frankfurt School is first and foremost a multi-plicity; it is an event that brought a diverse range of scholars together in a historically specific and interesting time period between the First and Second World Wars. There is no space in this chapter to introduce the Frankfurt School and its history in any great detail. Many useful books have been written fulfilling this task (see, for example, Hoy and McCarthy, 1994; Jay, 1973; Rush, 2004).

A range of organization theorists have drawn on the critical theory of Frankfurt School scholars in various ways. Here we can mention, for example, Burrell (1994), Burrell and Morgan (1979), Hancock and Tyler (2001), Hassard (1993), Jermier (1998) and Parker (2002). Noteworthy is also the special issue of the *Journal of Organizational Change Management* (2000) on 'critical theory and the management of change in organizations'. Again, my task here is not to engage with these useful contributions. It is simply to acknowledge that there have been a variety of readings of critical theory in organization theory, although on the whole the study of the works of Frankfurt School scholars has been rather limited.

What is striking is that most students of organization are introduced to critical theory through the writings of Alvesson and Willmott. In their textbook, *Organization Theory*, for example, Crowther and Green (2004) rely almost exclusively on citations to the works of Alvesson, Willmott and their co-authors. Let us be empirical about this: in their section 'Critical Theory – The Frankfurt School' (Crowther and Green, 2004: 119–126) 'Willmott' is cited six times, 'Alvesson and Deetz' are cited four times, 'Deetz' is cited twice, and 'Alvesson and Willmott' are cited once. Besides one reference to Marcuse, there are four references to only one of Habermas' books. Although Adorno and Horkheimer are briefly discussed (Adorno's work is introduced in two short sentences), Crowther and Green (2004) fail to include even one reference to their many writings. While the failure to mention Benjamin and others who have been associated with the Frankfurt School is perhaps excusable, Crowther and Green's reading becomes highly questionable when they give the impression that Lukács, Gramsci as well as Deetz were or are members of the Frankfurt School.

While this episode may tell us something about the level and quality of Crowther and Green's (2004) scholarship, it points perhaps more generally to the state of reading in organization theory. Of course, it is slightly unfair to pick a student textbook published by the Chartered Institute of Personnel and Development as a 'straw man' here. But given that this textbook aims to introduce theory to students of organization in a different way than most other books (Crowther and Green, 2004: 5), I think it is appropriate to put this alleged difference to the test. While the responsibility for such a poor reading of critical theory certainly lies with Crowther and Green, it is important not to individualize or even psychologize this episode. That is, what I would like to argue now is that their scholarship – or rather the lack of it – can be perhaps traced to the way influential organization theorists, such as Alvesson and Willmott, themselves have read critical theory. Reading is not something one does on its own. Reading is a social and relational event. Reading occurs in a community of theoretical practice, and it is for this very reason that it is important to engage, trace, contextualize, translate, reread – that is, critique – other people's readings.

ALVESSON'S AND WILLMOTT'S INTEREST IN CRITICAL THEORY

Mats Alvesson's and Hugh Willmott's collaboration goes back to the mid-1980s (Alvesson and Willmott, 1996: ix). Both had a background in the critical studies of work, control, ideology and the labour process (Alvesson, 1987, 1991; Knights and Willmott, 1989, 1990). As Professor in the Department of Applied Psychology at the University of Lund, Sweden, in the 1980s, Alvesson was interested in how psychological investigations could be brought together with sociological analyses in order to theorize work and gender subjectivities (Alvesson, 1987; Alvesson and Billing, 1992). Similarly, throughout the 1980s Willmott's project was about broadening the question of subjectivity beyond traditional approaches in labour process theory (Knights and Willmott, 1985, 1989, 1990; Willmott and Knights, 1982).

At the end of the 1980s both Alvesson's (1987, 1991) and Willmott's (Knights and Willmott, 1989, 1990) writing projects were concerned to show that workers' subjectivities and social reality as a whole are products of a plurality of conscious and unconscious processes of symbolization as well as power and knowledge, rather than simply determined by the rational, economic laws of the capital–labour relationship in the workplace. As Knights and Willmott write, power cannot be 'reduced to a property of persons, a dominant class, a sovereign or the state. Rather, it is dispersed throughout the social relations of a population in a diverse set of mechanisms and a multiplicity of directions' (1989: 553). Following Foucault, they continue that 'forms of power are exercised through subjecting individuals to their own identity or subjectivity, and are not therefore mechanisms directly derived from the forces of production, class struggle or ideological structures' (Knights and Willmott, 1989: 553).

Similarly, for Alvesson (1991), ideology is not simply a result of economic workplace relations, but determined by a complex set of conscious and unconscious processes of symbolization. For him, an 'increased awareness of the symbolic nature of organizations . . . and the symbols' role in the reproduction of a certain social order and certain ways of conceptualizing social life, might be an important element in the process of emancipation' (Alvesson, 1991: 223). Both Alvesson's and Willmott's projects are hence related to an expanded understanding of control mechanisms of workers' subjectivities beyond psychological and economic deterministic explanations. What is evident in their individual writing projects in the 1980s is that, for them, workers' emancipation cannot simply be an individual, egoist outburst of self-determined agency, nor can emancipation simply come through a resolving of the contradictions of the labour–capital class relationship.

It is precisely through these concerns that Alvesson and Willmott became interested in, and sensitized by, the critical theory of Frankfurt School scholars. In the early 1980s, Willmott and Knights (1982) had already engaged more closely with the work of Erich Fromm — who was associated with the Frankfurt School mainly in the 1930s. What Willmott and Knights (1982) saw in Fromm (1977) is the attempt to merge Freudian psychoanalytical studies with Marx's economic analyses of capitalist relations of power, which was a concern shared by many Frankfurt School scholars. Willmott and Knights (1982) were interested in Fromm because of his critique of the notion that psychology is geared only towards the uncovering of individual psychological traits. Instead, Fromm wanted to develop a social psychology that would decentre human consciousness by placing it into specific historical processes. Yet, despite this historicization of human subjectivity, Fromm was interested in retaining the human ability and capacity for agency. For Fromm, one of these agencies is the faculty of critical thinking:

> Critical thinking is the only weapon and defense which man has against the dangers in life. If I do not think critically then indeed I am subject to all influences . . . Critical thinking is not something which you apply as a philosopher . . . Critical thinking is a quality, is a faculty, it's an approach to the world, to everything; it's by no means critical in the sense of hostile, or negativistic, of nihilistic, but on the contrary critical thought stands in the service of life, in the service of removing obstacles to life individually and socially which paralyze us.
>
> (Fromm, 1994: 168–169)

While Fromm's faculty of critical thinking may sound like a voluntaristic cry for freedom, he was careful to problematize traditional conceptions of emancipation and freedom. What interested Willmott and Knights (1982) in Fromm's (1977) analysis is the notion that individuals may also have a 'fear of freedom'; people are thrown into this world, and often the easiest and most convenient thing to do is to not emancipate oneself or be critical or explore all possibilities to become free (see also O'Doherty, 2005: 151).

FROM CRITICAL THEORY TO 'CT'

Alvesson and Willmott pick up this important concern for a conceptualization of emancipation in their joint writing at the beginning of the 1990s. In their influential article, 'On the idea of emancipation in management and organization studies' published in the *Academy of Management Review* in 1992, emancipation is described as 'the process through which individuals and groups become freed from repressive social and ideological conditions, in particular those that place socially unnecessary restrictions upon the development and articulation of human consciousness' (Alvesson and

105

Willmott, 1992b: 432). What Alvesson and Willmott try to do in this article is 'to reevaluate the concept of emancipation, developed by the Frankfurt School and other proponents of Critical Theory (CT) in the light of recent critiques from poststructuralism, especially Foucault' (Alvesson and Willmott, 1992b: 432). This is, in fact, the first sentence of their article, and it introduces not only their article but also the way Alvesson and Willmott engage with critical theory and philosophy as such.

While Willmott and Knights' (1982) paper on Fromm is a more or less careful engagement with the arguments put forward by one Frankfurt School scholar, Alvesson and Willmott's (1992b) article is characterized by gross generalizations in terms of how critical theory and the concept of emancipation are represented (see also Jones in Boje et al., 2001). Let us look at a few examples. They write: 'The intent of CT is to facilitate clarification of the meaning of human need and expansion of autonomy in personal and social life' (1992b: 432). Here, critical theory becomes a homogenous signifier, an acronym, 'CT'. The multiplicity of writings of scholars associated with the Frankfurt School is forced into an essentialist language that makes claims about critical theory as a whole. To be fair, Alvesson and Willmott are aware of this limitation; in the first footnote they write: 'We acknowledge the danger of lumping together members of the Frankfurt School who developed distinctive positions' (1992b: 432, fn 1). While every text involves processes of simplification and abstraction, it is surprising that Alvesson and Willmott think that this disclaimer can simply let them 'off the hook', that is, allow them to represent critical theory in the generalizing and essentializing way they do.

Given their treatment of critical theory, it seems plainly self-contradictory when Alvesson and Willmott claim that the Frankfurt School's critique is 'totalizing' (1992b: 438) and that 'CT has assumed a highly abstract, inaccessible form of communication that is easily perceived to express an elitist, pontificating attitude toward understanding people and change' (1992b: 437). They go on to maintain that critical theory has an 'inclination to reduce or totalize phenomena so that they fit into the interpretive powers of a single, integrated framework' (1992b: 440), without providing any textual evidence for their totalizing critique. Their essentialist claims continue when they critique critical theory for having an 'essentialist idea of an integrated, coherent, homogeneous individual' (Alvesson and Willmott, 1992b: 440). Where exactly does 'CT' say this? Which scholar associated with the Frankfurt School do they talk about? Did Alvesson and Willmott not first become interested in Fromm and other critical theorists because of their historical and non-essentialist conceptions of subjectivity?

But these reductionist and essentialist readings of critical theory are not only confined to Alvesson and Willmott's *Academy of Management Review* article. In their edited collection, *Critical Management Studies* (1992a), as well as their research monograph, *Making Sense of Management: A Critical Introduction* (1996), which have both been influential reference points for many critical organization theorists, critical theory is again treated as an homogeneous body, which is often represented as 'CT': 'CT contends that emancipatory progress has been made in the past and, potentially, can be made in the future' (Alvesson and Willmott, 1996: 14); 'It is this that provides the foundations of CT' (Alvesson and Willmott, 1996: 73). And even their introduction to the newest collection, *Studying Management Critically* (2003), does not fare much better: 'CT aspires to provide an intellectual counterforce to the ego administration of modern, advanced industrial society' (Alvesson and Willmott, 2003: 2). 'CT is saying this'; 'CT is maintaining that'. At no point do Alvesson and Willmott problematize this signifier 'CT'. While my argument is not that texts cannot or should not involve any abstractions, because of the lack of textual engagement with the actual writings of critical theorists, it is very difficult for the reader to see how Alvesson and Willmott have come to make their statements about 'CT'.

HABERMASING CRITICAL THEORY, OR, FORGETTING CRITICAL THEORY

At the rare occasion when Alvesson and Willmott do engage with the actual texts written by critical theorists and provide textual evidence for their claims, it is apparent that the work of Jürgen Habermas provides the greatest inspiration for their views on, and critiques of, critical theory. For example, in Chapter 3 of *Making Sense of Management* – a chapter that is entitled 'Critical theory: Development and central themes' – Alvesson and Willmott (1996) refer almost exclusively to Habermas' textual apparatus. Again, let us be empirical about this: in this chapter there are about twenty direct page references to Habermas' texts, while Adorno and Horkheimer's (1979) *Dialectic of Enlightenment* and Marcuse's (1969) *An Essay on Liberation* are cited only once each. There is no evidence at all for an engagement with the plentiful texts written by Adorno, Horkheimer, Fromm, Marcuse – and Benjamin is not even mentioned once. While this quantifying exercise might sound pedantic to some, this shows clearly that Habermas can be seen as the monopolizing voice in terms of how critical theory is represented by Alvesson and Willmott. What is even more unfortunate is that Frankfurt School associates, such as Benjamin, seem to be completely written out of Alvesson and Willmott's version of critical theory.

Although Benjamin was never formally involved with the Institute for Social Research, he shared a lot of its philosophical and political concerns, which are expressed, for example, in a lively exchange of letters between Adorno and Benjamin (2003), which began in 1928 and lasted until Benjamin's death in 1940. This correspondence reveals interesting insights into their analyses of capitalist society as well as their understanding of critique as an immanent and speculative yet affirmative technique. While Adorno was firmly embedded in the German university system and one of the central figures in the Frankfurt School, Benjamin operated at its fringes. Benjamin never held an academic position – his text, *The Origin of German Tragic Drama* (1998), was not accepted by the University of Frankfurt as a habilitation thesis, which

107

at that time meant that he could not become a university professor. Yet, as Brodersen (1996) and others argue, Benjamin had a significant influence on Frankfurt School scholars. Particularly Adorno, who called Benjamin 'the dialectician of the imagination' (1967a: 240), was deeply indebted to him, as they were both interested in developing 'a philosophy directed against philosophy' (Adorno, 1967a: 235).

Alvesson and Willmott manage to at least mention Benjamin once in their latest book collection (2003: 2), but they are not on their own in their lack of recognition of his contribution. Besides a few recent engagements with his work (see, for example, Burrell and Dale, 2003; Carr and Zanetti, 2000; Sørensen, 2004; Styhre and Engberg, 2003; ten Bos, 2003) and my own efforts in this direction (Böhm, 2002, 2006, 2007), organization theorists have tended to ignore Benjamin's critical theory. In their attempt to critique critical theory (that is, Habermas) and its supposedly 'totalizing attacks on the prevalent social order', Alvesson and Willmott (1996: 180) could have made productive use of Benjamin's philosophy. They go to great length to argue that post-structuralism (note that this becomes 'PS' in their writing) – particularly the work of Foucault – emphasizes micro-political 'studies that explore and critique particular, local practices without losing sight of the relevance and potency of more "global" insights' (Alvesson and Willmott, 1996: 180). While this is a useful insight, they did not need to employ Foucault to make this point. Both Benjamin's and Adorno's critical theory is precisely about the dialectical relationship between, and critique of, local practices and global insights.

Benjamin's *Arcades Project* (1999b), for example, is a dialectical critique of the cultural and material specificities of Parisian modernity of the mid-nineteenth century. Rather than making grand claims about modernity and possibilities for 'grand projects' of social change – as Alvesson and Willmott frequently accuse critical theory of doing (for example, 1996: 186) – Benjamin engages in a careful textual analysis of the rise and fall of the Parisian architectural phenomenon of the arcade, which he links to the emergence of capitalist mass-consumer culture. Similarly, Adorno's *Minima Moralia* (2005) is a devilish engagement with, and critique of, the dull realities of modern life produced by the culture industries. Like Benjamin's *Arcades Project* as well as his 'One-way Street' (1999c), Adorno's text immerses itself right into the specific materialities and images of modernity: homes and property, marriage, children, sex, intellectuals, music and cars. Here, critical theory is not about 'grand claims', as Alvesson and Willmott often claim in a rather grand way. Instead, Benjamin's and Adorno's critical theory is what Alvesson and Willmott might have in mind when they talk about Foucauldian micro-political and micro-emancipatory engagements with, and critiques of, social relations. Both Benjamin and Adorno called it 'immanent critique'.

IMMANENT CRITIQUE, OR, FROM FRANKFURT TO PARIS AND BACK AGAIN

For both Adorno and Benjamin 'immanent critique' is a critique that does not come from above, from an idealist, essential category. Instead it must be immanent in the sense that it is embedded in a specific societal and political reality and its dynamics (Adorno, 1998: 14). 'Immanent critique of intellectual and artistic phenomena seeks to grasp, through the analysis of their form and meaning, the contradiction between their objective idea' and their ideological presentation (Adorno, 1967b: 32, translation modified). According to Adorno, critique must be immanent; it must come from the inside, which also involves the suffering of being embedded in the very ideological structures and practices one aims to critique. 'The dialectical critic of culture must both participate in culture and not participate' (Adorno, 1967b: 33). That is, in order to critique an ideological content, one must be involved in a process of repeating that content, in order to hope that this repetition would eventually unravel and change that ideology. 'Immanent critique' asks how a phenomenon – for example, a phenomenon of organization – stands in relation to the antagonisms of society, and whether there are any techniques to confront and overcome these antagonisms. Only if one is immanently involved with these antagonisms one can speculate about a way beyond them.

Does this conception of 'immanent critique' not sound curiously alike what Alvesson and Willmott see and value in the approach taken by Foucault and 'what he termed the microphysics of power, that is, power as exercised in the context of a complicated network of power relations and struggles rather than as a purely repressive mechanism originating from a single unified source' (Alvesson and Willmott, 1992b: 442)? And is this not close to what they might have in mind when they call for 'microemancipation' (1992b: 446)? By not immersing themselves into the texts of critical theorist such as Adorno and Benjamin, Alvesson and Willmott miss an important point: perhaps there are not so many dividing boundaries between Frankfurt and Paris, between 'CT' and 'PS'. If they would look beyond their acronyms for critical theory and post-structuralism, that is, if they would read the multiple and diverse texts produced by scholars associated with these philosophical categories, they would notice that there are many connecting lines between these German and French philosophical traditions. As Foucault stated himself:

> When I recognize all these merits of the Frankfurt School, I do so with the bad conscience of one who should have known them and studied them much earlier than was the case. Perhaps if I had read those works earlier on, I would have saved useful time, surely: I wouldn't have needed to write some things and I would have avoided certain errors.
>
> (Foucault, 1991: 119)

109

Perhaps organization theorists need to learn from Foucault's experience and go back to studying the texts produced by Frankfurt School scholars more closely. This reading would enable organization theorists to go beyond the crude and 'jargon-ridden' (Fournier, 2002: 177) categorizations that are usually associated with both critical theory and post-structuralism. One can refer here to Alvesson and Deetz (2000) who have come up with typologies that press critical theory as well as post-structuralism into static compartments, which the organization theorist is then supposed to apply to practical problems in organization and management research. Alvesson and Deetz (2000) present us with four alternative discourses that offer different, but not competing, approaches to conduct critical organization research: normative (determinism, functionalism), interpretive (social constructionist views), critical (politics, struggle and domination) and dialogic (postmodernism that reclaims conflict and sees otherness). Here, critical theory is part of a supermarket shelf of different research approaches, which the organization theorist can choose from, depending on the practical relevance and usefulness of their methodologies (Alvesson and Deetz, 2000: 39).

Such pragmatism arguably has nothing to do with 'immanent critique' or indeed a Foucauldian approach to research. In their work on emancipation, Alvesson and Willmott (1992b, 1996) call for 'new styles of writing' and 'emancipatory elements in texts'. What Alvesson and Deetz produce with their paradigmatic research typology is the opposite: text is squeezed into prefabricated and pragmatic categories, which kills the event of reading and tries to make philosophy consumable for organization theory. Adorno was, of course, very critical of these developments to making philosophy pragmatic. In his view, a pragmatic philosophy tries to eternalize the here and now by basing all its analytical power on existing relations to make them consumable and practicable. For Adorno, the problem with such a practical approach is that it 'remains under the spell of disaster unless it has a theory that can think the totality in its untruth' (Adorno, 1998: 14).

The pragmatism practised by Alvesson and Willmott and their colleagues is in line with their (1992b, 1996) critique of what they call the 'negativism' of critical theory. In their view, critical theory research is often 'one-sided, negative, and unconstructive' (1992b: 442), and they claim that the 'reluctance of CT researchers to engage in a dialogue with mainstream, technicist, objectivist, and promanagerial researchers has contributed to its marginalization' (1992b: 443). Therefore, Alvesson and Willmott (1992b: 443) as well as Alvesson and Deetz (2000: 47) call for a more practical critical theory that is able to engage with managerialist discourses and go beyond antagonisms and political differences by way of open participation, information sharing and interpretation. Adorno's response to such a pragmatist reading of critical theory would point out that a critical engagement with the world cannot come through a positive reaffirmation of what is, but only through speculative, negative thinking.

Thought as such, before all particular contents, is an act of negation, of resistance to that which is forced upon it . . . Today, when ideologues tend more than ever to encourage thought to be positive, they cleverly note that positivity runs precisely counter to thought and that it takes friendly persuasion by social authority to accustom thought to positivity. The effort implied in the concept of thought itself, as the counterpart of passive contemplation, is negative already – a revolt against being importuned to bow to every immediate thing.

(Adorno, 1973: 19)

Thus, the 'negativism' Alvesson and Willmott bemoan is, in fact, a negative dialectics that Adorno deploys in order to resist the positive, pragmatic reality that we are always already encouraged to accept and follow. Adorno's negative dialectics precisely tries to question and go beyond the type of categorical and practical readings Alvesson and Willmott employ. But this negative, critical thinking is not simply a 'negativism'. On the contrary, this negative thinking involves an immanent critique of society, which is a positive movement in itself, as it aims to present a new knowledge of society.

READING PHILOSOPHY AND ORGANIZATION

This book is about the relationship between philosophy and organization. What I have tried to do in this chapter is to read critical theory as well as critique the way critical theory has been read in organization theory. We can see in the writings of Alvesson and Willmott that critical theory has often been read in quite simplistic ways; it is seen as a homogeneous, well-packaged body of work that can be critiqued from the 'outside'. The outside from which Alvesson and Willmott critique critical theory is post-structuralism, which again is presented as a homogenous body of work, albeit one that is somewhat superior and more advanced in its thinking than critical theory.

There is a certain idea of progress built into the way Alvesson and Willmott critique critical theory through post-structuralist concepts. Perhaps this is the 'storm of progress' Benjamin writes about in his 'Theses on the Philosophy of History'; the storm that 'irresistibly propels' us 'into the future' (Benjamin, 1999a: 249). For Benjamin, this storm of irresistible progress is the storm of history, which has 'become a tool of the ruling classes' (1999a: 249). What Benjamin is concerned about is this 'history making' that we are constantly subjected to. History is made by dominant voices by categorizing the past into homogenous packages that do not present a threat to the present. Rather than reading the works of Frankfurt School scholars in detail, critical theory is presented as 'CT', a category that can then be easily subjected to a universalizing critique from a historically progressed and progressive position.

For both Benjamin and Adorno a reading of philosophy has to be done differently. 'Instead of reducing philosophy to categories, one would in a sense have to compose it first. Its course must be a ceaseless self-renewal, by its own strength as well as in

111

friction with whatever standard it may have' (Adorno, 1973: 33). So, rather than seeing critical theory as a pre-composed category, it is our task to continuously renew philosophy. That is, we are called upon to read critical theory in ever new ways, precisely because

> if thinking is to be true, if it is to be true today, in any case – it must also be a thinking against itself. If thought is not measured by the extremity that eludes the concept, it is from the outset in the nature of musical accompaniment with which the SS liked to drown out the screams of its victims.
>
> (Adorno, 1973: 365)

While Adorno and other critical theorists faced the horrors of the SS and Nazism, the political task of philosophy as well as organization theory remains: to continuously think against itself – that is, negate itself – in order to put into question all seemingly positive or pragmatic systems, whether this is Nazism, Stalinism, capitalism, neo-liberalism or other 'isms'. Such critique cannot come from above as an idealist, essential category. Instead, it must be immanent in the sense that it is embedded in the specific societal and political reality and its dynamics.

As Benjamin says, the true historian reads 'what has never been written' (Benjamin, 1974: 1238). It is thus our task – and this is indeed a joint, social affair – to read critical theory the way it has never been written and read by organization theorists. To fail this task, according to Benjamin, implicates the reader with the barbaric history of the past. History must therefore be 'wrested away' from those who simply want to progress and carry on with history in a positive and pragmatic way. Benjamin says: 'In every era the attempt must be made anew to wrest tradition away from a conformism that is about to overpower it' (1999a: 247). But this 'wresting away' cannot be done from outside tradition, precisely because we are part of that very history. It is for this reason that this 'wresting away' has to also include philosophy itself. Critical theory is part of the history that needs to be 'wrested away' from those who simply want to embed critical theory into a continuous, categorized history. Adorno is therefore interested in developing 'a philosophy directed against philosophy' (1967a: 235). He calls on us to face 'the problem of a liquidation of philosophy' (Adorno, 2000: 29).

This presents us with the following problem. The relationship between philosophy and organization cannot be a linear one, as 'philosophy' and 'organization' themselves are not given constructs. That is, before we can even problematize this relationship, we have to first envisage the destruction of philosophy and organization. In the first instance this involves the destruction of the leading representatives of critical theory in organization theory. This is why I have engaged with Alvesson and Willmott in this chapter. I hope that my writing has not been elitist or come from 'above', as my intent was to engage in an immanent critique of Alvesson's and Willmott's writings, among which there have been important contributions to the field of organization theory.

The destruction of their work attempted here should not be read as something negative. Not at all. Both Adorno and Benjamin are quite clear that a negative dialectics is an engagement with a work that aims to produce affirmative knowledge. Critique is an affirmative, theoretical practice (see also Jones, 2004: 42). Only if we destruct, that is negate, established writings on, and readings of, critical theory, are we able to produce a different, affirmative future of and for organization.

ACKNOWLEDGEMENT

I would like to thank the editors of this book for their useful comments on earlier drafts of this chapter.

REFERENCES

Ackroyd, S. (2004), 'Less bourgeois than thou? A critical review of *Studying Management Critically'*, *ephemera: theory and politics in organization*, 4(2): 165–170.

Adorno, T. W. (1967a) 'A portrait of Walter Benjamin', in *Prisms*, trans. S. Weber and S. Weber. Cambridge, MA: MIT Press.

Adorno, T. W. (1967b) 'Cultural criticism and society', in *Prisms*, trans. S. Weber and S. Weber. Cambridge, MA: MIT Press.

Adorno, T. W. (1973) *Negative Dialectics*, trans. E. B. Ashton. London: Routledge & Kegan Paul.

Adorno, T. W. (1998) 'Why still philosophy', in *Critical Models*, trans. H. W. Pickford. New York: Columbia University Press.

Adorno, T. W. (2000) 'The actuality of philosophy', trans. B. Snow, in B. O'Connor (ed.) *The Adorno Reader*. Oxford: Blackwell.

Adorno, T. W. (2005) *Minima Moralia: Reflections from Damaged Life*, trans. E. Jephcott. London: Verso.

Adorno, T. W. and W. Benjamin (2003) *The Complete Correspondence 1928–1940*, ed. H. Lonitz, trans. N. Walker. Oxford: Blackwell.

Adorno, T. W. and M. Horkheimer (1979) *Dialectic of Enlightenment*, trans. J. Cumming. London: Verso.

Alvesson, M. (1987) *Organization Theory and Technocratic Consciousness: Rationality, Ideology, and Quality of Work*. Berlin: de Gruyter.

Alvesson, M. (1991) 'Organizational symbolism and ideology', *Journal of Management Studies*, 28(3): 207–225.

Alvesson, M. and Y. D. Billing (1992) 'Gender and organization: Towards a differentiated understanding', *Organization Studies*, 13(1): 73–103.

Alvesson, M. and S. Deetz (2000) *Doing Critical Management Research*. London: Sage.

Alvesson, M. and H. Willmott (1992a) 'Critical theory and management studies: An introduction', in M. Alvesson and H. Willmott (eds) *Critical Management Studies*. London: Sage.

Alvesson, M. and H. Willmott (1992b) 'On the idea of emancipation in management and organization studies', *Academy of Management Review*, 17(3): 432–464.

113

Alvesson, M. and H. Willmott (1996) *Making Sense of Management: A Critical Introduction*. London: Sage.

Alvesson, M. and H. Willmott (2003) 'Introduction', in M. Alvesson and H. Willmott (eds) *Studying Management Critically*. London: Sage.

Benjamin, W. (1974) 'Anmerkungen der Herausgeber [Comments of the editors]', in *Gesammelte Schriften*, Vol. 1.3, ed. R. Tiedemann and H. Schweppenhäuser (with T.W. Adorno and G. Scholem). Frankfurt/M: Suhrkamp.

Benjamin, W. (1998) *The Origin of German Tragic Drama*, trans. J. Osborne. London: Verso.

Benjamin, W. (1999a) *Illuminations*, ed. H. Arendt, trans. H. Zohn. London: Pimlico.

Benjamin, W. (1999b) *The Arcades Project*, trans. H. Eiland and K. McLaughlin. Cambridge, MA: Belknap Press.

Benjamin, W. (1999c) 'One-way Street', in *Selected Writings, Vol. 1, 1913–1926*, ed. M. Bullock and M. W. Jennings, trans. E. Jephcott. Cambridge, MA: Belknap Press.

Böhm, S. (2002) 'The consulting arcade: Walking through fetish-land', *Tamara: Journal of Critical Postmodern Organization Science*, 2(2): 20–35.

Böhm, S. (2006) *Repositioning Organization Theory: Impossibilities and Strategies*. Basingstoke: Palgrave Macmillan.

Böhm, S. (2007) 'The carousel event', in P. Case, S. Lilley and T. Owens (eds) *The Speed of Organization*. Copenhagen: Copenhagen Business School Press.

Böhm, S. and S. Spoelstra (2004) 'No critique', *ephemera: theory and politics in organization*, 4(2): 94–100.

Boje, D., S. Böhm, C. Casey, S. Clegg, A. Contu, B. Costea, et al. (2001) 'Radicalising organisation studies and the meaning of critique', *ephemera: critical dialogues on organization*, 1(3): 303–313.

Brodersen, M. (1996) *Walter Benjamin: A Biography*, ed. M. Dervis, trans. M. R. Green and I. Ligers. London: Verso.

Burrell, G. (1994) 'Modernism, postmodernism and organizational analysis 4: The contribution of Jürgen Habermas', *Organization Studies*, 15(1): 1–19.

Burrell, G. and K. Dale (2003) 'Building better worlds? Architecture and critical management studies', in M. Alvesson and H. Willmott (eds) *Studying Management Critically*. London: Sage.

Burrell, G. and G. Morgan (1979) *Sociological Paradigms and Organizational Analysis*. London: Heinemann.

Carr, A. and L. A. Zanetti (2000) 'The emergence of a surrealist movement and its vital "estrangement-effect" in organizational studies', *Human Relations*, 53(7): 891–921.

Crowther, D. and M. Green (2004) *Organization Theory*. London: Chartered Institute of Personnel and Development.

Foucault, M. (1991) *Remarks on Marx: Conversations with Duccio Trombadori*, trans. R. J. Goldstein and J. Cascaito. New York: Semiotext(e).

Fournier, V. (2002) 'Theory and practice', *Organization*, 9(1): 176–179.

Fournier, V. and C. Grey (2000) 'At the critical moment: Conditions and prospects for critical management studies', *Human Relations*, 53(1): 7–32.

Fromm, E. (1977) *The Fear of Freedom*. London: Routledge & Kegan Paul.

Fromm, E. (1994) *The Art of Listening*. London: Constable.

Grey, C. and H. Willmott (eds) (2005) *Critical Management Studies: A Reader*. Oxford: Oxford University Press.

Hancock, P. and M. Tyler (2001) *Work, Postmodernism and Organization: A Critical Introduction*. London: Sage.

Hassard, J. (1993) *Sociology and Organization Theory*. Cambridge: Cambridge University Press.

Hoy, D. and T. McCarthy (1994) *Critical Theory*. Oxford: Blackwell.

Jay, M. (1973) *The Dialectical Imagination: A History of the Frankfurt School and the Institute of Social Research 1923–1950*. Boston, MA: Little, Brown.

Jermier, J. M. (1998) 'Introduction: Critical perspectives on organizational control', *Administrative Science Quarterly*, 43(2): 235–257.

Jones, C. (2004) 'Jacques Derrida', in S. Linstead (ed.) *Organization Theory and Postmodern Thought*. London: Sage.

Journal of Organizational Change Management (2000) 'Critical theory and the management of change in organizations', 13(3).

Knights, D. and H. Willmott (1985) 'Power and identity in theory and practice', *Sociological Review*, 33(1): 22–46.

Knights, D. and H. Willmott (1989) 'Power and subjectivity at work: From degradation to subjugation in social relations', *Sociology*, 23(4): 535–558.

Knights, D. and H. Willmott (eds) (1990) *Labour Process Theory*. London: Macmillan.

Marcuse, H. (1969) *An Essay on Liberation*. Boston, MA: Beacon Press.

O'Doherty, D. (2005) 'David Knights and Hugh Willmott: The subjugation of identity and . . . and . . . and organization-to-come . . .', in C. Jones and R. Munro (eds) *Contemporary Organization Theory*. Oxford: Blackwell.

Parker, M. (2002) *Against Management: Organization in the Age of Managerialism*. Cambridge: Polity.

Rush, F. (ed.) (2004) *The Cambridge Companion to Critical Theory*. Cambridge: Cambridge University Press.

Sørensen, B. M. (2004) *Making Events Work, or, How to Multiply your Crisis*. Copenhagen: Samfundslitteratur.

Styhre, A. and T. Engberg (2003) 'Spaces of consumption: From margin to centre', *ephemera: critical dialogues on organization*, 3(2): 115–125.

ten Bos, R. (2003) 'Business ethics, accounting and the fear of melancholy', *Organization*, 10(2): 267–285.

Thompson, P. (2004) 'Brands, boundaries and bandwagons: A critical reflection on critical management studies', in S. Fleetwood and S. Ackroyd (eds) *Critical Realist Applications in Organisation and Management Studies*. London: Routledge.

Willmott, H. and D. Knights (1982) 'The problem of freedom: Fromm's contribution to a critical theory of work organisation', *Praxis International*, 2(2): 204–225.

Chapter 7

Why feminist ethics?

Janet Borgerson

INTRODUCTION

In offering contributions from feminist ethics to organization studies, this chapter draws out crucial distinctions between feminist ethics, 'care ethics' and essentialist forms of feminine ethics, and, moreover, addresses researchers' frequent failure to differentiate among these discrete fields. The failure to differentiate between, for example, *feminist* and *feminine* ethics has resulted in misapprehension, theoretical misunderstanding and, most importantly, missed opportunities to benefit from the resources of *feminist ethics*. In extending the context for feminist ethical interventions, the discussion reveals that far from being limited to discussions of gender differences feminist ethics provides frameworks for recognizing, evaluating and addressing ethical dilemmas generally. Thus, feminist ethics engages broader issues of interest, motivating powerful concepts and novel ways of thinking and providing diverse approaches to central concerns in business ethics and organization studies (Calás and Smircich, 1997; Derry, 2002).

The field of feminist ethics draws upon and develops theoretical foundations that question and pose alternatives to traditional ontological and epistemological assumptions, invoking fundamental reflection and unveiling productive possibilities. Feminist ethics articulates, theorizes and works to understand modes of exclusion, subordination and oppression – and the damage inflicted by these processes and practices – often against the backdrop of traditional ethical theories' marginalization of females generally. However, females have not been the only segment – nor the private domestic sphere the only arena – marginalized, or excluded from, the traditional vision of moral theory (Tong, 1993: 224). Understandably, then, the concerns of feminist ethics exceed focus upon women's oppression and engage the welfare of other groups, as well.

Indeed, as Alison Jaggar argues, the concepts of traditional moral theory were often 'ill-suited to the contexts under discussion', *failing to account for the experience of many* within those contexts (Brennan, 1999: 861). Reflection upon embodied lived experience may generate instances of previously unrecognized diversity and variation – frequently evoking, demonstrating and elaborating alternative ontological and epistemological mappings that provoke rethinking of typical mainstream understandings of meaning, being, interaction and theorizing itself. Moreover, embodied experience of marginalized existence often produces observations on and insights into living with, enduring and attempting to resist forms of exclusion, subordination and oppression.

The tendency to critical inquiry, especially regarding the frequently forgone 'givens' of particular situations marks feminist ethics *not* as a list of essential sex-based ethically relevant traits or a set of predetermined gender-based applicable principles, but rather as an intervention that calls for active engagement in dilemmas. Feminist ethicists have insisted that 'The process by which a community arrives at its standards or moral norms is itself open to moral scrutiny' (Brennan, 1999: 864), forcing attention upon the context and structure of moral reflection and judgement and attending to signs of oppression. After offering a brief background for feminist ethics and feminist ethical theory, I discuss fundamental insights emerging around concepts of relationships, responsibility and experience. Then, I deepen the understanding of feminist ethics through a critical appraisal of Levinas' motivation of intersubjectivity, and conclude by articulating the notion of feminist ethical ontology. First, however, I give some context for the underestimation of feminist ethics in business ethics.

FEMINIST ETHICS IN BUSINESS ETHICS

Many researchers in business ethics have yet to recognize that care ethics is not constitutive of feminist ethics; nor are all versions of care ethics founded upon feminine traits and characteristics (Nunner-Winkler, 1995; Tronto, 1993). Business ethics textbooks provide obvious, yet not inconsequential, sites of analysis for relevant confusions regarding feminist ethics. Take for example, *Business Ethics: A European Perspective* by Andy Crane and Dirk Matten (2004). Although presenting the familiar ethical perspectives arguably relevant for business ethics – utilitarianism and deontology – the authors also include short sections on 'virtue,' 'feminist,' 'discourse' and 'postmodern' ethics. Business ethics desperately needs this augmentation. However, the Crane and Matten text inaccurately reduces feminist ethics to 'care ethics' and, moreover, mistakenly grounds care ethics in a 'feminine approach'.

Feminist ethics, a field of philosophical research in itself, appears – somewhat misleadingly – within *Business Ethics: A European Perspective* under the heading of 'contemporary ethical theories', defined as those theories that include 'consideration of decision-makers, their context, and their relations with others as opposed to just abstract universal principles' (Crane and Matten, 2004: 95). In short, such a theory would offer consideration for ethics emerging from concrete positions and particular situations, rather than prescribe preordained principles or duties in choosing, or judging, the good or right thing to do. Thus, traditional ethical theories, and more recent versions derived from them (for example Rawls, 1971), are set against

117

contemporary ethical theories: contemporary ethical theories often retain aspirations for seeing the bigger picture yet, at the same time, take seriously details that traditional ethics' approaches have been known to distain and disregard. However, as the following discussion illustrates, the impetus to collapse the field of feminist ethics into a 'theory' that reduces to a common ontological trope of essentialized female traits and characteristics – assumedly drawn upon in ethical 'consideration' – explains much about the remarkable underestimation of feminist ethics in business ethics.

It is a theoretical error to speak of a universally recognizable male or female mode of ethical reflection, response or action – essentialist notions of 'being' male or female are rejected in feminist ethics. Within Crane and Matten's (2004: 97–98) short section on 'Feminist Ethics', 'male approaches' are directly contrasted with 'feminist perspectives': such an opposition suggests a lack of understanding around the basic distinction between sex and gender. Employing coherent concepts in the explication of feminist ethics as a contemporary ethical theory requires marking masculinity's distinction from the male and femininity's distinction from the female. Indeed, in the wake of feminist ethics' ontological and epistemological shifts, the impact of such essentialist assumptions would emerge as a site for critical analysis. Moreover, various contradictions arise in attempting to generalize 'effects' of a certain ethic, or ethos, on all others and in all situations.

The 'feminist' term in 'feminist ethics' designates a theoretical position distinct from both a 'female perspective' or a 'feminine' perspective. Indeed, a more accurate introduction to feminist ethics would interrogate why aspects of stereotypical femininity, such as being passive, emotional or other-focused – often expected of, imposed upon and developed in female bodies in certain groups, times and places, including contemporary western society – are more likely to coordinate with and express a 'care ethic', than are corresponding 'masculine' aspects. This likelihood of embodied females taking on, exhibiting and acting out – often subordinating – feminine traits in a sexist context is recognized as a problem with which feminist ethics has been particularly concerned. In addition, notions of female 'intuition' – presented by Crane and Matten (2004) as a source of feminist ethics' ethical response – reduces 'feminist ethics' to an informal process of applying feminized female common sense. This diminutive characterization exacerbates the underestimation of feminist ethics.

Furthermore, many of the insights credited to 'postmodern ethics' (Gustafson, 2000: 21, cited in Crane and Matten, 2004) could be derived from work in feminist ethical theory, and indeed often emerged earlier within feminist thought. In equally relevant exclusions, critical race theory (Gordon, 1997) and disability studies (Shildrick and Mykitiuk, 2005) raise crucial, complex issues of identity, intersubjectivity and agency, and – this should be obvious – not only as a result of specific engagement and ideological agreement with post-structural theory or thinkers. Insights that have emerged from the experiences, innovations and theorizations of marginalized groups – such as women, racial minorities and disabled people – often are ascribed solely to what is known as postmodern theory and post-structural theorists. Such careless attribution both reveals and breeds ignorance (and worse) and serves to reintroduce the marginalization such theory often seeks to acknowledge.

Considerable development in various disciplinary territories has been cultivated with insights derived from theorizing multiple and particular experiences of living in divergent societies, places, times and bodies. Yet, recognition of such fundamental data tends to vanish in attempts to maintain the status of an abstract and authoritative voice. Given this observation, it is not surprising that a certain kind of discourse intimately connected to, and privileged by, this 'tradition' continues processes of exclusion and marginalization.

Whereas feminist ethical theory does share some fundamental assumptions with post-structural theory – a ground for so-called postmodern ethics – this emerges not because all feminist theory, and therefore feminist ethics, is derivative. Rather, many feminist philosophers and theorists, as well as their critical race theory and disability studies colleagues, have trained in similar intellectual traditions – philosophical phenomenology, epistemology and semiotics – as, for example, have Foucault, Deleuze and Derrida (Borgerson, 2005). Sharing, then, academic heritage and disciplinary genealogies, feminist ethical theory has, in some instances, exploited derived tools to develop conceptual and practice-based contributions often along lines of gender, theoretically understood (Alcoff, 1988; Diprose, 1994; Walker, 1998). Such work includes attention to the intersecting meanings, instantiations and functionings of hierarchical dualisms in lived human experience, and thus has implications beyond gender difference (Borgerson, 2001).

It may be prudent at this juncture to mention that Crane and Matten's (2004) articulation of contemporary ethical theories has ontological, as well as methodological, implications. Their representation of feminist ethics focuses upon *who* or what *type* of person is the source of judgements – grounded in 'consideration of decision-makers, their context, and their relations with others'. Accordingly one is twice removed from the action, reflecting uncritically instead on the agents who – in the process of concluding good or bad, right or wrong – draw upon certain traits or identity-based considerations. This understanding obscures the provocative and fundamental tenuousness that feminist ethics locates in notions of essentialism, necessity and universality. Ontology, the study of being, abjures any necessity or essentialism, and hence examines all notions of being and existence including being's dislocation, absence or lack. Notable and coinciding methodological, and interwoven epistemological, questions emerge. For example, how might one recognize, document, describe or judge the embodied, lived experience of one who comprehends and ethically values a decision-maker's particular contexts and relations?

If we hope to perceive how feminist ethics can contribute to business ethics and organization studies, we must move beyond seeing feminist ethics as a 'contemporary ethical theory'. This brief chapter will not explore what abstracted, essentialized female traits might offer business ethics. Instead, it will seek to clarify what business ethics can learn from feminist ethics – understood in a robust way that makes an educated exploration of resources beyond care ethics and uncritical notions of femininity.

FEMINIST ETHICS: ACCESSING THE FIELD

The word ethic, derived from the Greek *ethos*, refers to the disposition, character or fundamental value peculiar to a specific person, people, culture or movement, and usually is conceived of as a set of principles of right conduct or a theory or system of moral values. Such an understanding clearly evokes an array of questions. How does an ethos make itself known? How is the ethos experienced in day-to-day life? Or in law? Why do some people or groups have one ethos rather than another? Claudia Card, articulating the work of feminist ethics, writes, 'oppressive sexual politics sets the stage for ethical inquiries into character, interpersonal relationships, emotional response, and choice in persistently stressful, damaging contexts' (Card, 1991: 5). Thus, feminist ethics states a motive for investigating the ethics of an ethos itself.

A thorough genealogy of feminist ethics would require an extensive and complex review. For the purposes of this chapter, however, psychologist Carol Gilligan remains a relevant starting point. Focused upon moral development – as exhibited in decision-making around ethical dilemmas – Gilligan's (1982) research challenged attributions of moral superiority usually granted to those research subjects who solved the dilemmas by referring to abstract values derived from universal principles. Her work responded, for example, to psychologist Lawrence Kohlberg's influential hierarchical scale of moral maturity, based in dominant Kantian notions of rational morality. Gilligan's early studies revealed 'different' approaches, perspectives or voices, including the voice of 'care', in her subjects' ethical deliberations that defied abstract, universal positioning. Kohlberg's scale would judge them inferior, yet Gilligan argued that these voices deserved recognition for mature moral reasoning: a care perspective was different, yet equally capable of morally mature judgement.

These alternative ethical considerations – centred around values of care and heard most often in Gilligan's female subjects' voices – have been misapprehended as expressing an essentially female ethos, or women's natural way of being. In fact, Gilligan never identified the caring voice with the voices of all, and only, women. Whereas sexual dualism and female gender roles increase the likelihood that a female 'voice' expresses care, great variation persists in who voices care and why.

In later research, Gilligan (1995) made a crucial distinction between a feminine ethic and a feminist ethic. Conceptions of femininity – understood theoretically as the subordinated element in the gender binary masculinity/femininity – carry meanings derived from often associated essentialized female traits, such as passivity, irrationality and desire to nurture even at the expense of self. A *feminine* ethic in a patriarchal social order is an ethic of 'special obligations and interpersonal relationships'. Gilligan writes, 'Selflessness or self-sacrifice is built into the very definition of care when caring is premised on an opposition between relationships and self-development' (Gilligan, 1995: 122). To put this another way, a relationship informed by so-called feminine traits emerges as fundamentally unequal – a one-sided concern with the well-being and development of others that demands prior assumption of female sacrifice made unproblematic by essentialist claims. In other words, combining traditional modes of femininity with notions of responsibility and caring puts into play a particularly debilitating permutation of ethical agency, where agency is understood as action that 'transcends its material context' (McNay, 2000: 22). In short, the ability to act suffers under a feminine ethos, or feminized way of being.

On the other hand, by remaining reflective upon potential sites of oppression and subordination, feminist ethical theory informs care ethics' focus on relation differently. A *feminist* ethic 'begins with connection, theorized as primary and seen as fundamental in human life' (Gilligan, 1995: 122). In this context, 'disconnection' and expectations of autonomy appear as problems. Such a perspective shares conceptual points with Emmanuel Levinas' model of responsibility; but as I argue later, adaptations of Levinas' ethical model often underestimate feminist ethics' fundamental contribution. Feminist ethics bears witness to intersubjectivity while maintaining or developing 'the capacity to manage actively the often discontinuous, overlapping or conflicting relations of power' (McNay, 2000: 16–17).

Feminist ethics places the tendency to value connection – and demonstrate alternatives to traditional notions of autonomy – outside conventional visions of a natural or an essential female-gender based, or essential human, way of being in the world. Feminist ethics turns instead to concrete and particular, yet theoretically elaborated, cultural and historical understandings of diverse marginal or subordinated groups' experience. Focusing upon feminist ethics as a feminine trait-based ethic of care concerned with 'harmonious and healthy social relationships', and relying upon 'personal, subjective reasoning' (Crane and Matten, 2004: 98), underestimates and undermines the critical power of feminist ethic's analytical examinations and philosophical arguments around unequal power relations, agency and identity formation, and systemic subordination. By motivating an investigation of feminist ethics' insights, a stronger and expanded contribution from feminist ethics will be forthcoming.

FEMINIST ETHICAL THEORY

Generally, feminist ethical theories are those that aim 'to achieve a theoretical understanding of women's oppression with the purpose of providing a route to ending women's oppression . . . and . . . to develop an account of morality which is based on women's moral experience' in the sense that, previously, women's experience has been excluded (Brennan, 1999: 860). However, this attempt to gather and comprehend varieties of experience in particular contexts – that formerly remained beyond philosophical ethics' consideration – is not a claim about how women naturally, and hence necessarily, experience the world. Indeed, what we want to be cautious of in the present endeavour is that 'in our efforts to explain various realities that are saturated with the weight of the interests that created them, we often present "neat" versions of reality to suit our agendas' (Gordon, 1995: 133).

Rosemarie Tong has condensed the most important feminist ethical contributions into what she calls 'challenges to the assumptions of traditional ontology and epistemology' (Tong, 1993: 49–77). Ontologically, the dualism of self versus other, or individual versus community – in which the discrete existence of each element is linked to conceptions of autonomy – becomes a question of relationships between self and other and responsibilities of self to the other, and vice versa, in particular contexts. That is, feminist ethics attempts to account for intersubjectivity, or interrelations between moral agents even as the boundaries between these become blurred. These interactions include situations of inequality, and power, rather than contracts among assumedly equal partners. In addition, traditional oppositions in epistemology, such as, abstract versus concrete knowledge, universal versus particular standpoints, impartial judgement versus partiality, and reason versus emotion also fall under scrutiny. The epistemological shifts in feminist ethics require a sensibility that maintains a closer contact with practice and the particular and, hence, remains receptive of concrete experience's details and insights.

Investigations undertaken from a feminist ethical perspective are less likely to accept elements and structures of a dilemma as given. To put this another way, feminist ethical theories often spur expansion of the contexts in which problems are to be understood, allowing a broader range of problem recognition, possible solutions and, moreover, pre-emptive work. So, for example, whereas research in business ethics has explored the phenomenon of 'ethical sensitivity' (for example, Collins, 2000: 11) as a gender difference issue that expresses aspects of apparently natural female, or sex-based, virtues, feminist ethics refuses to essentialize, or treat as naturally occurring, so-called 'women's experience', thus provoking productively alternative inquiries into 'ethical sensitivity'. As Card (1991) suggests, feminist ethics calls upon us to interrogate the very occurrence and manifestation of such 'sensitivity'.

INSIGHTS FROM FEMINIST ETHICS

For present purposes, three main theoretical contributions may be discerned as central to feminist ethics: these include attention to responsibility in conjunction with the recognition of relationships' primacy – including aspects of intersubjective agency – and a focus upon particular experience in context. These contributions' conceptual richness open new possibilities for the impact, complexity and usefulness of business ethics. For example, whereas business scenarios often call for attention to experience and the context at hand, traditional ethical considerations that aim at principle-based objectivity and universality often judge such experience inappropriately subjective and unworthy of consideration in solving problems and coming to terms with conflicts of interest.

Moreover, in traditional ethical discourse, concepts of responsibility usually function in reference to fulfilling duties and obligations. Responsibility's more comprehensive and insightful modes – for example, as a context for agency based in relationships that are developed and borne out intersubjectively – have little hope of emerging within traditional discussions of business ethics and corporate social responsibility, yet emerge readily in feminist ethics.

RELATIONSHIPS

Arguments have been made in business ethics stating that autonomy must be the basis for ethical action and reflection – with a focus on recognizing the sight of agency, decision-making and, of course, blame tending to minimize incidences of multiple influence, manipulation and chance. Alternative articulations of autonomy, as well, reflect on the interference presented by relationships or intersubjectivity (Lippke, 1995). Stephen Darwall (1998) points to the distinction between acknowledging the fundamental role of relationships and accepting a more vulgar understanding of an almost democratically compromised autonomy:

> The idea is not that we should involve others in our deliberations because they will help us come to the right decision. Rather, because the question is always what to do in light of the various relationships we have to others, there is no way of specifying the right decision independent of others' input. And since the relevant relationships are often reciprocal, appropriate deliberation must often be collective.
>
> (Darwall, 1998: 224)

Traditionally, relationships might be hypothesized as between autonomous individuals (agents), or between agents who themselves are the products of relations and therefore represent some modified version of autonomy. These relationships could be understood as formed between the self, or subject, and some other, in and across a hypothesized gap that separates these agents and protects their status as independent, responsibility-bearing decision-makers. The interactions and exchanges form the basis of relations, and, moreover, provoke questions such as, 'How should the self treat the other?' 'How can the self know the other?' and vice versa.

Feminist ethical notions of self–other relations – as Tong's (1993) notion of ontological shifts suggests – are largely intersubjective and interdependent: that is, self and other are conceived of as developing in relation with each other. Indeed, calling attention to intersubjectivity and interdependence raises varying degrees of doubt about the very nature of the distance that supposedly separates self and other, and this

123

provides a critical context for interrogating autonomy. In ethical theory, relationships have often appeared threatening to autonomy and moral integrity because of the role strict boundaries in individual rational decision-making and choice have played in making one's decisions one's own (see Card, 1996: 21–48). Feminist ethical theory faces this threat to the perceived site of agency, examining and observing revealed contradictions and emergent insights, yet acknowledging that relationships – actual or imagined, lived or theoretically conceptualized – form the foundation for notions of responsibility.

Paying greater attention to the fundamental role of relationships in human existence invokes notions of responsibility to and for others beyond traditional moral contract-based and principle-justified duties and obligations. Furthermore, human agents may be conceived of as 'having' or 'taking' responsibility. Manifestations of this discussion are wide-ranging and complex, and will be developed later in this chapter. Basic insights for business ethics guide the following section.

RESPONSIBILITY

As Darwall (1998) notes above, human embeddedness in relationships, our intersubjectivity, cannot be disregarded in discussions and elaborations of responsibility. Claudia Card writes:

> The challenge is to show how the importance and point of responsibility can survive the realization that the quality of our character and our deeds is not entirely up to us as individuals.
>
> (Card, 1996: 22)

Responsibility is often understood to describe an ability to respond to a situation – whether this involves another person, a group or simply a scenario in which one acts to accomplish an action – and may take the form of recognizing or refusing ties, duties or obligations that we have in relation to this world around us. Such a notion may also be expanded to include possibilities of responsibility to self.

Card (1996) argues that whereas someone or something may *have* responsibility for a set of situations or actions, *taking* responsibility requires a centre of agency, a choosing to act or follow through in a certain way. 'We may be given responsibility, assigned it, inherit it, and then accept or refuse it' (Card, 1996: 29). Card states, 'Agents are more responsible when they take responsibility in a sense that shows more initiative than when they do not.' Card (1996: 28) designates four different dimensions of taking responsibility each with its own related accomplishments:

1 *Administrative* or *managerial* – estimation and organization of possibilities, deciding which should be realized and how;

2 *Accountability* – being answerable or accountable, either through specific agreement or 'finding' oneself such, for something and following through;

3 *Care-taking* – a commitment of support or backing of something or someone, and holding to the commitment;

4 *Credit* – taking the credit or blame for something that did or did not happen, 'owning up'.

These four senses of responsibility require an active willingness to take such responsibility: and what kind of agent manifests such willingness again becomes an issue for investigation. Of course, some people, or agents, may not be willing to 'take' responsibility in these ways if as a result they incur more burdens or blame than they would have had otherwise. There is, then, a potential flight from responsibility – or bad faith – that remains troubling. Levinas, for example, engages this concern, attempting to place ethics and relations of responsibility beyond human choice. Feminist ethics, instead, tends to elaborate on being a certain kind of agent, and, thus, having particular kinds of experiences.

EXPERIENCE

Feminist ethical theory may push us to critically reflect on a phenomenon rather than simply assume its merits, and hence interrogate the emergence and effects, for example, of 'ethical sensitivity'. Larry May (1992) has argued that sensitivity to the lives of others and their particular experiences can serve as an opening to acting ethically in relation. Whereas sensitivity to others has often been understood as feminine gender's domain, May does not find such an essentialized limitation necessary, rather regarding sensitivity a basic human capacity that can be cultivated.

Recalling Hobbes' statement in *Leviathan*, May points out that the opportunity to learn and develop from experience is one of the fundamental equalities that exists in the state of nature (May, 1992: 130). Clearly, such an opportunity is altered by prevailing experiential circumstances, and ultimately, some people seem to learn more than others from the lessons of their lives and even succeed in applying these to solve future dilemmas. Moreover, there is no guarantee that the lessons learned point toward 'ethical' behaviour and actions, sensitive or otherwise, as life is not an ethically reliable teacher.

Yet, knowledge gained in situations not generally regarded as morally relevant nevertheless generates ways of functioning and modes of decision-making that have broad ethical import. Feminist ethics has taken a special interest in the understandings acquired by particular, often marginalized, groups and individuals. Ethical investigations that include such perspectives require listening to other's voices and emphasizing a broader acknowledgement of human interaction and attention to the lives people lead.

Such a focus on acknowledgement of lived experience and learning invites a distinction between the 'natural' and 'unnatural' conditions under which people make choices, including recognition of how histories of oppression circumscribe the contexts in which relationships and responsibility emerge. Card writes,

> It is not enough to confront the inequities of the 'natural lottery' from which we may inherit various physical and psychological assets and liabilities. It is important also to reflect on the unnatural lottery created by networks of unjust institutions and histories that bequeath to us further inequities in our starting positions and that violate principles that would have addressed, if not redressed, inequities of nature.
>
> (Card, 1996: 20)

Being born into a situation may be a 'natural fact', but how the nation or race into which one is born has been treated historically and how various effects emerging from these historical variables will place a newborn are not natural facts. Contingent – though not necessarily accidental – historical circumstances, shaped and held in place by systems of power and status, may be ascribed to the just and unjust functioning of 'institutions': such institutions may be as intimately related to an individual as his or her family relations, skin colour, and gender.

SHARED CONCERNS: REVISITING 'ETHICAL SENSITIVITY'

The emphasis upon relationships, responsibility and lived experience found in feminist ethics provides penetration into the realm of business and organization that traditional moral theories may fail to accomplish. Indeed, feminist ethical theory proves useful in understanding the issue of 'ethical sensitivity' mentioned earlier, offering insight into, and tools to address, the concern that 'many gender studies lack a theoretical framework that predicts when and why women are more ethically sensitive than men' (Collins, 2000: 11). The *Journal of Business Ethics* has given witness to the role that ethical sensitivity plays in ethical dilemmas in business contexts (Collins, 2000). Ethical sensitivity has been defined as 'an ability to recognize that a particular situation poses an ethical dilemma', and exemplifies intolerance toward unethical behaviours, and a proneness to do the right thing (Collins, 2000: 6).

Ethical sensitivity has often been examined in terms of gender differences, in particular an interest in whether women's so-called feminine characteristics, including caring traits, form the foundation for greater ethical sensitivity. As Collins has noted, the results and conclusions have been mixed. Conceptual innovations and analysis motivated by feminist ethics suggest that ethical sensitivity could be studied as a matter of attention to certain details, more obvious, compelling, and relevant to some ethical agents than to others. Recall that feminist ethical conceptualizations support the conclusion that context matters. That is, feminist ethical theory encourages us to explore why it is that agents with experience of certain kinds – for example, a lived awareness of intersubjectivity and particularity arising in daily life practices and culturally socialized ways of being still regularly expected of and manifested in women in contemporary western cultures – are more likely to be ethically sensitive. (What such agents ultimately do, of course, is a different question.)

The contributions of feminist ethics push us beyond an essentialist view of gender difference – that bases female predilection for ethical sensitivity on an unfathomable natural, or even cognitive, difference – to conceive, perceive and construct alternative and supplementary understandings that can be mobilized, theorized and applied in future scenarios. Thus, the phenomenon of ethical sensitivity emerges as an outcome of specific epistemological and ontological assumptions and cultural preconceptions that play out in lived experience of being female, or conversely male, at a historically specific time and place. That is, ethical sensitivity derives from experience generally and, further, out of experience in relationships of responsibility with others. Such critical reflection gives us a depth of perspective regarding ethical tendencies and traits. The following section explores what is at stake in ignoring theoretical and conceptual distinctions from the field of feminist ethics.

INTERSUBJECTIVITY AND SUBORDINATION

The debate over which characteristics are crucial for ethical agency has been around for some time; yet the attempt to privilege so-called feminine virtues without careful consideration of their context defies the wisdom of centuries of anti-sexist work (Wollstonecraft, 1975; Young, 1990: 73–91). Feminist criticisms of feminine trait-based ethics have raised crucial questions about damaging relationships, desirable boundaries and ethical agency under oppressive conditions (Borgerson, 2001). In western patriarchal culture and in other cultures as well, being has traditionally been divided into two. This binary mode has given rise to well-recognized, hierarchically ordered dualisms of meaning and being: the self/other, white/black, heaven/earth, civilized/primitive, rational/irrational, finite/infinite dichotomies that Val Plumwood (1993: 51–55) finds implicated in the 'logic of colonialism'. The field of feminist ethics recognizes that related processes of ontological 'othering' have perpetuated and reinforced historically evident privileging of the male, the white and the rational (Goldberg, 1993).

Traditionally philosophers have granted ethical superiority to traits and behaviours arising from a stereotypically masculine way of being. Kant, for example, in his *Observations on the Feeling of the Beautiful and the Sublime* insists upon maintaining the 'charming distinction that nature has chosen to make between the two sorts of human beings' (Kant, 1960: 77). In this context, men exemplify capacities for depth, abstract speculation, reason, universal rules and principles. Women are modest, sympathetic,

127

sensitive and capable of particular judgements, but not principles. In Kant's philosophical universe, this 'charming distinction' leaves women unilaterally unable to attain full ethical agency. Feminist ethics has attempted to confront the impact of such sexist dualisms.

However, given this traditional underestimation, should not feminist ethics welcome the opportunity to award female contributions and feminine characteristics their long overdue recognition of moral or ethical worth? After all, the re-evaluation of ghettoized caring traits has opened up discussions of the role of care-taking and relationships with others within ethics generally, including a much-heralded challenge to notions of disembodied, contextless, autonomous agents. Moreover, women's experience of relationships seem to suggest the permeable nature of boundaries between individual beings, self and other, pointing out possibilities for communication between persons, rather than contracts (Held, 1993: 28). Nevertheless, designations of 'typical' feminine or masculine habits of deliberation, no matter how apparently virtuous, maintain a troublesome and damaging sexist dualism not extinguished even as the value of traits shift. Socialized female and stereotypical feminine traits have long been valued by philosophers as 'charming distinctions' appropriate to women's ways of being, yet this valuing has not changed the overall judgements of female ontological and epistemological potential (see, for example, Card, 1996: 49–71; Sherwin, 1996: 49–54).

Thus, in the field of ethics, and western philosophy generally, the legacy of hierarchical dualism dominates, even in the work of those who in other contexts seem extraordinarily concerned with power, subordination and marginality. For example, Levinas-inspired ethicists elaborating responsibility for, and response to, the Other have not listened to the feminist call for full consideration of histories of subordination both in theory and lived experience. In *Closeness: An Ethics* (Jodalen and Vetlesen, 1997), philosophers working in the 'ethics of proximity' reassert a kind of essential human responsiveness in the face of the Other, but disconnect the apparently related human traits from sexist and racist dualisms.

The ethics of closeness, or proximity, emerge from a phenomenological conceptual lineage, especially from the apparent move beyond phenomenology by Levinas. From this perspective, human beings express their freedom in their response to the Other, not in a cognitive process, not as a matter of contract or reciprocity, but as a precondition to being human (Jodalen and Vetlesen, 1997: 1–19). 'Responsibility means to respond, to respond to the call for responsibility issued wordlessly from the Other and received pre-voluntarily by the subject' (Jodalen and Vetlesen, 1997: 9). This formulation, an example of 'having' responsibility, raises an interesting paradox. The manner of response that a Levinas-inspired intimate ethic lauds is precisely the kind of response demanded of subordinate being, evoking a traditional feminine caring or mothering model (see, for example, Gilligan, 1982; Noddings, 1984). Caring – in particular, feminine trait-based caring – often opposes concern for self with concern for other (Card, 1996), evident when a self-forgetting caring response is held in contrast to alternative modes of being.

Yet, Levinasian responsibility is proposed as simply human (cf. Nietzsche, 1998: 36–37; see also Borgerson, 2001: 82–84). The lack of reflection upon such essential 'responsibility' and, moreover, the failure to acknowledge the shared oppressions of subordinated peoples leaves crucial domains of ethics untouched by the 'bare givenness of intersubjectivity', or a Levinas-inspired vision of human relation (Jodalen and Vetlesen, 1997: 7). To put this another way, the one who must answer *the call* becomes uncritically *feminine* invoking the interrelations of oppressions that share position and characterization in semiotically and existentially relevant dualistic hierarchies.

Indeed, work in feminist theory and philosophy of race suggests that other-centeredness will be recognized most readily in semiotically associated oppressed groups (Gordon, 1997; Stack, 1993). Arguably, the ironic outcome of Levinas' ethics, then, is that the most freedom is found in the groups that have been most enslaved. Whereas this may prove a neat paradox, those who experience embodied lives in oppressive contexts that block human development may well miss the philosophical elegance. In ignoring the critical discourse from, specifically, the field of feminist ethics, proponents of ethical closeness have steered clear of acknowledging the relation between the mode of being they celebrate and the actual circumstances of those who have modelled and still model – willingly or not – those behaviours, regardless of whether there is anything essentially ethical about them (Bell, 1993: 17–48). In other words, the 'proximity ethics' interpretation of Levinas – and arguably Levinas himself – fails to incorporate insights from feminist ethics into the notion of an ethos based in uncompromising intersubjectivity, ignoring the ethical implications of being a particular human being, or kind of agent, in contexts of marginalization, subordination and oppression.

CONCLUSION: FEMINIST ETHICAL ONTOLOGY

In pursuing ethical guidelines and addressing ethical practices, feminist ethical ontology maintains a concern for the existential phenomenological experience of particular forms of being in the process of embodying ethical relations (for example Whitbeck, 1983). Thus, feminist ethical ontology brings feminist ethics' awareness of the subjugated status of certain forms of being to an articulation of ethical theory (Borgerson, 2001). This occasions the conjunction of feminist investigations and existential-phenomenological experience with what Judith Butler has called 'moral ontology' – that is, 'a theory about what a being must be like in order to be capable of moral deliberation and action, in order to lead a moral life and be a moral personality' (Butler, 1999: 5). This requires noting that lack of boundaries between self and Other may have dangerous effects and, moreover, forms the typical situation of oppressed groups.

Feminist ethics and the critical awareness of feminist ethical ontology do more than displace traditional ethical voices, only to assert a 'different' voice with alternative concerns. As illustrated in the preceding discussions, simply asserting the primacy of relationships, recognizing the existence of permeable boundaries between the self and the non-self and questioning the site of agency may fail to attend to the existential-phenomenological realities of intersubjectivity and responsibility – including issues of power – that shed light on business ethics and organizational environments. Moreover, the field of feminist ethics' insistence on residing closer to understandings of lived experience may have a particular attraction – challenging, yet making sense to, those who work in organizational contexts, and who can be expected to invoke on-site experience-based insights that traditionally trained business ethicists may lack.

The underestimation of feminist ethics in business ethics could be viewed as in unfortunate continuity with modes of traditional, privileged, hegemonic philosophical discourse that have ignored, excluded and subordinated marginalized alternative views of the world for too long. Organization studies, a field with its own shadowed subordinations and feminized margins, may well defy the underestimation of feminist ethics, recognizing powerful philosophical opportunities and conceptual innovations.

REFERENCES

Alcoff, L. (1988) 'Cultural feminism versus post-structuralism: The identity crisis in feminist theory', *Signs*, 13(3): 405–436.

Bell, L. (1993) *Rethinking Ethics in the Midst of Violence: A Feminist Approach to Freedom*. Lanham, MD: Rowman & Littlefield.

Borgerson, J. (2001) 'Feminist ethical ontology: Contesting the "bare givenness of Intersubjectivity" ', *Feminist Theory*, 2(2): 173–189.

Borgerson, J. (2005) 'Judith Butler: On organizing subjectivities', in C. Jones and R. Munro (eds) *Contemporary Organization Theory*. Oxford: Blackwell.

Brennan, S. (1999) 'Recent work in feminist ethics', *Ethics*, 109(July): 858–893.

Butler, J. (1999) *Subjects of Desire: Hegelian Reflections in Twentieth-Century France*. New York: Columbia University Press.

Calás, M. B. and L. Smircich (eds) (1997) 'Predicando la moral en calzoncillos: Feminist inquiries into business ethics', in A. Larson and R. E. Freeman, *Business Ethics and Women's Studies*. Oxford: Oxford University Press.

Card, C. (1991) *Feminist Ethics*. Lawrence, KS: University Press of Kansas.

Card, C. (1996) *The Unnatural Lottery: Character and Moral Luck*. Philadelphia, PA: Temple University Press.

Collins, D. (2000) 'The quest to improve the human condition: The first 1500 articles published in *Journal of Business Ethics*', *Journal of Business Ethics*, 26: 1–73.

Crane, A. and D. Matten (2004) *Business Ethics: A European Perspective*. Oxford: Oxford University Press.

Darwall, S. (1998) *Philosophical Ethics*. Boulder, CO: Westview.

Derry, R. (2002) 'Feminist theory and business ethics', in R. Fredrick (ed.) *A Companion to Business Ethics*. Oxford: Blackwell.

Diprose, R. (1994) *The Bodies of Women: Ethics, Embodiment and Sexual Difference*. London: Routledge.

Gilligan, C. (1982) *In a Different Voice: Psychological Theory and Women's Development*. Cambridge, MA: Harvard University Press.

Gilligan, C. (1995) 'Hearing the difference: Theorizing connection', *Hypatia*, 10(2): 120–127.

Goldberg, D. (1993) *Racist Culture: Philosophy and the Politics of Meaning*. Oxford: Blackwell.

Gordon, L. (1995) 'Rethinking ethics in the midst of violence: A feminist approach to freedom', *Sartre Studies International*, 1(1–2): 133–150.

Gordon, L. (1997) *Her Majesty's Other Children: Sketches of Racism from a Neocolonial Age*. Lanham, MD: Rowman & Littlefield.

Gustafson, A. (2000) 'Making sense of postmodern business ethics', *Business Ethics Quarterly*, 10(3): 645–658.

Held, V. (1993) *Feminist Morality: Transforming Culture, Society, and Politics*. Chicago, IL: University of Chicago Press.

Jodalen, H. and A. Vetlesen (eds) (1997) *Closeness: An Ethics*. Oslo: Scandinavian University Press.

Kant, I. (1960) *Observations on the Feeling of the Beautiful and the Sublime*, trans. J. T. Goldthwait. Berkeley, CA: University of California Press.

Lippke, R. (1995) *Radical Business Ethics*. Lanham, MD: Rowman & Littlefield.

McNay, L. (2000) *Gender and Agency: Reconfiguring the Subject in Feminist and Social Theory*. Cambridge: Polity.

May, L. (1992) *Sharing Responsibility*. Chicago, IL: University of Chicago Press.

Nietzsche, F. (1998) *On the Genealogy of Morality*, trans. M. Clark and A. Swensen. Indianapolis, IN: Hackett.

Noddings, N. (1984) *Caring: A Feminine Approach to Ethics and Moral Education*. Berkeley, CA: University of California Press.

Nunner-Winkler, G. (1993) 'Two moralities? A critical discussion of an ethics of care and responsibility versus an ethic of rights and justice', in M. J. Larrabee (ed.) *An Ethic of Care*. New York: Routledge.

Plumwood, V. (1993) *Feminism and the Mastery of Nature*. London: Routledge.

Rawls, J. (1971) *A Theory of Justice*. Cambridge, MA: Harvard University Press.

Sherwin, S. (1996) 'Feminism and bioethics', in S. M. Wolf (ed.) *Feminism and Bioethics: Beyond Reproduction*. Oxford: Oxford University Press.

Shildrick, M. and R. Mykitiuk (eds) (2005) *Ethics of the Body: Postconventional Challenges*. London: MIT Press.

Stack, C. B. (1993) 'The culture of gender: Women and men of color', in M. J. Larrabee (eds) *An Ethic of Care: Feminist and Interdisciplinary Perspectives*. New York: Routledge.

Tong, R. (1993) *Feminine and Feminist Ethics*. Belmont, CA: Wadsworth.

Tronto, J. (1993) *Moral Boundaries: A Political Argument for an Ethic of Care*. New York: Routledge.

Walker, M. (1998) *Moral Understandings: A Feminist Study in Ethics*. New York: Routledge.

Whitbeck, C. (1983) 'A different reality: Feminist ontology', in C. C. Gould (ed.) *Beyond Domination*. Totowa, NJ: Rowman & Allenheld.

Wollstonecraft, M. (1975[1790]) *A Vindication of the Rights of Woman*, ed. M. Brody Kramnick. London: Penguin.

Young, I. M. (1990) *Throwing Like a Girl and Other Essays in Feminist Philosophy and Social Theory*. Bloomington, IN: Indiana University Press.

131

Chapter 8

Race, revolution and organization

Stefano Harney and Nceku Q. Nyathi

INTRODUCTION

What is the relation between race and revolutionary thought? This question has been crucial to the advance of revolutionary thought since at least the 1930s, and it had been moving to the centre of such thought at least since Marx and Engels began to reconsider their position on revolution in Ireland. The double movement of this relation is perhaps best displayed in the intellectual career of W. E. B. DuBois (1970), whose analysis of the colour line prompted him to move toward a revolutionary position on race from the 1930s onward, and whose subsequent achievements also changed the nature of revolutionary thought. After him, as C. L. R. James (1993) would often put it in his own seminal contributions, it became just as impossible to think of race without class, as to think of class without race (Buhle, 1986).

This is not to say that thought did not continue to disable itself by trying to separate these categories, but more on that in a minute. The relations between race and revolutionary thought has subsequently been considered positively, and negatively. Positively it became anti-colonial thought. Here one thinks of a line of thinkers from Jose Rizal (1997) a contemporary of DuBois, in the Philippines, to Frantz Fanon (1963, 1967) perhaps the most exemplary thinker on this relation, to the anti-racist revolutionaries today like Angela Davis (2005) and Mumia Abu-Jamal (2001) in the United States, or the Zapatistas in Mexico, or indeed those parts of the movement of movements from the Global South who insist on autonomy and separation from their Northern comrades.[1] In all of this thought, despite its diversity, the histories of slavery, indenture, colonialism, imperialism and their sciences, their ethics, and their aesthetics, to say nothing of their sexualities and drives, provide the grounds for struggle, rebellion, revolution.

If the positive consideration of this relation produced anti-colonial thought, the negative consideration of this relation produced postcolonial thought. But this is by no means a slight to postcolonial thought. Indeed keeping these consideration together in a relation is the task of anyone interested in revolutionary thought today.[2] But postcolonial thought has been bequeathed the question of how race, and its sciences, ethics, aesthetics, sexualities and drives thwarted a revolution against human history's most total assaults on social being in the name of private gain. This was the project that first came into focus in the universities with Edward Said's (1978) work on orientalism and Gayatri Chakravorty Spivak's (1988) work on the subaltern. The best subsequent work in postcolonial theory would follow the example of these theorists by asking how to think the question of the relation.

ENTER ORGANIZATION STUDIES

Now all of this thought has been marginal to the development of organization studies and in its relation to an undesignated philosophy, the subject of this book. But of course an important lesson of postcolonial theory has been to teach us to ask how the marginal might be of more than marginal importance. This is the hard lesson of marginalizing race in revolutionary thought, and the not very less hard lesson of marginalizing revolution in the thought of race. One thinks of what 'whiteness studies' (Ignatiev, 1996; Ignatiev and Garvey, 1996) has taught us about the damage done to solidarity by marginalizing anti-racist thinking in the first instance (Roediger, 1999). And one thinks of the appropriation of multiculturalism in the second instance (Gordon and Newfield, 1996). So it is probably worth asking why organization studies as it evolved in the 1970s and 1980s did not develop as a discipline dedicated to the relation between anti-racist thinking and what one might call the thought of revolutionary organizational futures, in the positive sense, or between racism and the dominance of the antisocial organizational form, in the negative sense.[3]

Most histories of this relatively young discipline locate its institutional origins in the rise of the British business school drawing together the labour of industrial sociologists, organizational psychologists, and sociologists of organization into a common orbit. The deeper intellectual origins of this discipline follow every academic discipline in being simultaneously 'contested' as Westwood and Clegg (2003) observe and forgotten as Parker (2000) recalls. But we are less interested to start with what is proper to organization studies as it develops, than what is improper to it. Some of these sociologists and psychologists were sympathetic to a revolutionary perspective, and in many cases they were directly influenced by Marxism, especially through the work of Harry Braverman (1974) and sometimes because of contact with radical trade union movements in Britain (Thompson, 1997). And yet if one looks at one major source for an archaeology of organization studies, the papers collected each year from the labour process conferences held in various British universities in the 1980s and 1990s, one cannot argue that the relation of race and revolution prevails or indeed even appears (Knights and Willmott, 1990, but cf. Burawoy, 1982). Race remains improper to the development of organization studies.

In fact looking back at these collections, or the early issues of journals in the field, this now looks like an unreasonable expectation. Why would this relation figure centrally? Yet here it would be necessary to read into the record the postcolonial corpus of writing on 'reason' and the 'reasonable'. Because in fact an academic worker, interested in revolution in the 1970s and into the 1980s in Britain, might well have made this relation central to his or her research. Indeed many did so. One thinks of the founding of the journal *Race & Class* in this period, or classic studies like *Policing the Crisis* (Hall et al., 1978) produced by University of Birmingham's cultural studies researchers, or the sudden growth of Marxist development studies at this time. There is in fact nothing 'unreasonable' about asking why organization studies did not see the centrality of race to revolutionary thought and revolution to anti-racist thinking. It would be difficult, without psychologizing individual researchers, to say why the founders of organization studies made the decision not to move with A. Sivanandan (1982, 1990), Stuart Hall, and so many other researchers who were their contemporaries in this direction. But with Rock Against Racism and the Brixton and Toxteth riots at the beginning of the 1980s, through the Soweto massacre and the genocidal war against indigenous people in Central America in the middle of the 1980s, all the way up to the brutal regimes of the International Monetary Fund at the end of the decade, the choice of direction cannot be put down to parochialism. One could not easily miss the legacy of colonialism, indenture and imperialism in the decades of organization studies' consolidation.

THE FUTURE LASTS FOREVER

Whatever the reasons, this sense of the proper seems to have sealed the fate of organization studies over the next twenty years. Of those thinkers who would have a central influence on the development of organization studies, and could be considered interested in revolution in some sense, none would help organization studies bring together the real question of the twentieth century. Neither Harry Braverman nor Michel Foucault nor Gilles Deleuze stand up very well to a postcolonialist critique. One thinks of Joy James' (1996) work on Foucault, or of Spivak's (1988) famous rebuke to both Foucault and Deleuze. Despite Foucault's brilliant analysis of the founding of nation as race war, he rarely pursued the sciences, ethics, aesthetics and desires that turned up in his archives to their origins in the colonized world (Almond, 2004). And Deleuze's preference for capitalism as desire rather than fetish works better in the superabundance of the overdeveloped world than the scarcity of the underdeveloped world. As for Braverman (1974), his lack of interest in wildcat action is well known, but somehow less often acknowledged is that as scholars from Frederic Jameson (1988) to Fred Moten (2003) have pointed out, the high point of this wildcat action occurred among African American workers, as Braverman was writing his book, a book in which this relation does not feature.

Now one could take issue with any of these critiques. One thinks of the useful way Ann Stoler (1995) reads Foucault to understand desire on the plantation in Sumatra. One could say these thinkers have themselves become marginal in a field increasingly technocratic in its scholarship. But it would be harder to argue that these thinkers have been helpful to organization studies in shining a light on this central relation of race and revolution, anti-racist thought and revolutionary thought. Thus a certain path dependence in the development of the discipline requires now that this discipline regard postcolonial theory as a newly arrived guest, and this indeed is how postcolonial studies have been 'introduced' in recent years into organization studies. This greeting is a strange anachronism, not so much because this guest has been forgotten, as because this guest who has produced this house by her absence is today invited in the front door (Karamali, 2007).

But if postcolonial studies is to be sat at the table, perhaps organization studies should at least be told what it has let through the door, if not told about the door itself. This guest brings not just the hard lessons of neglecting the relation of race and revolution, but also the revolutionary thought of attention to this relation, the positive impulse of the anti-colonial legacy, the potentiality of revolution out of race. Dinner conversation might start with some questions to the host from this inappropriate(d) other, as Trinh Min Ha (1989) once said. And the conversation might drift then toward a positive relation between race and the revolutionary organizing of the social individual, or if you like an organization studies to-come. Indeed the evening's conversation might unsettle the discreet charm of the occasion altogether.

AT TABLE

It might go something like this. To what extent can we understand the political position of the discipline today as the result of this historic neglect of the relation between anti-racist, anti-white-supremacist thought and revolutionary thought? Receiving no answer, our guest might begin: well, if one does not put race at the centre of analysis in the field, one can predict a number of consequences, not least of which will be that revolution too will slip away. First, without an attention to race, one misses the majority of revolutionary organizing that occurred in the second half of the twentieth century. This organizing took place in the developing world, and among developing peoples everywhere. Without attention to the developing world, one misses the majority of revolutionary organizational forms.[4] One misses revolutionary states, parties, movements, art forms and local associations, to name a few. One misses the majority of organizational forces too. Without race at the centre of the analysis, colonialism and imperialism, the forces by which most people in the world were organized in the twentieth century, can be reduced to just peripheral social phenomenon, certainly prior to the North's discovery of globalization four centuries on. Indeed it might be said that a lack of attention to race means despite its best intentions, organization studies never manages to keep its head above the sea of work organizations. The researcher never sees the shores of politics where all the other forms of organizing and organization operate, and therefore one could even say that the discipline's surrender to an overwhelmingly pro-capitalist perspective is less a lack of commitment than a lack of vision. Unable to see the revolutionary horizon that might give the research strength, the researcher drowns in the inevitable sea of the work organizations, never knowing that it was the implicit racism of the field that sealed his or her fate. One does not expect revolution from someone who is drowning.

But that is not all. Because if some researcher does struggle on to the shore and out of the swamp of capitalist inevitability, the habit of blindness continues to drive that researcher into the hands of the enemy. Because most of the lessons of the relation between the researcher and revolution require equal attention to the centrality of race. How to learn the value of indigenous knowledges without Vandana Shiva (1989)? How to explore the praxis of the intellectual without Jose Mariategui (1996)? How to learn about leadership without Paolo Freire (1972)? How to problematize the conditions of work (for instance the racial divide that sees European professors profit from degrees sold in the developing world) without Chela Sandoval (2000)? Even those organization studies researchers who reject the pro-capitalist and Eurocentric bias of their conditions find they have been denied a whole history of struggle upon which to draw for inspiration. They may wish to go forward, but first they would have to go back.

Thus today to seize on the movement of movements as some wish to and to study their form, or contribute to its development, comes with all these problems. The researcher is like an amnesiac in the face of these movements, unaware of the history of revolutionary organization beyond Europe that might help to explain their struggles. This seems particularly urgent now that this movement of movements has entered a kind of dormancy in the shell of the social forums. Equally, to suppose that all of this organizing could be brought into organization studies, instead of organization studies abandoning itself to all of this organizing, is to give the discipline a false sense of battle. Researchers end their days punching the dark, thinking the discipline is a contested terrain while all along the small cell of the discipline's history holds them prisoner.

But against this emerging genealogy of the discipline, the other side of the dialectic of anti-racist and revolutionary thought also comes into view. An embrace of race as the central problematic of the discipline of organization studies makes available an inspiring history of praxis, and makes possible organizational futures that move past the organization, and even more the work organization, as the normative form, and strive for organizing as the project of the discipline, and one might even say the fate of the discipline. It is difficult right now to see what that would look like, and organization studies is a long way from being convinced that it matters, and remains ill equipped for the task. So for those who want to pursue a link to these counter-globalization movements for instance, the danger is that their training tempts them to neglect the relation of anti-racist thought to revolutionary thought, a neglect that will make them quickly irrelevant to these movements, who must themselves struggle with this relation. On the other hand a pursuit of the organization of difference that through race retains its commitment to a critique of capitalism opens up the dialectic of difference and history, both for researchers and movements. It might even finally bring sexuality and feminine difference to the organizing moment that would be this discipline's object.[5] From there, a return to revolution through the study of the forces that organize these differences and the differences that organize these forces appears on the horizon. If organization studies comes to see that it dwells in a house that race built, all of this is possible.

NIGHT

But it is also possible that such a dinner would go badly. That the host would sense a lack of gratitude, a lack of appreciation for all the effort. An awkward silence might tell all it was time to go. Still, on the doorstep that night the guest might say one last thing to the host before going off into the night. The guest might say that race is the dominant organizational form of modernity, and what it does is always remind anyone who pays attention that the organization of the world, and the organizations of the world, are fundamentally antisocial, basically anti-human. Perhaps later that night the host will think about that.

NOTES

1 When we use the term anti-racist thought we mean to invoke a specifically anti-white-supremacist thought born of the struggle against modern colonialism, slavery, and imperialism, and developed in contemporary struggles against neo-colonial, crypto-fascist and continuing white-supremacist forces around the globe.
2 The incessant call for a return to the political in postcolonial studies, rehearsed again in the new collection by Ania Loomba et al. (2005), might be more productively understood as the tension of keeping this antagonism together.
3 Recently there has been some attention to postcolonial theory. See for instance Cooke (2003), Erney (2004), Jack and Westwood (2007), Linstead and Bannerjee (2004), Prasad (2003), Westwood and Clegg (2003). Stella Nkomo also wrote a pioneering anti-racist piece in 1992.
4 Martin Parker (2000) has called for the study of more kinds of organizations but perhaps there is a reason beyond the restriction of the business school workplace for this reticence.
5 For instance a new generation of scholars on slavery point to a dialectic of racial and sexual difference as stolen labour of production and reproduction, a theft that can show up at the heart of English literary fiction as easily as in the fiction of economic man.

REFERENCES

Abu-Jamal, M. (2001) *All Things Censored*. New York: Seven Stories Press.

Almond, I. (2004) 'The madness of Islam: Foucault's occident and the revolution in Iran', *Radical Philosophy*, 128(November/December): 12–22.

Braverman, H. (1974) *Labor and Monopoly Capital: The Degradation of Work in the Twentieth Century*. New York: Monthly Review.

Buhle, P. (ed). (1986) *CLR James: His Life and Works*. London: Allison & Busby.

Burawoy, M. (1982) *Manufacturing Consent: Changes in the Labour Process under Monopoly Capital*. Chicago, IL: University of Chicago Press.

Cooke, B. (2003) 'The denial of slavery in management studies', *Journal of Management Studies*, 40(8): 1895–1918.

Davis, A. Y. (2005) *Abolition Democracy: Beyond Prisons, Torture and Empire*. New York: Seven Stories Press.

DuBois, W. E. B. (1970) *WEB Dubois Speaks: Speeches and Addresses*. New York: Pathfinder.

Evney, H.-G. (2004) 'Postcolonial theory and organizational analysis: A critical engagement', *Organization Studies*, 25: 315–318.

Fanon, F. (1963) *The Wretched of the Earth*, trans. C. Farrington. London: Penguin.

Fanon, F. (1967) *Black Skin, White Masks*, trans. C. L. Markmann. London: Pluto.

Freire, P. (1972) *Pedagogy of the Oppressed*, trans. M. B. Ramos. London: Penguin.

Gordon A. and C. Newfield (eds) (1996) *Mapping Multiculturalism*. Minneapolis, MN: University of Minnesota Press.

Hall, S., C. Critcher, T. Jefferson and J. Clarke (1978) *Policing the Crisis: Mugging, the State, and Law and Order*. London: Macmillan.

Ignatiev, N. (1996) *How the Irish Became White*. New York: Routledge.

Ignatiev, N. and J. Garvey (eds) (1996) *Race Traitor*. New York: Routledge.

Jack, G. and Westwood, R. (2007) *International and Cross-Cultural Management: A Postcolonial Reading*. London: Macmillan.

James, C. L. R. (1993) *Beyond a Boundary*. Durham, NC: Duke University Press.

James, J. (1996) *Resisting State Violence: Radicalism, Gender and Race in US Culture*. Minneapolis, MN: University of Minnesota Press.

Jameson, F. (1988) *Cognitive Mapping in Marxism and the Interpretation of Culture*. Urbana, IL: University of Illinois Press.

Karamali, E. (2007) 'Has the guest arrived yet? Emmanuel Levinas, a stranger in business ethics', *Business Ethics: A European Review*, 16(3).

Knights, D. and H. Willmott (eds) (1990) *Labour Process Theory*. London: Macmillan.

Linstead, S. and B. Bannerjee (2004) 'Masking subversion: Neocolonial embeddedness in anthropological accounts of indigenous management', *Human Relations*, 57(2): 221–247.

Loomba, A., S. Kaul, M. Bunzl, A. Burton and J. Esty (eds) (2005) *Postcolonial Studies and Beyond*. Durham, NC: Duke University Press.

Mariategui, J. C. (1996) *The Heroic and Creative Meaning of Socialism: Selected Essays of Jose Carlos Mariategui*. Atlantic Highlands, NJ: Humanities Press

Moten, F. (2003). *In the Break: The Aesthetics of the Black Radical Tradition*. Minneapolis, MN: University of Minnesota Press.

Nkomo, S. (1992) 'The emperor has no clothes: Rewriting "race in organization" ', *Academy of Management Review*, 17(3): 487–514.

Parker, M. (2000) 'The sociology of organization and the organization of sociology:

Some reflections on the making of a division of labour', *Sociological Review*, 48(1): 124–146.

Prasad, A. (ed.) (2003) *Postcolonial Theory and Organizational Analysis: A Critical Engagement*. New York: Palgrave Macmillan.

Rizal, J. (1997) *Noli Me Tangere*. Honolulu, HI: University of Hawaii Press.

Roediger, D. (1999) *Wages of Whiteness: Race and the Making of the American Working Class*. London: Verso.

Said, E. (1978) *Orientalism: Western Conceptions of the Orient*. London: Penguin.

Sandoval, C. (2000) *Methodology of the Oppressed*. Minneapolis, MN: University of Minnesota Press.

Sivanandan, A. (1982) *A Different Hunger: Writings on Black Resistance*. London: Pluto.

Sivanandan, A. (1990) *Communities of Resistance: Writings on Black Struggles for Socialism*. London: Verso.

Spivak, G. C. (1988) 'Can the subaltern speak?', in N. Cary and L. Grossberg (eds) *Marxism and the Interpretation of Culture*. Urbana, IL: University of Illinois Press.

Stoler, A. L. (1995) *Capitalism and Confrontation in Sumatra's Plantation Belt, 1870–1979* (second edition). Ann Arbor, MI: University of Michigan Press.

Thompson, P. (1997) *The Nature of Work: An Introduction to Debates on the Labour Process*. London: Macmillan.

Trinh Min Ha (1989) *Woman, Native, Other: Writing Postcoloniality and Feminism*. Bloomington, IN: Indiana University Press.

Vandana, S. (1989) *Staying Alive: Women, Ecology and Development*. London: Zed.

Westwood, R. and S. Clegg (eds) (2003) *Debating Organization: Point-Counterpoint in Organization Studies*. Oxford: Blackwell.

Part Three

Illuminations

Chapter 9

Workers of the world . . . relax!

Introducing a philosophy of idleness to organization studies

Norman Jackson and Pippa Carter

INTRODUCTION

Overwork is a problem, and constitutes the underlying cause of manifold further problems in contemporary society. This much is relatively uncontentious, as evidenced by a voluminous literature rehearsing these ills and/or proposing ameliorations from the palliative to the surgical (see, for example, Bunting, 2004; Hardt and Negri, 2000; Thoburn, 2003). The important point here concerning this literature is that it does not belong to, is not admissible to and does not inform the discourse of organization studies. It would seem that these issues ought to be central to organization theory yet it and the discourse of organization studies (OS) more generally – including much of what describes itself as critical management studies – has little to offer other than coping strategies (see Fuglsang, Chapter 4 in this volume).

An obvious potential solution to the ills of work and overwork might be to do less of it, but this possibility remains generally unarticulated within that discourse. This is hardly surprising since the critical issues that prefigure any kind of solution – most importantly, the interrogation of the general principles that inform the organization of work – also remain unarticulated, indeed inadmissible. The discourse of OS, thereby, even lacks a language with which to express either the problems or their possible solutions. By reference to the exposition of Deleuze and Guattari (1994), of 'small p' philosophy, we suggest a means to introduce a language of relevant concepts to the discourse of OS. As an example, we explore the qualities of idleness, as developed in Russell's (1935) essay, as a concept, and its possible utility in addressing the problems of work and overwork. We suggest that idleness has the potential to be precisely the sort of 'small p' philosophical concept that should gain presence in organization theory to enable more 'workable' solutions to a problem that the discourse of OS *claims* the prerogative to solve.

What do we mean by *work*? Obviously, it is a very complicated concept and

143

activity. For our purposes here, it is important to distinguish between work as the expenditure of energy and work as it is associated with 'waged labour', organized work, employed work. It is this latter that is particularly relevant to the well-known depredations of work, psychologically, socially, economically, environmentally, and it is in this sense that we use the term. What do we mean by *overwork*? This term signifies work required beyond what is necessary, however that is defined, and characterized in concepts such as surplus repression (Marcuse, 1969) and dressage (Foucault, 1977; Jackson and Carter, 1998) and 'production for production's sake' (Thoburn, 2003: 2). There are two particular issues to be considered in the problem of overwork: the hours spent working and the intensity of work in those hours.

Both issues are intimately connected to questions of what is necessary and what is unnecessary work. The matter of hours spent working has been the principal site of contestation, especially over the past 250 years, as control of the work process became a function of capital rather than of labour. Every attempt to reduce working hours meets the same furious resistance – this is certainly characteristic of the present era, where, whenever reductions in working hours have been achieved (as in the case of the 35-hour week in France, for example) or seem to be about to be achieved (as in the case of the European Union's Working Time Directive, for example), this provokes attack, expressed in the rhetorical language of incontrovertible truth that we cannot 'afford' it, we must work more, not less. Some commentators argue that a 'natural' reduction in the demand for work will occur, driven by, say, developments in technology (see, for example, Beck, 2000). However, there is little evidence that the absolute demand for labour is reducing. Freeing up labour for 'not-work' would seem to go against the carceral and governmental roles of work in helping to create 'docile bodies', at a time when such control tends to be increasing rather than decreasing (Foucault, 1991; Jackson and Carter, 1995). Witness also the proposals currently in the United Kingdom to curtail early retirement and to delay the normal retirement age. But, if overwork is a problem now, even keeping things as they are, much less demanding more work, is not going to solve those problems.

WORK: VIRTUE OR VICE?

An important factor in the problem of finding a positive language with which to talk about not-work, and in the problem of the admissibility of such a language to the discourse of OS, is the elevation of work to the status of an essential good in itself. It could be suggested that, over time, this essential goodness of work has accumulated more and more layers of justification and legitimization. To start with, there was the idea that work was a moral duty – the means of entry into Heaven and eternal bliss – particularly associated with, for example, the Protestant Work Ethic. By the nineteenth century the doctrine of self-improvement saw work as not only a moral duty but also the means to economic betterment for the individual. The twentieth century saw a refinement of the idea that work is simply a means to an end – work became not only the source of moral and economic benefit but also a source of psychological benefit. Two examples are worthy of note. The now ubiquitous concept of self-actualization symbolizes the idea that the creative urge is to be satisfied through, and at, work. Another accretion, sometimes referred to as 'the latent functions of work', is the idea that it is through work that we find the means to satisfy our duty and desire to contribute to society. Jahoda (1979) implies that we need work to give our lives structure and order and to enable us to gain a positive 'civic identity'. By now, work is a total product – it gets you into Heaven, it is the means for improving your material situation, it makes you happy and a virtuous citizen. It is, now, not only for social benefit, but also for your own well-being, morally, materially and psychologically. So, we are told, the more of it the better!

Freud also notes the significance of work, as necessary for society to function and, for the individual, to attach one to 'reality', but, most importantly, as a channel for using up libidinal energy. But he also notes that 'as a path to happiness, work is not highly prized by men. They do not strive after it as they do after other possibilities of satisfaction' (Freud, 1963: 17 n1). How can this be so? Not surprisingly, however, there is an equally long, parallel, tradition of thinking which offers a rather different understanding of the impact of organized work. There is, for example, the Catholic tradition, in which work might be encouraged to enrich the Church, though for mammonish reasons rather than theological ones, but was not seen as directly relevant to morality or to salvation. By the nineteenth century the social reform movement was seeking to improve conditions of work and of workers to resemble more closely the enlightened ideal of modern society and included in its ranks many industrialists and employers. In the twentieth century the argument that the concept of the essential goodness of work is merely part of an ideology whose function is to legitimate, and gain acceptance of, control and repression, both at work and in society more generally (for example, Anthony, 1978; Bendix, 1966; Doray, 1988) has gained many adherents. Throughout there has been a veritable litany of the profound dysfunctions of the way work is organized, nowadays almost daily rehearsed in the news, as well as in learned publications.

There seems to be an utterly unbridgeable gap between these two traditions. They seem to exist almost independently of each other, the critical view being simply the negative of the positive view. There is little, if any, debate between them. Of course, those who manage work, whoever they may be, are not totally blind to the possibility that organized work has some undesirable impacts, but their response comes principally in the form of coping strategies. These may range from teaching people to manage their stress, or their time, to strategies such as empowerment (see, for example, Collins, 2000), and the encouragement to be wholly committed to 'the organization', so that, perhaps, whatever the costs of work and overwork might be, they seem to be worth it! These strategies, on one hand, merely address the symptoms of the problem and, on the other hand, normalize it, reinforcing the dogma that

145

work is a good in itself. They mask the nature of the problem and shift responsibility for it from manager to managed. Instead of being a problem of managerial exploitation, overwork becomes a problem of worker inadequacy. These strategies reinforce the positive view of work, which is, in any case, dominant. And, because of the majoritarian position of the status quo, it can safely ignore any minoritarian challenge presented by the critique of it (Carter and Jackson, 2004).

Why are we so willing to work so hard and so long? Why are we so willing to believe, or to be persuaded, that the costs are worth the benefits? Why are we so willing to cooperate in our own repression? Deleuze and Guattari (1984) offer the explanation that people (are persuaded to) pursue their (manufactured) desires even though these desires conflict with their interests – with the effect that 'desire is determined to desire its own repression' (1984: 372). Accepting that benefits do accrue from (employed) work itself, it can be demonstrated that not only does intensified work not bring intensified benefits, but also it actually depletes such benefits. Even if, for example, it is accepted that work links one to reality, more work makes this link more tenuous, rather than stronger, since one of its effects is that one only has time to experience the hyper-reality of organized work. As regards satisfactions, Cooper (1974) points out that they are not an issue of 'productivity outcomes'. As long ago as the 1920s, Myers demonstrated that intensifying work beyond a certain point would lead to negative benefits (see, for example, Rose, 1978). (As far as entry into Heaven is concerned, however, we are not able to comment.) There is, of course, the economic argument that more work equals more money. But this link is by no means inevitable, especially where the issue is intensification, and as Deleuze and Guattari (1984: 373) point out, even where 'wage increases and increases in the standard of living are realities . . . exploitation grows constantly harsher'. In other words, the price of betterment is more repression!

THE WORK OF PHILOSOPHY

For all that is known about work from these two polar positions, it is still not possible to answer the question 'How much work should we do?' Could Philosophy help? The problem for Philosophy as a discourse is that it has never produced a transcendent explanation, only a wide range of incommensurable interpretations of the world. In an epoch in which knowledge is judged by the dominant criteria of science and of utility, this has led to it becoming discredited – the 'end of philosophy' argument (see, for example, Baynes et al., 1987) – and perceived as inferior to science, if not actually useless and irrelevant. Whereas Science could produce demonstrable answers to (technical) problems, all Philosophy could do was to produce an apparently chaotic spectrum of generally undemonstrable propositions. In Philosophy there is no common purpose, it inevitably generates an expanding multiplicity of claims to represent Truth. This is a difficulty for Philosophy as a discourse because of the ways in which that discourse has defined its task. It has construed itself as the guardian of rules, standards and norms for thinking, and its purpose as 'the search for unchanging truth, that it assigns eternal values, and that it is the determination of a foundational Absolute or invariable transcendence' (Hayden, 1998: 69). This vision of the role of Philosophy is one which, according to Deleuze, 'stops people from thinking' (Deleuze and Parnet, 2002: 13).

During the Modernist epoch, characterized by the search for universal truth(s) embodied in the laws of nature, the contradictions of Philosophy were both unhelpful and inadmissible. But, with the postmodern abandonment of the search for truth in nature, the potential multiplicities inherent in Philosophy can be seen as not just unproblematic, but both inevitable and positively necessary. The very quality of Philosophy which had been seen as its fatal weakness can be reconstrued as its special strength. Ironically, it is not just a generalized strength, but also a strength vis-à-vis Science, since it is now more readily recognized that there are problems to which Science cannot provide an answer but to which a philosophical approach at least might offer a range of possibilities within which an answer might be found. This, however, is not simply to rehabilitate Philosophy as a discourse, which largely remains a cacophony of competing claims to represent Truth. The postmodern view of Philosophy is not merely to welcome a manifestation of pluralism within which there is a potential, dialectically or otherwise, to resolve differences towards a rationally achieved consensus (though this seems to remain a discursive ideal) — for example, from a poststructuralist viewpoint, such a consensus would simply become another version of discursive domination. This view is one that welcomes not outcomes, but *process*. In the phrase of Deleuze and Guattari (1994: 17), philosophy should be 'the expression of a possible'.

PHILOSOPHY AND PHILOSOPHY

It might be said that (big P) Philosophy (following Rorty, 1982) is concerned with meta-theorizing, with grand narrative, with the search for ultimates, and it is these concerns that serve as constraints on the kinds of explanation that it is able to offer. This Philosophy exhibits all the characteristics of a Foucauldian discourse, with its rules of inclusion and exclusion, rules about who can speak, what can be said and how it can be said. Like a Kuhnian normal paradigm, it has become institutionalized. As in any discourse, the concern with enforcing the rules limits utility for solving problems because the rules are not only about knowledge, but, especially, about power. Deleuze comments that this Philosophy is repressive and 'a formidable school of intimidation' (Deleuze and Parnet, 2002: 13). It is precisely this utility that is recaptured by thinking about (small p) philosophy as a process, and this is the particular radical rethinking of philosophy that is offered by Deleuze and Guattari (especially 1994). For them, philosophy is definitely not 'contemplation, reflection and communication'

(1994: 6), it is a profoundly creative and constructive process with the sole purpose of contributing to the solution of problems. Because of this focus, philosophy also *cannot* be about fitting explanations, ideas and concepts into some greater unity: 'philosophical concepts are fragmentary wholes that are not aligned with one another so that they fit together. . . . They are not pieces of a jigsaw puzzle but rather outcomes of throws of the dice' (1994: 35). 'Small p' philosophy is minoritarian (see also Thoburn, 2003) and so 'by definition has no model; it is itself a becoming or a process' (Smith, 1998). It is 'the theory of multiplicities' (Deleuze and Parnet, 2002: 148). This is what we signify when we call 'small p' philosophy 'philosophy as a process'.

'Small p' philosophy performs the crucially necessary task of creation of *concepts*. While in Science the concept is reductive and fixed, itself an end state, measured against Science, for philosophy the concept is never fixed, always becoming, measured against potentiality rather than against discursive authority. Concepts are not, and should not aspire to be, simple, they are multiplicities, and multiplicities are not just given, they must be made. Concepts are rigorous and internally consistent, each distinct but not discrete because they are related, internally and externally, historically and paradigmatically, with other concepts. Concepts should be innovative in the sense that they create a new 'event', perhaps that they stimulate a new awareness or way of thinking about a problem. As Deleuze and Guattari note, 'we require just a little order to protect us from chaos' (1994: 201), and this is the very function that the concept performs: 'it refers back to a chaos made consistent, become Thought. . . . And what would *thinking* be if it did not constantly confront chaos?' (1994: 208, emphasis in original). The concept is a window onto chaos, not to order it or to reduce it, but to recognize it, to make it sensible – perhaps, thinkable.

It is because concepts have history as well as becoming that thinking about philosophy as a process is not about discarding the many philosophies that are contained within Philosophy, the discourse. But it *is* about re-examining them to recover their potential, their vitality and mobility, to undermine their alleged canonical status – it is, perhaps, to recognize that they are texts. In this way, texts can be released from the constraints of discourse, because, above all else, for Deleuze and Guattari (1994: 22), philosophy is *non-discursive*. It is, and should be, an integral component of all knowledges, its purpose to reveal possibilities. It is not about replacing Science, it is there to do what Science cannot do, there not to reflect what is, but for the continuous production of difference, and to be critical. Philosophy should concern itself with 'critique of transcendent realms, causes, values, principles, and affirmation of a dynamic, fluid and immanent world where humans exist and create diverse ways of living' (Hayden, 1998: 68). But, as philosophy should be a rigorous and creative process *oriented* to the solving of problems, it cannot merely content itself with critique, it must also generate new concepts and ideas with which to think the possible. And critique cannot concern itself only with manifest problems, or indeed problems that are defined as problems by, for example, those with power, or Others.

148

It should also, perhaps especially, question the taken-for-granted. As Marks (1998: 23) notes, for Deleuze and Guattari, 'philosophy is a matter of posing questions rather than proposing solutions' (see also Spoelstra, Chapter 3 in this volume).

WOULD IT WORK?

It is worth noting that Philosophy and philosophers have had a long tradition of reflection on organization in general, and on work in particular. More recently, however, organization and work, and the organization of work, as objects of study, have become 'ghettoised' in the discourse of OS, which has claimed them as part of its prerogatives and has excluded philosophers as legitimate contributors to the discourse (see also Burrell, 1988). It might be claimed that philosophy has re-entered the discourse of OS through the contemporary development of the field of organiza-tional/managerial ethics, and ethics does have much to say about how people should be treated at work. But the contribution of ethics to *this* discourse obviously needs to legitimize itself through organizational and managerial utility, and does not generally deal with the topic of work itself.

Yet overwork is a well-known phenomenon, and work more generally is notorious for the dysfunctions that it produces, for people and for society. While this is recognized within the discourse, the best that it is able to offer as remedy are palliative strategies which address symptoms rather than causes. To suggest that to generate genuine remedies it may be necessary to address the fundamental principles govern-ing the organization of work itself is, so far, inadmissible within the discourse because these principles have, effectively, been placed beyond question. While the organization of work at the micro level is, and has been, much debated within the discourse – it might be said that it is *the* topic of significance in some aspects of the discourse, such as organizational behaviour – the macro level principles of the organization of work are very rarely interrogated and, in almost all speculations about how work might be organized and what criteria should be included, this is taken-for-granted. The debates usually come down to arguments about how the costs and benefits, both material and immaterial, should be distributed. Whatever might be done to increase productivity or to overcome the dysfunctions of work and overwork, for example, must be accom-plished within that unquestioned, and unquestionable, framework. But perhaps there cannot be an effective remedy without such questions.

The most parsimonious solution to the dysfunctions of work is to do less of it. The difficulty with this kind of proposal, however, is that it questions the a priori place of the role of labour in capitalist production and is therefore part of the inadmissible in the discourse. The limited vocabulary of the discourse does not allow space or opportunity for discussion of such a contraposition. This is why there is a need to turn to 'philosophy as a process'. If the disconsolations of work are to be alleviated, rather than merely coped with, concepts from outwith the boundaries of the discourse of OS need to be appropriated. And such concepts *are* to be found, new to OS, but not in themselves new. The opportunity is there to recapture such concepts, to interrogate their components in terms of their potential applicability to the increasingly urgent problems of work and overwork. If, for example, these problems were re-expressed as over-exploitation of a resource, then immediately a large range of concepts becomes available to explore the issues – ironically, most, if not all, of these concepts refer to the over-exploitation of natural resources and have not crossed over into possible application to 'human resources'. As if humans are unnatural!

A particularly relevant case is that of extensification of resource usage prominent in agriculture, where it is recognized that there are benefits to be gained, both socially and to the resource itself, by deliberately reducing the exploitation and productivity of that resource below what is actually possible. So, for example, the medieval practice of allowing fields to lie idle periodically was a response to awareness of the dysfunctions of over-exploitation. The American dustbowl of the 1920s was clearly attributable to over-cropping, arable and animal, later regarded as catastrophic. Contemporary practices such as set-aside are recognized as having a range of benefits, including aesthetic value, as well as reducing production. The popular shift to organic and free-range farming benefits both consumer and resource – interestingly, the factory farming of animals is seen as cruel, unhealthy and degrading, while the 'factoryization' of humans barely raises an eyebrow. It is increasingly widely accepted that, systemically, there is synergy to be gained from the extensification of agricultural resources (apart, of course, from labour). Why should not these benefits be generalized to include the world of work?

Within the discourse of OS, 'work' is an object that is well defined, well understood and freely spoken of, but its opposite, 'not-work', is notable by its absence. Certainly, there are ideas such as 'leisure', but this is seen as exogenous to work, to which it can be accommodated. For example, it is important that leisure activities do not impinge on the ability to work; workers can be refreshed by 'sensible' leisure activities; provision of corporate leisure facilities can encourage loyalty, and so on. Phenomena such as laziness and idleness, on the other hand, are not acceptable – they should not occur, they should be proscribed. A lazy worker is a functional pathogen and must either be 're-educated', or excised. Idleness is a deadly sin, acedia, against both God and Capitalism. According to Seneca, 'nothing is so certain as that the evils of idleness can be shaken off by hard work'. So, by this creed, labour intensification combats evil! The manager who requires work *forte et dure* is a virtuous person, preventing workers from falling into wicked ways! So it is hardly surprising that words such as 'lazy' and 'idle' cannot be spoken positively within the organizational discourse. How transformative it would be, then, if a concept that claimed that the dysfunctions of work could be 'cured' by the simple strategy of requiring less work to be done – labour extensification, for example[1] – were to appear within the discourse. Should such a concept become legitimized within the discourse, related concepts would lose their terrors (see, for example, Carter and Jackson, 2005). If it might be a good thing to ask people to do less, laziness and idleness could become just available 'tools' for achieving this end, some among other possibilities. As Deleuze and Guattari note (1994: 19), concepts contain other concepts that can be liberated from the historically negative usage that has defined them. And, crucially, new concepts will introduce new thinkers.

WORKING ON IDLENESS

Though the discourse of OS is, as yet, a barren ground on which to look for a viable and critical language of not-work, there is work of potential value in generating such a language to be found in Philosophy. Among others, there is Lafargue, whose humorous and ironic 1883 pamphlet, *The Right to be Lazy*, was immensely popular (Derfler, 1991). Lafargue is particularly eloquent on the collusion of workers in overwork: 'A strange delusion possesses the working classes of all nations where Capitalist civilisation holds sway . . . This delusion is the love of work' (Lafargue, 2002: 9). His description of the problems and impacts of over-production and over-consumption could, in some respects, have been written yesterday. However, we have selected another example – Russell's 'In Praise of Idleness' (1935) – to illustrate. This might be regarded as an unusual choice, because Russell's particular brand of Philosophy is, perhaps, the one least amenable to metaphysical speculation, logical positivism (and it is certainly interesting to reflect on whether Russell would have been able, given time and inclination, to validate his claims in this essay in terms satisfying the imperatives of logical positivism). But perhaps 'In Praise of Idleness' should not be seen as Philosophy at all? Perhaps this is Russell the social commentator, rather than Russell the philosopher? Perhaps these are just labels? Do these labels matter, in this context? We would suggest not. On one hand, 'In Praise of Idleness' is a text, available to be used as required, and on the other hand, from the perspective of philosophy as a process, what does matter is the *concept*, rather than any specification of where it should be located within the discourse. The concept of idleness is not an integrated, integumented entity to be described, but a potential multiplicity to be explored for its possibilities and for what it might contribute to understanding, in this case, the problems of work and overwork. Russell does not take the status quo of practice regarding work as something merely needing fine-tuning to be perfected, but proposes a radical reassessment as a way of addressing the recognized ills of work. In particular, he offers a language with which to talk about not-work, and has something to say about the values that might inform the application of Science in this respect, especially about to whom the benefits of Science should accrue, and how they should be distributed.

Russell's view is that work is just a necessary evil: 'a great deal of harm is being done in the modern world by belief in the virtuousness of WORK, and . . . the road to happiness and prosperity lies in an organized diminution of work' (1935: 13,

151

emphasis in original). He argues that this belief is merely the product of the powerful convincing the powerless that it is their duty to work hard, that the powerless should prioritize the interests of their masters rather than their own because their masters' interests are identical with the 'larger interests of humanity' (1935: 15). He further notes that the 'necessity of keeping the poor contented . . . has led the rich, for thousands of years to preach the dignity of labour, while taking care themselves to remain undignified in this respect' (1935: 21)! In summary, Russell's argument is that a certain amount of work is necessary, but that it should be kept to a minimum. It should be shared out and rewarded equitably, rather than, as is the case both then and now, doing more work than is necessary and distributing both it and its rewards inequitably. In this respect he identifies three groups: the rich, who do little work and get a disproportionately high share of the benefits, a large group who do most of the work but receive only a small share of the benefits, and unemployed people, who are not allowed to do any of the work or to share in the benefits, other than as recipients of the largesse of the state. The contribution of Science, Russell argues, should be to reduce the amount of necessary work, not to find 'better' ways of doing ever more work. This is not shocking or subversive. What Russell proposes is, simply, a 'rational' allocation of the costs and benefits of work throughout society. In Russell's argument, the time freed up by this minimization of time and effort spent at work would enable everyone, rather than just the privileged few, to pursue 'the good life' – what would, in another (philosophical) language, be called authentic existence.

Thus, significantly, what Russell means by 'idleness' is absence of employed work, *not* absence of activity. The central tenet of his argument is that people should have the freedom to 'spend' the benefits that they gain from employment in any way that they might choose. Some might choose to sit in the sun, some 'self-improvement', some to pursue dreams. In any case, work should be recognized for what it is, a means to some other end, not the be-all and end-all of existence that it is, explicitly or implicitly, claimed to be. In any case, since work as it is currently organized is profoundly alienated – for example, working for someone else's benefit – this ought to be seen as, at least, a demoralizing, if not actually an immoral, claim. Russell suggests that four hours per day is probably enough work to satisfy the requirements of comfortable survival and there is some empirical, as well as anecdotal, evidence to support this figure – as well as a manifest desire on the part of some workers to achieve a four-hour day (see, among many examples, www.iww.org and www.fourhourday.org). It must be acknowledged that Russell addresses only the issue of reduction of hours of attendance at work, and does not venture into the question of the intensity of work during that attendance. Nonetheless, there is here the basis of a philosophy of labour extensification.

Of course, all this might be seen as utopian (small u). However, Marcuse (1988), for example, is not alone among critical thinkers in arguing that we need to be *more* utopian, not less so. While cautious about particular usages, such as transcendent, or authoritarian, utopias, Deleuze and Guattari (1994) argue:

Actually, *utopia is what links* philosophy with its own epoch . . . it is with utopia that philosophy . . . takes the criticism of its own time to its highest point. . . . The word utopia therefore designates *that conjunction of philosophy, or of the concept, with the present milieu.*

(Deleuze and Guattari, 1994: 99–100, emphases in original)

There may also be, perhaps, some resonance with what Smart (1992) terms 'realistic utopias', associated, for example, with Gorz (for example, 1989). These utopias do not seek to envisage ideal forms of life but to identify 'scope and potential for considerable improvement in the condition of humanity' (Smart, 1992: 67). The point is that things could be 'better' than they are, and it is important to think both desirable ways of defining better and means to achieve this. Russell's (1935) proposals do offer possibilities.

Whatever the particular heritage of Russell's essay on idleness, it can be argued that in the idea of idleness itself there is potentiality for the development of a *concept* appropriate to philosophy as a process and relevant to the discourse of OS. It addresses the problems of the dysfunctions of work and overwork and is innovative in its potential to ask new, different and critical questions about the intrinsic values of work and its organization, thus offering the possibility of a different, and new, range of solutions to these problems. At the same time, it has a history (which can also, potentially, be adduced to address these problems), as part of a significant critique of the organization of work, a critique long excluded from the discourse of OS on grounds of admissibility in respect of its 'form', but which is of direct relevance in respect of its 'content' to the problems that the discourse claims to address. Its critique of what is, is complemented by a creative speculation on what could be. It resists the reductionism characteristic of much of the discourse, of seeing the person who works as no more than 'a worker', and seeks to reinstate a much more complex and multiple view of the components which should inform our understandings of work and its organization. In the process, it also offers a rigorous distinction between imposed work and work in itself, a distinction long elided within the discourse by the assumption that work is only to be understood as employed work in the service of capitalism. In particular it opens to question the hitherto usually unquestioned governmental principles of the organization of work.

WE CAN WORK IT OUT

It is no use looking to management or organization theories to ask questions about how much work we should do, because it is simply not (yet) admissible in that discourse to raise such questions (or, if it is, it is assumed that the answer must be *more*). Russell's essay is not didactic, in that it proposes that we should all work less, but does not try to specify how that might be organized. This ought to be of interest to anybody, both in terms of how much work one might need to do and, for managers and potential managers additionally, in terms of how much work it is reasonable to demand from others. If it can be demonstrated empirically that managers demand too much work from people, as the acknowledged occurrence of dysfunctions suggests, then the question of how much work is reasonable inevitably raises important further questions about, for example, what might be a persuasive characterization of the role of managers – disinterested technicians contributing to social and economic betterment? Agents of ownership? Crucial elements, wittingly or otherwise, of the Foucauldian system of governance? Administrators of the carceral function that work organizations might be argued to serve? These questions ought to be of major significance, especially to managers and potential managers, not least because they represent existential issues related to their sense of self – decentred or otherwise. It must be possible to question the catechism of the supposed verities of work as a good in itself, to say the unsayable, to admit the inadmissible, to challenge the regime of truth.

There are many concepts that the discourse of OS seems to seek to exclude automatically, but which are of direct relevance to the issues and problems that the discourse claims to address. Yet the magnitude of these problems suggests that discursive niceties ought to be less important than consideration of any possibilities which might contribute to their solution. What (management) Science has been unable to achieve might be facilitated, or even just illuminated, by Philosophy, especially, we have proposed, by the particular sense of philosophy developed by Deleuze and Guattari, philosophy as a process.

The majoritarian meta-theory of work as a good in itself is one that, rhetorically, presents itself as Truth – indeed, as Truth so obvious that it does not need to be spoken. What is needed, however, is precisely that this supposed Truth be reopened to question. These are not trivial matters. The implication of Russell's (1935) essay is that questions about how much work is necessary and/or reasonable are based on questions about the 'meaning of life' itself, Is life to be lived, or to be spent? Russell offers the potential, in an average working life, to remit twenty years of work, or to gain twenty years of 'idleness'. Can this really be such a repellent proposition? What about gaining some time to think about some genuine and profound change?

NOTE

1 Labour extensification does already exist as a term, though rarely used, that refers to lengthening the working day, while labour intensification, as a term, generally refers to the rate at which work is performed. Thus, both terms refer to the requirement to produce more and we intend to consider them both as intensification. This releases the term labour extensification to refer to any effort to reduce the amount of work done, which could be achieved by reducing the number of hours worked and/or the rate at which it is done. This brings it more into line with the sense of resource extensification in agriculture, from which we take our inspiration.

REFERENCES

Anthony, P. D. (1978) *The Ideology of Work*. London: Tavistock.

Baynes, K., J. Bohman and T. McCarthy (eds) (1987) *After Philosophy*. Cambridge, MA: MIT Press.

Beck, U. (2000) *The Brave New World of Work*, trans. P. Camiller. Cambridge: Polity.

Bendix, R. (1966) *Work and Authority in Industry*. New York: Wiley.

Bunting, M. (2004) *Willing Slaves: How the Overwork Culture is Ruining our Lives*. London: HarperCollins.

Burrell, G. (1988) 'The absent centre: The neglect of philosophy in Anglo-American management theory', *Human Systems Management*, 8(4): 307–313.

Carter, P. and N. Jackson (2004) 'Gilles Deleuze and Felix Guattari', in S. Linstead (ed) *Organization Theory and Postmodern Thought*. London: Sage.

Carter, P. and N. Jackson (2005) 'Laziness', in C. Jones and D. O'Doherty (eds) *Manifestos for the Business School of Tomorrow*. Turku: Dvalin (www.dvalin.org).

Collins, D. (2000) *Management Fads and Buzzwords*. London: Routledge.

Cooper, R. (1974): *Job Motivation and Job Design*. London: Institute of Personnel Management.

Deleuze, G. and F. Guattari (1984) *Anti-Oedipus: Capitalism and Schizophrenia*, trans. R. Hurley, M. Seem and H. R. Lane. London: Athlone.

Deleuze, G. and F. Guattari (1994) *What is Philosophy?*, trans. H. Tomlinson and G. Burchell. London: Verso.

Deleuze, G. and C. Parnet (2002) *Dialogues II*, trans. H. Tomlinson and B. Habberjam. London: Continuum.

Derfler, L. (1991) *Paul Lafargue and the Founding of French Marxism 1842–1882*. Cambridge, MA: Harvard University Press.

Doray, B. (1988) *From Taylorism to Fordism: A Rational Madness*, trans. D. Macey. London: Free Association Books.

Foucault, M. (1977) 'The eye of power', in C. Gordon (ed.) *Power/Knowledge*, trans. C. Gordon, L. Marshall, J. Mepham and K. Soper. London: Harvester.

Foucault, M. (1991) 'Governmentality', trans. C. Gordon in G. Burchell, C. Gordon and P. Miller (eds) *The Foucault Effect*. Chicago, IL: University of Chicago Press.

Freud, S. (1963) *Civilization and its Discontents*, ed. J. Strachey, trans. J. Riviere. London: Hogarth Press.

Gorz, A. (1989) *Critique of Economic Reason*, trans. G. Handyside and C. Turner. London: Verso.

Hardt, M. and A. Negri (2000): *Empire*. Cambridge, MA: Harvard University Press.

Hayden, P. (1998) *Multiplicity and Becoming*. New York: Peter Lang.

Jackson, N. and P. Carter (1995) 'Organisational chiaroscuro: Throwing light on the concept of corporate governance', *Human Relations*, 48(8): 875–889.

Jackson, N. and P. Carter (1998) 'Labour as dressage', in A. McKinlay and K. Starkey (eds) *Foucault, Management and Organization Theory*. London: Routledge.

Jahoda, M. (1979) 'The impact of unemployment in the 1930s and the 1970s', *Bulletin of the British Psychological Society*, 32: 309–314.

Lafargue, P. (2002[1883]) *The Right to be Lazy and Other Studies*, trans. C. Kerr. Amsterdam: Fredonia.

Marcuse, H. (1969) *Eros and Civilization*. London: Penguin.

Marcuse, H. (1988) *Negations: Essays in Critical Theory*, trans. J. J. Shapiro. London: Free Association Books.

Marks, J. (1998) *Gilles Deleuze*. London: Pluto.

Rorty, R. (1982) *Consequences of Pragmatism*. Minneapolis, MN: University of Minnesota Press.

Rose, M. (1978) *Industrial Behaviour*. Harmondsworth: Penguin.

Russell, B. (1935) 'In praise of idleness', in *In Praise of Idleness and Other Essays*. London: Unwin.

Smart, B. (1992) *Modern Conditions, Postmodern Possibilities*. London: Routledge.

Smith, D. W. (1998) 'Introduction', in G. Deleuze, *Essays Critical and Clinical*, trans. D. W. Smith and M. A. Greco. London: Verso

Thoburn, N. (2003) *Deleuze, Marx and Politics*. London: Routledge.

Chapter 10

Messing up organizational aesthetics

Samantha Warren and Alf Rehn

INTRODUCTION

It is virtually a truism that philosophy represents purity. It is the search for the true nature of things, and the final word on a subject. Its unequivocal logic in argument and premise is a kind of thinking 'beyond the veils', trying to find the Wizard if you will. In this view, philosophy stands as a form of monomaniacal thinking of the kind where a philosopher can spend a lifetime pondering the minutest thing in all its sublime variations and forms. This might not be the only way to think the nature of thinking, but it is a powerful one which has provoked many of the most profound critiques of philosophy – such as those of Ludwig Wittgenstein (1958), Gilles Deleuze (1990) and Richard Rorty (1979).

Some common ways of viewing philosophy (or even Philosophy) seems to be about not being distracted by the variations inherent in a thing, but to cut through to its essence – philosophy as divine reduction (cf. Badiou, 1999). Such reduction is, for some, right and proper when it comes to philosophical thinking as it keeps us focused – keeps the baby in the bath-water where it is supposed to be. At the same time, regarding philosophy as a single, simple thing may be a somewhat romantic view of the activity of thinking. Such a view sees it as an interesting but inert phenomenon, rather than as a manifold of energies, and thus assumes that there is a way to utilize philosophy to reach the philosophical, with no cost or translation involved along the way. In other words, it thinks philosophy as an efficient thing – an economical process.

Our claim is that this is exactly the problem with philosophy harnessed for the sake of organization studies – that it has been seen as philosophy '*in use*', and has been thought of as a pure and economical process. Our contention is more in line with that of Ruud Kaulingfreks (Chapter 2 in this volume), that philosophy shouldn't be understood through the category of use and that, strictly speaking, perhaps it can't be used for anything other than generating more concepts and questions.

But we wish to take this argument further and point out that when philosophy *is* used, as despite our protestations it will inevitably be, it shows us another aspect of itself, namely that of the manifold. Rather than thinking of philosophy-in-use as a tool for 'cutting to the quick', we argue that what makes this such a forceful mode of thinking is the sheer spectrum of illuminations it brings – some murky, some radiant – and not the way in which it can penetrate an issue. Paraphrasing Ludwig Wittgenstein, the light of philosophy (in use) is much like that of a reading lamp. This illumination is not the glare of the flashlight but more like that of a candle, always bringing flickering shadows and tricks of light. It is a manifold light, lighting, obscuring and creating new visions all at once. This is the strength and weakness of philosophy, and our interest lies with one instance of this manifold.

This instance refers to a kind of switcheroo, where one mode of argumentation almost imperceptibly carries another one with it. Although the various subfields of philosophy seem to refer to neatly delineated spheres of potential human knowledge – areas such as the theory of knowing, the theory of argument, the theory of the good life and so on – this holds true only in a very limited sense, and the reality of philosophical argument is that it continuously mixes these spheres, creating hybridity. Looking to the history of thought, this is evident and even laudable. The early stages of Western thought clearly didn't play with boundaries, and as for instance Nietzsche (2000) intimates in *The Birth of Greek Tragedy*, the separation between wise person, prophet and art critic is a late invention. Still, it is an invention that has gained great currency, as is evident in the increasing fragmentation of knowledge in post-industrial society. Indeed, many do not only treat the fields of knowledge as discrete and bounded, but also extend this purification into the separation of yet smaller subfields.

Herein lies a rub, and again the thinking of Wittgenstein (1958) may be of some service. He noted that although words and concepts may seem like separate things, they shared what he called 'family resemblances'. In the same way two sons may both look like their father – in a way conceptually carrying him – but still not look alike, concepts sometimes almost blur into one another so that the only way to tell them apart is to observe their use and context. The same word, even denoting the same kind of concept, may mean different things depending on the place they occupy in a language game. For instance, somebody saying 'Oh, your argument is simply sublime!' may do so in a sycophantic, adoring or highly ironical manner, but nothing in the word or the statement (or even the inflection) will tell us which. The word 'sublime' can thus carry several meanings, and often more than one at the same time – for example, the satirical use of the word depends on there being a possible non-satirical usage. Something similar can happen with philosophical arguments. By necessity, their status as statements means they carry with them certain other sentiments and notions through family resemblances, for example: the non-problematic, taken-for-granted assumptions that make it possible to share meaning and understand each other. Consequently, the perfectly formed argument may well be a fairly marginal phenomenon, if it exists at all. It is perhaps more realistic to recognize that most philosophical statements are likely to carry with them unvoiced philosophical claims – babies with the bath-water.

We will work with one form of such bath-water in particular – aesthetics – and the attempt to use this in organization studies. Our claim here will be that the usage of this field of philosophical theorizing to grasp issues in and concerning organizing processes has, unwittingly, brought in much that was never (consciously) planned to be part of the discourse. More to the point, we will argue that the baby in this aesthetic bath-water can be named, and that her name is Ethics, second name Ideology (and such a lovely girl too).

ORGANIZATION STUDIES AND AESTHETICS

It is no exaggeration to state that the philosophical subfield of aesthetics has become quite fashionable in organization studies. With books such as Rafael Ramirez's (1991) *The Beauty of Social Organization*, Antonio Strati's (1999) *Organization and Aesthetics*, the works of Pierre Guillet de Monthoux (1993, 2004), as well as collected editions by Linstead and Höpfl (2000) and Carr and Hancock (2003), the field has been blessed with seminal works, discrete schools, and the potential for splintering. Both lauded as an important avenue for development, and chided for being naive and superficial, the art and aesthetics movement in organization studies has managed to position it as, at the very least, a discussion to be engaged with. Still, the aesthetics-in-organization-theory debate has suffered from being less than clear as to what its aims are.

In part this is obviously due to the problem of defining aesthetics, and the poly-valence of this concept. However, referring yet again to Wittgenstein, we argue that this is a non-problem. As with all abstract concepts, the word 'aesthetics' contains a multitude of understandings, most overlapping and some even contradictory. But despite the frenzy for definition among some scholars, this is not a real philosophical problem. Rather, it represents the normal state of language which is never at rest even though thought may try to be. Instead, we have to operate with the manifold directly. Non-scholastic engagement with such concepts deal with the myriad of understand-ings and the continuous slippage from one definition to another, so why shouldn't we? This said, it is important to acknowledge the different meanings that aesthetics has been imbued with by the field of organization theory, in order to get a feel for the ways this philosophical construct has been employed. Among these we can find *at least* the following: aesthetics as shorthand for knowledge derived from the senses, as a specific research methodology, as a specific literature/theoretic debate, as simply 'Art', as the theory of beauty, and so on. To try to find some common definition that would adequately encompass all these is as futile as the idea of the perfect definition is fallacious (cf. Welsch, 1997; Wittgenstein, 1958). Thus, we are here concerned only with delineating some of the fault-lines in the discussions regarding aesthetics and organizing, while trying to inquire into their specific underlying themes.

One distinct dividing line in this discussion is drawn through the concern with art. On the one hand, there are those who simply wish to bring the techniques and presence of Art into the sphere of Management which is assumed to be sterile and defined by calculative rationality. Although a blind belief in the panacea of art is sometimes blatantly essentialist, this is also a mode of argumentation that tries to link management to the romantic tradition of *Bildung* – furthering the humanist tradition in general. On the other hand, there are attempts to utilize aesthetics as a way to engage with organizing phenomena, i.e. the application of the philosophy of art and beauty to the organized world. This part of the debate has engaged with philosophical works in a more sustained and stringent fashion, and quite a lot of the argumentation within this field has built on the idea that a specific aesthetic philosophy can be deployed within the sphere of organization theory. For instance, Pierre Guillet de Monthoux has, in his works, consistently argued for Kantian aesthetics as a way to understand value-creation, while Carter and Jackson (2000) argue that a philosophically informed reading of aesthetics can be used to understand distancing and alienation in contemporary capitalism. Such a view works less from an understanding of art or the production thereof, and more from the analytical possibilities we can find in what is assumed to be a subset of philosophy. Thus, this latter mode adheres to a specific tradition in organization theory, namely the 'poaching' of theory from other academic disciplines and suggesting ways in which insights from these can be utilized in the study of organizing.

Now, what is interesting here is that both these approaches, which often have a somewhat antagonistic relationship to each other, actually build on a similar notion, for both assume that the curious manifold of knowledge and experience that can be lumped together under the heading of aesthetics can be utilized in organizations – or at least in the study thereof. Succinctly put, regardless of approach, the assumption is that aesthetics can be used to achieve some other, higher end. We will return to this point.

In addition, or in parallel, to the division between Art and aesthetics we can find a separation that, for example, Strati (2000) has insisted on. On one hand, we have a discourse on the aesthetic qualities of *objects*, where aesthetics is something which is tied into things, as properties. On the other we have the aesthetic sensation of a *person*, so that aesthetics refers to something within the individual – such as a feeling, an emotional engagement, desire and so on. Interestingly enough, and for want of better words, this 'separation' between the internal and the external aspects of aesthetics neatly coincides with a number of similar inside–outside pairings in organization and management discourse and of course attests to the fact that Cartesian ideals still live on in our conceptualizations. Important here, however, is how aesthetics has been seen as something that can have all of organization as its domain, from the common thing to the highest faculties of human cognition. Through this insistence on these aspects, aesthetics is imbued with at least the potential to be a master-concept, encompassing all. Even the indiscriminate use of it would thereby be acceptable due to the total character of its domain.

A third, and for our present interest more pertinent, set of differences can be identified through the general timbre of the argument – by ascertaining whether a scholar views aesthetics and organization in an optimistic or a pessimistic light. More specifically, one of the main (if often tacit and implicit) criticisms of aesthetics as a project within organization studies has been that it adopts an uncritically optimistic view of what can be achieved by using such a framework. Aesthetics has, in this mindset, become a way to make organizations 'better', or at least improve living conditions for those within them. Indeed, some organizational scholars seem to have a boundless faith in the potential for art to improve and develop organization and the organized. Reading some of the contributions to the debate on organizational aesthetics, one is left with the feeling that some scholars honestly believe that allowing for finger-painting, improvised theatre, or jazz, one could abate or cure most if not all organizational ailments. This has led the field (somewhat but not completely unfairly) to be lumped together with various New Age-movements and Potato-Printing-for-Profit!-workshops.

Not unsurprisingly, the field has reacted with its own backlash, specifically by way of adopting a far less cheery outlook on organizational aesthetics. This pessimist mode of organizational aesthetics has more of a cachet, but comes with its own problems. Here, critical engagement and speaking truth to power is seen as more philosophically astute than the somewhat frivolous praising of beauty and sensuous knowledge. Aesthetics has become yet another thing to be picked apart for signs of oppression, hegemony and general corporate malfeasance. Superficially, this critical turn would seem more theoretical and reflective than its happily upbeat counterpart, indeed this has been its main rhetorical weapon: silly optimism combated by serious doubting and the wrinkling of brows.

However, from a philosophical standpoint, little seems to separate these approaches. For instance, even though the later, critical writings of Philip Hancock (2002, 2005) stand in stark contrast with *The Art Firm* (Guillet de Monthoux, 2004), there is one common thread to these works. Both want to present a specific picture of the world using aesthetics to further that goal. For Guillet de Monthoux aesthetics stands for a better future world, one where art is the corporations' major value-producing function and galleries are the business schools. For Philip Hancock, aesthetics stands for a way in which the corporate colonization of everyday life is being increasingly effected and thus can effectively be analysed through that lens. Even though the two may disagree on why aesthetics is important, and whether the attitude towards it should be celebratory or wary, both nonetheless strive to utilize it for some other goal – to make organizations good, or as a reason why they are bad.

Unfortunately, here be monsters. Aesthetics in and of itself is obviously insufficient for such claims and, as for example, Immanuel Kant argues in *The Critique of Judgment*, the philosophic field of aesthetics does not deal in purposes, but in encounters with objects that are 'purposive without purpose' (Kant, 1952). By contrast, the field of organization studies is *all about* purpose: describing, explaining, understanding, contesting, challenging and attributing meaning to processes of organizing *for a reason* and not just because we think it is a nice thing to do in and of itself. Therefore, the idea of apprehending something for its own sake and free from personal motive sits uneasily with the goals of organization studies. It also cuts to the heart of our argument, as discussed below and beginning with a brief excursion through Kant's 'analytic of the beautiful' (Kant, 1952).

KANT, AESTHETICS AND ORGANIZATION STUDIES

For Kant, there are four conditions for our appreciation of beauty, which he describes as 'moments'. Although discussed separately, these four concepts are evoked simultaneously in the aesthetic judgements: disinterest, universality, finality and common sense.

- *Disinterest* As noted above, true philosophical aesthetic judgement (which Kant calls 'the beautiful') is in essence 'disinterested' and therefore independent of any personal motive or desire, or indeed any consideration of the conceptual/ontological properties of the object itself. This quite obviously makes the implicit claims of organizational aesthetics inherently problematic.
- *Universality* In Kant's second moment of beauty resides the claim that true aesthetic judgement is universal. According to Kant, everyone will react in some way when confronted with an aesthetic object since they are apprehending it without personal motive. Therefore, although the experience is a uniquely subjective one (because it is experienced by the subject) it is also universal. So long as an aesthetic experience is a 'pure' one (free from individual motive or interest), then it logically follows that the experience will also be a universal one: for example, everyone will feel *something* even if those somethings differ.
- *Finality* The third moment of beauty is the principle of finality; the idea that aesthetic experience exists for its own sake and no other purpose. 'We *dwell* on the contemplation of the beautiful because this contemplation strengthens and reproduces itself' (Kant, 1952: 64, emphasis in original). It is perhaps this moment of Kantian aesthetics that has held the most sway among organizational scholars, since it is a lack of purpose that seems to clearly mark out the aesthetic from other judgements made on the basis of sense perceptions. Strati (1999: 82) talks of this in terms of what he calls 'sensible finiteness' to distinguish the aesthetic from those emotionally infused experiences which are end directed. He gives the example of workers who arrange their work instruments in a pleasing manner and suggests that they are organizing the objects in their surroundings simply because it is pleasing to do so and not because it makes their job more straightforward or their endeavours more efficient.
- *Common sense* Kant's fourth moment of beauty deals with the *necessity* of common sense in the universal properties of aesthetic judgement sketched out above. Universality does not rest on the fact that there are inherently 'beautiful' aesthetic properties *in* objects themselves that are independent of the subjects who

apprehend them, only that some reaction – of whatever kind – is felt. The precise attractiveness (or otherwise) of objects is shaped by what Kant calls 'common sense' and we might call intersubjectivity. To reiterate the difference between universality and common sense for clarity, we can read the universal as meaning that everyone who apprehends an object aesthetically will have some kind of reaction, whereas common sense refers to the categorization of those reactions as beautiful or ugly, for example.

It is the import of this 'common sense' and the problems of defining aesthetic experience in terms of disinterestedness that our argument in this chapter turns upon, and here that we also diverge from Kantian ideals. Throughout Kant's philosophy there is an insistence on separation and boundaries, for example: the divide between a priori and a posteriori truths, between that which can be reasoned from thought alone and that which can be known through the senses – objectivity–subjectivity, concepts–empirics. Indeed, his forceful argument for the universality of morality and the categorical imperative stands tantamount to his belief that pure (practical) reason is untainted by the relativist concerns of the empiricist. By contrast, our argument rests on the assumption that outside of the philosopher's thought experiment, these spheres cannot be delineated so neatly. Therefore, while we embrace the undoubtedly comprehensive *structure* of Kant's aesthetic theory, we see perversions in the application of these ideas in organization studies.

What we want to argue is that philosophy-in-use is never simple, and that 'doing philosophy' is always a play with manifolds. Philosophical statements are often highly impure, amalgams of several statements where ethics, aesthetics, politics, power relations, logic and irrationality (to name a few) coexist and co-influence. That we could approach the disinterestedness of, for example, Kantian aesthetics when making claims in organization studies is not only overly optimistic, it may point to a critical fault-line between the two fields, and the very thought of a field such as organizational aesthetics (ethics, or anything else for that matter), divorced from the other aspects and parts of philosophy, is thus highly suspect. What is needed, then, is reflection as to what the manifold of philosophy means, and how the utilization of aesthetics should be understood. We are not, however, condemning the use of philosophy in organizational analysis, or the application of ideas about aesthetics either; we are merely reacting on the problem of dragging in a set of notions about the world only to assume that one has total control of what this subset means and how it works. To do so would be to take an *un*-philosophical approach to philosophy, and imagine that the manifold can be put under the same managerial auspices organization studies subjects everything else to.

ORGANIZATIONAL AESTHETICS AND IMPURITY

Indeed, it seems perfectly clear to us that there can *be* no aesthetics without ethics and associated political concerns and, likewise, aesthetics cannot be divorced from the particular ideology that the aesthete is embedded within. Making judgements about the world that meets our senses is to discriminate between different categories of thing. To implicitly or explicitly pigeon-hole people, events, things, happenings and so on as either beautiful, pleasing, fun (= good), or ugly, dull, repulsive (= bad) is a matter not only of aesthetics, but of ethics too. Of course, none of this would be important if judgement calls were morally innocent and had no ethical repercussions, but they do — and so by extension does aesthetics. A simple example is that 'good art' is worth a lot of money and 'bad art' is not. Likewise, organizations in a contemporary, aestheti-cized, image-driven economy that have the right look and feel to their product/brand (read: most-likely-to-result-in-more-profits) can surely add several zeros to the bottom line of their balance sheets.

It may be true to say that there is a certain category of sensations we might call aesthetic experiences that — in extreme cases — move us into a state of sublimity or rapture. These fleeting instances lead to conjecture that there can exist a kind of pre-reflexive aesthetic purity, free from the concerns of either ethics or ideology. These experiences may indeed form the proper stuff of Kantian aesthetics, duly purposeless, non-end-directed, existing 'just because' and connecting us in universal appreciation to the noumenal world of forms (as when one 'goes off in one' gazing at the branches of a tree swaying in a summer breeze, for example). But, generally speaking, these experiences are not of especial interest to organization studies since they cannot generate knowledge of anything other than themselves. Of course, aesthetic sensations are experiential grist for the judgemental mill, but our point here is that such 'pure' experiences are not the only ingredient in the mix, nor are they terribly useful to the organizational scholar.

For example, in Strati's (1999) example given above about the arrangement of workspace, how can aesthetics be separated from the more practical issues of where someone places their tools and belongings at work? Moreover, to what extent is such a distinction *desirable* in organization studies? What use is a feeling that exists only for its own sake and doesn't refer to anything outside itself? Even scholars using organiza-tional aesthetics as a methodological tool (cf. Strati, 1999) need their subject matter to reveal *something* about organizational life. Surely, it is insights into the utilitarian, economic, moral and personal aspects of organization that we hope attention to aesthetics will provide. Strati (1999) advocates the aesthetic approach as a way to *know* organizations, to understand the actions, artefacts and events that make them up in a way that complements and/or challenges more logical or cognitive interpretations of them. If the end result of this knowledge is simply that one person finds an organiza-tional arrangement pleasing or displeasing, for example, then we have probably not learned very much by employing an aesthetic approach to our research. The key point is that, for our purposes as organizational scholars, we may not *want* to divorce the practical-utilitarian from the aesthetic in our respondents' experiences. As Worth (cited in Gagliardi, 1996) suggests, aesthetic appreciation is 'written into the eye' and thus what we consider to be pleasing (or displeasing) is inextricably caught up with psychological, cultural and practical factors. Consequently, if we explore *why* and *how* a person came to their judgement we may learn much about the politics, intricacies and detail of life in this organization.

Thus, it is aesthetic *judgements* and not experiences *per se* that most interest the scholar of organizational aesthetics. The beauty of a well-formulated strategy, the boredom of workday routines, the delight in the 'warmness' of a brand or embarrassment felt when dressed in frumpy corporate livery are all matters of taste that have a bearing on organizational life and do, of course, offer us valuable insights. But aesthetic judgements can never be pure in the sense that we might contend aesthetic experiences could (at least in theory) be. They implicate a whole host of other issues apart from the disinterested sensuous apprehension of an external object that characterizes aesthetic experience. This is key to our premise that philosophical thinking always entails bringing in more than is bargained for, bringing those babies in with the bath-water.

First, aesthetic judgements are ideological because they are learned reflections of particular cultures' preferences, reified matters of taste if you like, that are maintained and reproduced by those with the power to dominate such cultural motifs. The old adage about beauty being in the eye of the beholder is simply not true. Although there are undoubtedly differences in individuals' aesthetic preferences, people with similar habitus have remarkably similar tastes – after all, that is how fashion works and how aesthetics functions as a cultural code.

The argument has most notably been made in relation to the historical depiction of women in art as laid bare for the devouring male gaze (Berger, 1972) and the debate continues to rage in critical analyses of pornography, the portrayal of images of an idealized female form in fashion magazines, and the rise of the ubiquitous überthin Supermodel. We can also trace back the relatively modern aesthetic predilection for picturesque countryside and dramatic mountain scenes to the Victorian invention of travel with all its associated connotations of exploitation of natural resources and pollution/damaging of the environment (Featherstone, 1991). In neither of these examples are aesthetics pure or given outside the prevailing ideologies of the time and we would suggest, thinking of them as such ignores the ethical consequences of these judgements (see Eagleton, 1990).

Historically we might refer to the iconographic power of the Church or the art of the bourgeoisie as arbiters of cultured aesthetic tastes – today we are probably more likely to look to the videos of barely adolescent pop-stars, ring-tones of mobile phones, conspicuous clothes of the celebrity or latest redesign of a sports equipment manufacturer's logo as dictates of modern style. Regardless, our point remains that whoever and whatever inscribes the aesthetic code of the day they/it are acting from an ideological position that is inextricably bound up with the aesthetic produced or consumed – an observation that cannot help but crowd our bathtub.

Aesthetic judgements are also grubby in another sense. As eloquently observed by Martienssen (1979) in a now rather dated article in the *British Journal of Aesthetics*, knowledge of the aesthetic is simultaneously sensuous, emotional, intellectual and cultural with each element infusing the other in a continuous feedback loop – as we noted above, the experience of the aesthetic is something quite different to knowledge about it, especially in organizational settings rife with asymmetrical power relations and replete with moral and ethical concerns. Put another way, there can be no such thing as a purely aesthetic response in organizational or any other sphere of life because once the experience is recognized for what it is – a reaction to something, it becomes shaped, molded, infused and inscribed with everything we already know and think about that something. Translated into organizational terms, can corporate aesthetics – say McDonald's golden arches, Nike's swoosh, or Virgin's logo – ever be understood *outside* the web of cultural meanings they produce, engender and reflect? If that were the case then branding and the whole business of corporate aesthetics management would be a pretty useless activity – marketers absolutely rely on the fact that aesthetic symbols are decoded semiotically by their beholders to convey particular meanings – that's the whole point.

CONCLUSION: BRINGING IN BABIES

Most scholars of organizational aesthetics would accept that aesthetic signs and symbols can be manipulated for corporate ends – this is of course the assumption that underpins the critical camp we outlined above. What we find intriguing is that despite this, there seems to be an assumption in many corners that the aesthetic experiences of organizational members, or the researcher themselves are somehow free from these ideological pressures and that *their* experiences of the aesthetic are the pure ones, with no hidden agenda and no ethical implications. This seems to be compounded too by the difficulties of *expressing* aesthetic experiences in any authentic sense and the inadequacy of language in conveying what Suzanne Langer (1957) calls these 'felt meanings'. Even more astounding is the notion that organizational scholars could disengage themselves from their ideological and ethical frameworks, throw themselves into the purifying waters of the aesthetics, and emerge pure as the driven snow. Given the conventions of our discipline, all research accounts in the main are written texts (maybe with a few pictures thrown in for good measure). Language, as we know, is not neutral, and the language of the aesthetic, whether in music, painting, potato-printing or macramé is no different: it constructs a certain version of truth.

To conclude, what intrigues us here is that despite what we have argued in this chapter, the idea that the aesthetic (and perhaps more commonly art) opens out onto a space that is untainted, truly emancipatory and offering opportunities for authentic becoming and expression of the self is strangely pervasive in accounts of organization and aesthetics. Whether in the giddily celebratory parlance of Pierre Guillet de Monthoux's (2004) *The Art Firm* or the melancholic wariness of Philip Hancock's (2002) 'Beautiful Untrue Things' the possibility – in the first instance – of engendering such an authentic aesthetic and – in the second – of protecting it from valorization, is clutched onto with a vice-like grip.

Succinctly put, the crystal-clear water, that some seem to imagine will run into their tubs if they just turn on the right philosophical tap, doesn't exist. Of course, none of what we have argued here should be read as advocating that aesthetics or any other branch of philosophy should be kept out of organization studies. Neither are we suggesting that the examples and authors we have given here are particularly guilty while others lie blameless. Nor do we automatically see instrumentality in employing an aesthetic perspective as a problem, as we hope the foregoing shows. However, what we are calling for is a more informed importation of philosophy into organization studies, one that recognizes the manifold of the ideas entailed, emphasizes their interconnectedness and is not ignorant of the frictions produced as they rub up against one another.

So yes, aesthetics is imbued with ethics, much as ethics is imbued with aesthetics, and both are connected to logic as well as a whole host of power dynamics and issues of political economy. This is not a mistake, nor a weakness, but the very point of *using* philosophy, the thing that gives it strength and makes it an important endeavour. The path of philosophy when applied to organization studies, or any other aspect of life, is not simple or efficient. It will lead us wrongly, it will confuse us, it will mess us up. And this is good. The problem with organizational aesthetics is that it has often assumed that a slice of philosophy would bring greater purity and clarity to organization studies, when this simply isn't how philosophy works. On one level we agree with Wittgenstein's claim that philosophy can never do anything except try to bring peace of the mind to the philosopher. We also agree with his observation that believing philosophy solves problems beyond itself means that one simply doesn't understand it. However, this is the very nature of human thinking – endless dialogue and engagement with thought. The activity of thinking can call itself many things – the search for truth, the solving of the world's problems, the love of wisdom, Philosophy – but in the end, it is an activity that strives to understand what it means to be human, warts and all.

REFERENCES

Badiou, A. (1999) *Deleuze: The Clamor of Being*. Minneapolis, MN: University of Minneapolis Press.

Berger, J. (1972) *Ways of Seeing*. London: Penguin.

Carr, A. and P. Hancock (eds) (2003) *Art and Aesthetics at Work*. Basingstoke: Palgrave Macmillan.

Carter, P. and N. Jackson (2000) 'An-aesthetics', in S. Linstead and H. Höpfl (eds) *The Aesthetics of Organization*. London: Sage.

Deleuze, G. (1990) *The Logic of Sense*, trans. M. Lester. New York: Columbia University Press.

Eagleton, T. (1990) *The Ideology of the Aesthetic*. Oxford: Blackwell.

Featherstone, M. (1991) *Consumer Culture and Postmodernism*. London: Sage.

Gagliardi, P. (1996) 'Exploring the aesthetic side of organizational life', in S. Clegg, C. Hardy and W. Nord (eds) *Handbook of Organization Studies*. London: Sage.

Guillet de Monthoux, P. (1993) *Det sublimas konstnärliga ledning* [*The Artistic Management of the Sublime*]. Stockholm: Nerenius & Santérus.

Guillet de Monthoux, P. (2004) *The Art Firm: Aesthetic Management and Metaphysical marketing*. Stanford, CA: Stanford Business Books.

Hancock, P. (2002) 'Aestheticizing the world of organization: Creating beautiful untrue things', *Tamara: Journal of Critical Postmodern Organization Science*, 2(1): 91–105.

Hancock, P. (2005) 'Uncovering the semiotic in organizational aesthetics', *Organization*, 12(1): 29–50.

Kant, I. (1952) *The Critique of Judgment*, trans. G. C. Meredith. Oxford: Clarenden.

Langer, S. (1957) *Philosophy in a New Key* (third edition). Cambridge, MA: Harvard University Press.

Linstead, S. and H. Höpfl (eds) (2000) *The Aesthetics of Organization*. London: Sage.

Martienssen, H. (1979) 'A note on formalism', *British Journal of Aesthetics*, 19(1): 144–146.

Nietzsche, F. (2000) *The Birth of Tragedy*, trans. D. Smith. Oxford: Oxford University Press.

Ramirez, R. (1991) *The Beauty of Social Organization*. Munich: Accedo.

Rorty, R. (1979) *Philosophy and the Mirror of Nature*. Princeton, NJ: Princeton University Press.

Strati, A. (1999) *Organization and Aesthetics*. London: Sage

Strati, A. (2000) 'The aesthetic approach in organization studies', in S. Linstead and H. Höpfl (eds) *The Aesthetics of Organization*. London: Sage

Welsch, W. (1997) *Undoing Aesthetics*. London: Sage.

Wittgenstein, L. (1958) *Philosophical Investigations*, trans. G. E. M. Anscombe. Oxford: Basil Blackwell.

Chapter 11

Singular plurality and organization

Ignaas Devisch

INTRODUCTION

I remember a review a few years ago of a book on continental philosophy, criticizing it for using difficult words like 'singularity'. Besides the rather banal character of this remark, it is very much to the point that singularity is indeed a difficult and vague concept. Maybe its difficulty has something to do with the fact that it is well known. Well-known concepts always have a particular effect on readers and users of it: because it is well known, out of a sort of political correctness, we all have to pretend as if we understand what we are saying. Of course, we have to do this all the time, we all are liars in a sense, although it can never be our aim.

Above that, the French word *singulier* is used in diverse contexts. One look at the web and one finds within this category a design shop (www.singulier.com), an art gallery (www.art-singulier.com), a pottery, etcetera. The word 'singularity' is also an important concept in technological contexts, used in future studies, meaning the technological creation of smarter-than-human intelligence. There are many technologies in this genre, like artificial intelligence or direct brain–computer interfaces, biological augmentation of the brain, genetic engineering, and so on, brought to us by the Singularity Institute (www.singinst.org).

To summarize, one can say that 'singular' might mean everything, which is often the case with fashionable concepts. To give only one more example: in a cooking programme on TV, the local chef was quarrelling about the 'deconstruction of his menu'. Maybe within a few years, he will serve his guests 'singular beans' or 'buffalo mozzarella with singularized tomatoes'?

Let us therefore limit ourselves to contemporary continental philosophy in our search for the meaning of the word singularity and possible applications of it in the context of organization. Let us also, for the sake of the argument and maybe also for the sake of philosophy, at least pretend that we do not understand what singularity means, as if we are 'dummies'. Maybe this is a fruitful starting point to unravel this frequently used concept and to evolve in this topic from 'dummy' to 'smarty'.

To begin with, let us ask ourselves the question: 'What is singularity?' Although this seems at first sight to be the easiest way to know something about singularity, maybe the above question is too shorthanded. I know at least two persons who would erase it with all the means they have: Martin Heidegger and Jacques Derrida, two major figures of twentieth-century philosophy. Heidegger and Derrida were at their best when they analysed a philosophical question as such. From their work, we know that the way we question something always already determines our answer. To apply this immediately to our question: what would/could have been their objections?

I think it would be something like this: with asking for a 'what', we ask for an essence of something. If we ask, for example, 'What is a chair?' – we presuppose there is an essence of the object chair that can be denoted by a well-formulated description that makes mention of all the essential parts of the chair. Similarly, if we ask for the 'what' of singularity, we ask for its essence for we presume, like Aristotle would have done, that there is one to ask for. The question of the 'what' is therefore backed up by the ontological claim that things in the world have an essence and that man can grasp this essence by defining it.

Seen in the light of this, the question of what is maybe the worst one to describe singularity. If authors mention the word 'singular', most of the time they refer to something that is rather ungraspable and unique, something hasty or fluid. These are, of course, not characteristics that will lead us towards the substance or essence of singularity. It rather appears to be the other way round: the lack of any essence seems to be the only essence of singularity. But how then to describe it, if we cannot ask the question what it is? How to define something that disappears as soon as it is defined? Before despair takes us over, let us deal with two texts which possibly can clarify this 'aporia'. The first one is *Being Singular Plural*, a major study by the French philosopher Jean-Luc Nancy (2000), a thinker who has been, as far as I can see, largely ignored by organizational scholars (cf. ten Bos, 2006). The second text is by the same author and is called 'Un sujet?' (Nancy, 1992). Each of these texts reflects on singularity in a way which I consider to be characteristic for contemporary continental philosophy. Moreover, Nancy is in the discussion about singularity an outstanding voice. In this chapter, I will therefore refer to only a few other sources and focus on Nancy.

In a first step, I try to shed light on possible meanings of the concept under discussion here and the philosophical assumptions that go with it. In other words, we should ask ourselves why singularity is such a central and crucial concept in contemporary philosophy. Second, I want to clarify why singularity does not stand in oppositional relationship to concepts such as 'substance' or 'unity' but should rather be understood as an event, as something that happens or acts in such a unique and undividable way as to tell us something about existence in general. Third, I want to look at some questions that are relevant for the context of organization. I will argue that debates about singularity are very pertinent to the widespread attention of organizational scholars for issues relating to identity and subjectivity (for example Parker, 2000; Linstead and Linstead, 2005).

WHO COMES AFTER THE SUBJECT?

Assuming that singularity has no essence does not entail it is impossible to describe the concept. One of the most interesting descriptions, even though it is a rather negative one, comes indeed from Nancy:

> The singular is this indivisible unity, thus it is not something connected to an essence, be it a soul, the spiritual version, or a body, the material version. Its singularity is its unity as a unique existence. This is what is at stake with the decisive category of the singular, in so far as it is perhaps not even a category . . . The singular is not precisely classifiable, it is the act by which one leaves behind classification, by which one leaves the logical and cognitive order of substance.
>
> (Nancy, 1992: 99–100)

The implication of the quote is quite clear: singularity 'is not'. It is neither a substance nor an essence and perhaps it is not even a category. It is clear that Nancy works in the footsteps of Heidegger and Derrida. He stipulates here and there a few things, but like his teachers he refuses to ask for an essence and describes singularity primarily in negative terms. Nevertheless, with the above description, we know at least something. Singularity stands for an undividable unity and a unique existence that does not manifest characteristics which are oftentimes associated with concepts such as 'substance' or 'subject': a long-lasting unity, a self which endures for the time of its existence and which stands in opposition to the world. Nancy tries to point out something about the use of the word 'singular': the reason why it is so frequently used nowadays is related to the philosophical ways in which the subject has traditionally been understood. When one uses the word 'singularity', one oftentimes wants to make a philosophical statement against well-entrenched philosophical traditions.

Nancy argues that nowadays we can no longer unproblematically use the word 'subject' as a category that adequately describes our existence. Since Derrida, since Heidegger, and even since Kant, the category of the subject has been called into question. We can no longer deal with the subject as we did in the seventeenth century. Taking issue with rationalist or empiricist understandings of the subject, Nancy believes, should be a central task for contemporary philosophy and not only for philosophy. Looking at the titles of one of the books that he co-authored, *Who Comes after the Subject?* (Cadava et al., 1991), one gets an impression of how philosophy might perform this task. The question about what will come after the subject is also the main thread of 'Un sujet?' In order to shed light on singularity, we will have to go deeper into this discussion.

THE SUBJECT: THREE MOMENTS OF SUSPICION

According to Nancy, the subject is a self-productive entity which permanently grounds itself as the platform on which not only the outer world but also the self is presented. The subject can be seen as present-to-itself or as 'being-at-itself'. (In other words, it is a 'substance' or 'supposition of the self': Nancy, 1992: 53, 83). Connected to this description, Nancy specifies three moments in the history of Western philosophy during which the subject came under suspicion and he relates these moments to three authors: Kant, Heidegger and Derrida.

It is in Kant's work, Nancy argues, that the subject gets seriously hit for the first time. Due to the impossibility of knowing 'the thing as such' or the noumenal object, we will never know what is behind the empirical world which appears to us within the framework of the a priori categories. Thanks to this framework, we are able to understand the world as it appears to us, but this does not mean that we understand the world as such. Evidently, this also counts for the subject itself. It may fall back upon a transcendental self, but the self as such is unknowable to me. After Kant, the substantial subject is reduced to a strictly formal instance.

The second moment comes with Heidegger, who radicalizes Kant in that he bluntly postulates the worldliness of the 'subject'. Heidegger's concept of *Dasein*, being there, is not that of a subject which stands in opposition to a world of objects. Existing is always already being there, that is to say, it always already exposed to a world. *Dasein* is to be thrown *there*, right into a world, a throw that it can no longer ground or support.

Derrida builds upon this and constitutes the third moment identified by Nancy. 'I am', Derrida argues, is always caught in a differential movement of supplementary inscriptions through which the self is infected by what does not belong to the self. This differential movement permanently destabilizes the presence at itself. More precisely, before the self can be present to itself, it is always already seized by this difference. Here, Nancy argues, we finally witness nothing less than the end of the subject. The former subject, present to itself, has become an instance within a finite space and a finite time that can only exist as what is not present to itself. The former 'subject' was in various ways thought of as something that escapes material, transcendental or existential conditions. Now, the finite subject is exposed to others rather than merely present to itself and as such it can no longer be its own ground. It has, in other words, ceased to be a pure and transparent presence to itself. Therefore, it makes no use anymore to refer to this constant exposure of the self to the world in terms of a subject. Nancy concludes that the subject is occupied by a *singular* existence.

This conclusion, I believe, cannot but have the most relevant implications for the way we speak about identities nowadays, be it the identity of an individual or the identity of a collective. It is therefore more than necessary to know how singularity works, how it operates and what it does to us. Thus, our question is no longer 'What is singularity?' but 'How does singularity happen?'

SINGULAR PLURAL

In yet another text of Nancy, *The Experience of Freedom* (1993), we find an interesting passage that might help us to answer this question:

> For us, existence is above all what is singular. It happens singularly and only singularly. As for the existence, its own existence is above all singular, which means that its existence is not precisely its 'own' and that its 'existing' happens an indefinite number of times 'in' its very individuality (which is for its part a singularity). Singularity is what distinguishes the existent from the *subject*, for the subject is essentially what appropriates itself, according to its own proximity and law. Yet the advent of a subjectivity is itself a singularity.
>
> (Nancy, 1993: 190–191, n. 2)

To exist means above all to exist in a singular way. A singular existence stands for an existence which is no longer determined by an essence that grounds existence. Existence takes place only in a singular way. It is not a presence of an identity to itself. Existence *is* only in the countless singular moments that it comes to presence. My existence is singular in so far as it is not mine and in so far as it takes place numerous times 'in' my individuality.

This is not to imply that there is no self, but rather that the self exists without an essence. Nancy argues that existence, being yourself, is without an essence. The singular is not the result of the production or the auto-positioning of something or someone. Contrary to the subject, it has no final ground or first cause. What was once called *subiectum*, that is to say, the ground of every act of existence, *is* no longer. The singular is the unique act of existence without an essence, or in Nancy's own vocabulary, the coming into presence. The singular is not present to itself as a subject is, but comes each time again, with every act of existence, into presence. Its only presence is this coming into presence, each time again and in every act of existing. As being-in-the-world, it is exposed to other singularities, or to be more precise, to other singular moments. Being singular means being unique and undividable or, perhaps better, being singularized each time again. Singularity exists but in the act of singularization, the coming to presence rather than as presence to itself.

Nancy is not the only philosopher who toys with these non-characteristics of singularity. To accentuate the non-essential and temporary character of our identity as an individual or as part of a collective, a lot of contemporary continental thinkers have used the notion of singularity. Many of them are or have been looking for a suitable concept to think identity in a non-substantial or non-essential way. Agamben, Derrida and Deleuze, to mention just a few names, have tried to make progress in thinking our identity in this way. Why? Most of them have an almost inborn fear from the political, philosophical, and social claim that identity can be seen as something that one owns. This holds not only for an individual essence but also, and perhaps more urgently, for essences that believed to be shared collectively. Twentieth-century politics have shown all too clearly where the claim on substantial identities might lead to. Therefore, all of the thinkers named (and others) want to undo the possibility of this claim by thinking identity or existence in another way.

The specific touch of Nancy is the explicit relation he establishes between singularity and plurality. He argues that there is no singularity which is not plural and, the other way round, that there is no plurality which is not singular. *Being Singular Plural* is not by accident the title of one of his major studies, and it is one of the central research theses of his entire oeuvre: being is always being-with, singular is always singular plural, being one is always being more than one. Singularity *is* a plurality, with and between other singularities (which are, by the same token, also pluralities). Nancy speaks of the singular plural in such a way as to make clear that singularity is inextricably bound up with plurality. Singularity is being-with-many (Nancy, 2000: 32).

How should we understand this philosophical claim? From what we have seen so far, it should be clear that Nancy's writings operate on an ontological level. If we want to understand how singularity works, we have to deal with his conceptual apparatus to analyse our ontological condition. Let us therefore briefly sketch some major aspects this condition before we start to analyse the specific function or role of singularity in it.

BEING IS BEING-WITH

It is Nancy's conviction that Heidegger, in *Being and Time*, already opened the space for what can be called an analytic of the 'coexistential', that is to say, an analysis of how existence is always also coexistence. Unfortunately, Heidegger closed this space again by attaching being-with to notions such as 'destiny' and 'people'. Nancy unambiguously places the 'with' of the being-with back into the heart of being. In other words, at the point where Heidegger lost the thread, Nancy picks it up again to weave the question of being into the question of plurality. In *Being Singular Plural*, he is at pains to answer the question why plurality has been routinely subordinated by 'subject' or by 'being' throughout the entire history of philosophy. Nancy not only sheds light on this philosophical shortcoming, but also relates it to Heidegger's political pathos of destiny, people and authenticity. Heidegger could still understand an entire people as a subject because, as we will see later on, the radical question of a finite community is lacking in his work.

To radicalize Heidegger means in this context also to turn away strongly from his nationalistic pathos and from ensuing solidarities. However, Nancy's decision to develop a coexistential analytic is not simply a correction or improvement of Heidegger's work. On the contrary, he sort of recomposes *Being and Time* in such a way as to make being-with or singular plurality really co-essential and co-original with

Dasein. For Nancy, being is being-with or being singular plural. The primal onto-logical conditions of our existence are no longer conceived as the One, the Other, or the We, but as 'with', as 'singular plurality', or 'sharing' (*partage*). The question of being is therefore a question of being-with. So, Nancy sets out to 'unwork' Heidegger's 'infinite' determination of the 'with'. He wants to avoid a With or a We that functions as the Great Subject that swallows all individuality without entering in a political vacuity where only atomistic individuals reside. According to Nancy, Heidegger's ontological project must therefore become an ontology in which the question of the 'socius', the question of our being singular plural, has primary status.

Here the obvious question becomes: how does Nancy exactly think singular plural-ity? It is certainly not the possession of a common substance. Nor is it the juxta-position of pure exteriorities. For Nancy, singular plurality has to be thought as the only possible condition or structure of our being-in-the-world. The 'with' is not just a mode of being in the world. It is our 'quasi-transcendental' condition and as such anterior to any subject (an 'I' or a 'We'), to any presence, consciousness, or intention-ality. Up until now we are caught in an ontology of the same and the other: first, there is selfhood, then there is the other, be it a recognition of the other, my intention-ality towards the other, or my being questioned by the other. Not that Nancy's position is similar to what Emmanuel Levinas has proposed with his criticism of the 'Economy of the Same'. Nancy is not opting for an ethics of the Other beyond any form of ontology. On the contrary, he remains much more loyal to Heidegger's work in that he tries to radicalize ideas that are underdeveloped in Being and Time. As I have tried to make clear, Nancy argues that the concept of being-with conflates with or is co-original with that of *Dasein*.

Nancy thus starts from a singular plural being in the world where the 'with' is co-original with every 'there'. In order to articulate this structure or condition Nancy has developed several concepts and neologisms: 'being-in-common', 'coexistence', 'comparution', 'singular plurality', and so on. The relative structure of our singular plurality can be understood as transcendence in immanence or as what Nancy himself refers to as *transimmanence* (Nancy, 1998: 55): it is our ontological condition of being related to something or someone other than ourselves and yet constitutes ourselves. What opens us up to and exposes us onto the world, the 'co-' or the 'cum', is what discloses immanence. In other words, with a concept like transimmanence Nancy develops nothing but a resistance to a collective identity as a communion or closed community:

> Community means, consequently, that there is no singular being without another singular being, and that there is, therefore, what might be called in a rather inappropriate idiom, an originary or ontological 'sociality' that in its principle extends far beyond the simple theme of man as a social being (the *zoon politicon* is secondary to this community). For on the one hand, it is not obvious that the community of singularities is limited to 'man' and excludes, for example, the

'animal' . . . On the other hand, if social being is always posited as a predicate of man, community would signify on the contrary the basis for thinking only something like 'man'. But his thinking would at the same time remain dependent upon a principal determination of community, namely that there is no communion of singularities in a totality superior to them and immanent to their common being.

(Nancy, 1991a: 28)

In other words, plurality is the condition for every singularity to exist and the singularity of every plurality is the condition that makes a collective possible and at the same time prohibits it to become a closed community. For Nancy, singularity is the key term in thinking identity nowadays and our being singular plural is for him more than just a hint at the social or communitarian dimension of our existence. It is not a matter of putting the subject first, and 'intersubjectivity' or the 'primacy of the collective' second. The sociality of our existence is not something like a motif that takes place in the world, or, even weaker, something that results from altruism or a tolerant humanism.

Nancy's question is not whether humankind is behaving like a social being or not or whether we are multiculturalists or not. His analysis plays its role at a far more fundamental level, beyond any kind of moralizing about our behaviour towards 'the other'. His question is: how is it that we are singular plural? He works out our singular plural being as the essential ontological structure of how we exist. The singular plurality is the structure, the condition of being, of our existence as the each time temporary act of being singular plural. Our finite material-ontological condition has thrown us always already into a singular plurality, before every substantial primacy, be it that of the subject or of the collectivity. Anterior to any substantial identity, we already share (*partage*) — in the full ambiguity of the word: to partake in and to divide — our plural singularity to which we are exposed. This sharing is not a collective owning of some pre-given identity. Sharing is about acting rather than about substances. Being singular plural is not common to us as something that we could own or possess. That we are — and this is the condition of Nancy's social ontology — always singular plural through the act of sharing a world is the horizon out of which we have to think the question of singularity. In *The Inoperative Community* he writes:

A singular being does not emerge or rise up against the background of a chaotic, undifferentiated identity of beings, or against the background of their unitary assumption, or that of a becoming, or that of a will. A singular being *appears*, as finitude itself: at the end (or at the beginning), with the contact of the skin (or the heart) of another singular being, at the confines of the *same* singularity that is, as such, always *other*, always shared, always exposed.

(Nancy, 1991a: 27–28)

Being singular plural is Nancy's final comprehension of being. Being as a relational act of sharing is itself communal and every communal sharing does only exist in a singular way. Being forms the dynamic and relational structure in which we are always in a condition of singular plurality. In other words, the ontological question is the question of our singularity, or the other way round, the question of singularity is an ontological question. How we are is to be deduced from what singularity is, or better, from how it works. The time has come to answer that question in a very concrete way. How does singularity work? How do we have to understand singularities which are always embedded in a plurality?

SINGULARITY AS EVENT

Let me start with a substantial quote where Nancy specifies his conception of singularity in an exceptionally clear way:

> The concept of the singular implies its singularization and, therefore, its distinction from other singularities (which is different from any concept of the individual, since an immanent totality, without an other, would be a perfect individual, and it also assumes the togetherness of which the particular is a part, so that such a particular can only present its difference from other particulars as numerical difference). In Latin, the term *singuli* already says the plural, because it designates the 'one' as belonging to 'one by one'. The singular is primarily *each* one and, therefore, also *with* and *among* all the others.
>
> (Nancy, 2000: 32)

Singularity differs from the particular in a way that the particular presupposes the whole of which it is a part. In Nancy's words, the part-whole thinking is still caught in the ontology of the same or the other: either it puts forward the particular part (the same) or it transcends the particular in an overwhelming whole (the other). The singular *is* a plurality, with and between others. It can be each one. As Nancy puts it himself:

> The singular is a plural. It also undoubtedly offers the property of indivisibility, but it is not indivisible the way substance is indivisible. It is, instead, indivisible in each instance [*au coup par coup*] within the event of its singularization. It is indivisible like any instant is indivisible, which is to say that it is infinitely divisible, or *punctually* indivisible, but on the condition of *pars pro toto*: the singular is each time *for* the whole, in its places and in light of it. (If humanity is *for* being in totality in the way I have tried to present it, then it is the exposing of the singular as such and in general.) A singularity does not stand out against the background of Being; it is, when it is, Being itself or its origin.
>
> (Nancy, 2000: 32)

177

With the rise of every unique and indivisible act, the singular arises and it disappears with the falling of it. A singular existence is time and time again momentarily indivisible as the event itself of its singularization.

This event can be related to an individual, but can also operate on a infra-individual or trans-individual level. Friends meeting each other in a pub watching a football game or a festival of a local community are singular forms of being-together and not substantial collectives. In *A Finite Thinking*, Nancy tries to clear up this point a little bit:

> Existence is the sense of being. Not, however, according to a relation to 'being' in general (as if there was such a thing . . .), but in such a way that it concerns each time a (finite) singularity of being. Here 'singularity' isn't simply understood as the singularity of an individual (not simply as Heidegger's 'in each case mine'), but as the singularity of punctuations, of encounters and events that are as much individual as they are preindividual or common, at every level of community. 'In' 'me' sense is multiple, even if, here or there, this multiplicity can also comprise a sense that is 'my own': 'outside' 'me' sense lies in the multiplicity of moments, states, or inflexions of community (but equally, then, in what is always a singular 'we'). In any event, the singularity of the sense of being means that being's production of sense is not the being-self of essence. Essence is of the order of having: an assembling of qualities. By contrast, existence is itself its own essence, which is to say that it is without essence.
>
> (Nancy, 2003: 12)

Existence is without essence and that is what singularity is all about. If we all are singular and thus plural, we neither do have an essence nor are we substantial individuals:

> At this exact point, then, one becomes most aware of the essence of singularity: it is not individuality; it is, each time, the punctuality of a 'with' that establishes a certain origin of meaning and connects it to an infinity of other possible origins. Therefore, it is, at one and the same time, infra-/intraindividual and transindividual, and always the two together. The individual is an intersection of singularities, the discrete exposition of their simultaneity, an exposition that is both discrete and transitory.
>
> (Nancy, 2000: 85)

The singular is 'each time only this time' (*à chaque fois une seule fois*) (Nancy, 1993: 72). To singularize oneself means to be exposed to others and to differ from others. The relation between singularities is their incommensurability. They can never be reduced to one another, but their mutual differences never boil down to substantial characteristics which can lead towards the closure of a collective of similar singularities. We are different from one another, but not out of a substance or archetype. Characteristics like ethnicity or culture are contingent, in a way that they are not the exclusive and substantial key terms to include or exclude a person to a certain community or organization. Admittedly, there are Germans and others who are not, there are labourers and others who are not, or there are Muslims and others who are not, but here Nancy crucially points out these people do not differ in a substantial way from the others since there is no infinite and ever-lasting native essence called 'German', 'labourer' or 'Muslim'. Because of their singularization, identities differ from themselves and can no longer be thought of as a substance to which one, depending on whether one shares the putative essence of the collective identity, belongs or not. Identities, be it collectives or individuals, are contingent in a way that they change with every singularization. Each time again, they are recomposed, rebuilt and modified. Not that they are just like anything or anyone else. They are a 'self' but this self *is* only in its respective singular moments each time again different from the other moments.

Nancy wants us to believe that the social is all about singular differences: the infra-individual differences of a person which make him or her, time and time again different, plural, local and temporary, as well as the trans-individual differences of a group or organization which changes all the time. I differ not only from others, but also from myself. With friends, I am behaving in another way than with family. Or even with friends in different contexts, I can behave otherwise; indeed, I can *be* wholly otherwise. One does never meet person Y as such, but person Y with certain infra-individual characteristics, qualities and temper. People can therefore not be divided into separate groups on the basis of a common substance. There is no archetypical base or essence on the basis of which we can be compared with each other. The smile of an African girl does not follow from substantial attributes such as 'black' or 'African'. The smile characterizes her at that flashing moment when she smiles. Every new situation results in another smile (or tear) and thus in another singularization.

Let me provide one more example. In his book *Le Poids d'une pensée*, there is a text on 'Georges' (Nancy, 1991b: 113–124), a short text in which Nancy comments on a few pictures of an old man named Georges. With every picture a short description is added of the way Georges *is* at the moment. So, Georges is not the subject of the presentation. He differs again and again in every picture. He is nothing but the renewing singularity of his existence: someone who behaves differently, who is at one time drunk, at another time watches with a very melancholic gaze into the world or smiles like a newborn child. These everyday characteristics which differ across time, reveal what Nancy describes as singular plurality. At these moments, being singular plural happens.

179

SINGULARITY, SO WHAT?

Has something changed because of singularity? I want to make the claim that a lot has changed. It is another way of thinking subjectivity, of thinking individual or collective identity, and it changes the way we are positioned in the world as such. Identity is no longer a vast and steady entity, grounding itself and the world it perceives. Neither is a collective thought out in terms of a substantial criterion that allegedly marks the frontier between inner and outer. Both the individual and the collective exist in their respective singularizations. They change all the time and so do their characteristics.

What does this mean for organization? An organization is often argued to have indeed a kind of fixed identity, a set of essential characteristics that we might refer to as culture, and so on. Thinking these phenomena from the perspective of singularity means that they are no longer thought in terms of an unchangeable essence that stays the same forever. We do not 'own' ourselves, Nancy points out, and neither do collectives own themselves. Not that the result is a postmodern ontological conundrum that renders everything the same, that makes every truth merely relative and that leads us to believe that the world is too complex to be known and that it is therefore perhaps better to 'give me more wine, because life is nothing' (cf. Pessoa, 1993). We do have a self and others have one too and we are not the same.

Yet, many questions arise here. Before we try to answer them, it is important to acknowledge once more that for Nancy singularity works at many different levels: at the level of an individual, at the level of a collective, a culture, an organization, and so on. The whole difficulty is then of course how and when a culture or an organization can be called 'singular', or more exactly, how a culture, organization or society can singularize itself. How can an organization focus itself on singularity? Does the concept of singularity not in some sense belie the idea of organization? Since we are dealing here with something ungraspable, fluid, and hasty, should we not abandon hope that singularity can be organized? Maybe we should, but I want to suggest that one can at least pose the question and wonder about possible scenarios.

Let us, for the sake of the argument, start from the classical thesis in liberal democracy that the individual is prior to the collective. It implies that since every collective is added to this individual, the latter is situated in a context of alienation, supervision or obligation: the subject loses itself because of its alienation from something other than itself. Individual and collective are thus pinned down to a substantial criterion, an essence, a strong and steady 'self' by which they radically differ from each other. An unfruitful opposition is at work here: the collective, for example an organization, is seen as the enemy of the subject. For the organization, the subject is a strange entity it has to 'adapt' in order to make it functional for the organization.

But what if neither organization nor subject are that substantial? What would then be a possible outcome? A typical argument from a loyal worker who is asked to move to another working place is: 'I like it here, I don't want to move'. This answer is in a sense very substantial: the employee supposes that working culture, workfloor organization, and so on will stay the same during his or her whole career and that is why they do not want to leave. But those are conditions one can never be sure of.

The singularized answer would be more something like that: I like it 'here and now'. Because so many aspects and evolutions can impact on the job, it can be completely changed within even the shortest of periods. Organizations are not always places of stability (see also ten Bos, 2005). The reasons that employees offer when they refuse to go may not be available after change has set in: a new boss, a new colleague, other tasks to be carried out, a new owner of the organization, anything can happen. Within every change in conditions, we can potentially speak of a new constellation or singularization of the relation between the organization and the employee. The classic relation between them, often premised on concepts such as job security or lifelong loyalty, does no longer exist. Neither can we still speak of a relation between the whole and its parts, between the collective and its individual members. It is the temporary and unique constellations, based on the way employees behave, the policy of the organization, the traffic, the mood of the people at that very moment, the outside temperature, the loss by Manchester United the evening before in the Champions League, the whatever and many other aspects, that makes of an organization each time again a singularized entity. The collective *is* but its components with their singular traits at that very moment and these traits produce a singularized and thus necessarily temporary collective. Not that an organization is a 'whole' where workers substantially identify themselves with mission statements, the specific company cultures, or whatever. On the contrary, precisely the worker's singular characteristics at that very moment will potentially modify the whole as such. If you have to show some foreign visitors round your company and you are in a terrible mood that day, then you are for a great part the (bad) image of your factory. For them, the factory is what you tell them it is and the way you present it. So, even seen from this perspective alone (let us say: the perspective of 'image' or 'window dressing'), an organization has every reason to face the question of singularity.

Traditionally, an organization tries to suppress all these temporary influences of their employees and of the environment or society in general. An organization does not want the employee to malfunction because of the loss by Manchester United. It wants him or her to do the job, quite irrespective of whatever emotional state the employee is in. And the more structured and planned the acts of the employees are (do this, then this, . . .), the less singularity can play its role. As such this is a pity because one can also, besides the evident counterarguments, reveal many opportunities here where an organization could function better if it would be interested in singularity. It is in this optimistic vein that I want to end this chapter.

One can with concepts such as singularity think of a job or an organization in far less substantial ways. Every one of us has periods in our lives where we are creative and happy or when one is in an emotional crises or suffering from a complete burnout. When people have to do the same job during their whole life in the same way, one loses a lot. With some flexibility and the suitable incentives, one can stimulate employees in creative periods to fulfil other tasks, to work at other places in the factory, or to allow for the possibility to have people formulate novel ideas concerning the organization of their factory. In busy periods for employees (for example the nursing of little children at home), one can foresee the time and the place to step back for a period, be it part time, be it with letting them fulfil other tasks, and so forth. There are endless possibilities here. During certain periods, an organization needs more creativity, working hours or new ideas than during other periods of relative stability. Why not try to match these periods with the impulses coming from people working for the organization?

I am convinced that singularity can play a certain role in processes of organizational change and resist the idea that it should be suppressed at all cost in organizational settings. Why should not an employee or a manager learn to think in terms of jobs they can do rather than in terms of jobs they have to do? The more working places are organized in a bureaucratic and 'neurotic' way, the less they give singularity the space to develop the opportunities it can offer.

I am perfectly aware, of course, that singularity is not a magic formula that will somehow reorganize our whole society. Far from that. If it has a function to fulfil, that is to say, if we can allow it to happen – and this is what is at stake in Nancy's writing – it seems to play a rather 'modest' role. You cannot change a organization by the whim of a manager or the smile of a girl. But singularity does happen, also in organizations, and it has perhaps some potential to bring in new and creative ideas on law, work, labour, culture and so on. To allow it to happen rather than merely resisting it requires a rethinking of many of our frameworks that determine our views on work and organizations in general: the part-whole thinking or the substantial views on identities of subjects in general, and the emphasis on strong organizational cultures are only a few of them. A lot of thinking awaits us here, be it with or without Jean-Luc Nancy.

REFERENCES

Cadava, E., P. Conner and J.-L. Nancy (eds) (1991) *Who Comes after the Subject?* New York: Routledge.
Heidegger, M. (1996) *Being and Time,* trans. J. Stambaugh. New York: State University of New York Press.
Linstead, S. and A. Linstead (eds) (2005) *Organization and Identity.* London: Routledge.
Nancy, J.-L. (1991a) *The Inoperative Community*, trans. P. Connor, L. Garbus, M. Holland and S. Sawhney. Minneapolis, MN: University of Minnesota Press.
Nancy, J.-L. (1991b) *Le Poids d'une pensée*. Quebec: Le Griffon d'argile.
Nancy, J.-L. (1992) 'Un sujet?', in A. Michels (ed.) *Homme et sujet*. Paris: L'Harmattan.
Nancy, J.-L. (1993) *The Experience of Freedom*, trans. B. McDonald. Stanford, CA: Stanford University Press.
Nancy, J.-L. (1997) *The Gravity of Thought*, trans. F. Raffoul and G. Recco. Atlantic Highlands, NJ: Humanities Press.

Nancy, J.-L. (1998) *The Sense of the World*, trans. J. S. Librett. Minneapolis, MN: University of Minneapolis Press.

Nancy, J.-L. (2000) *Being Singular Plural*, trans. R. D. Richardson and A. E. O'Bryne. Stanford, CA: Stanford University Press.

Nancy, J.-L. (2003) *A Finite Thinking*, ed. S. Sparks. Stanford, CA: Stanford University Press.

Parker, M. (2000) *Organizational Culture and Identity*. London: Sage

Pessoa, F. (1993) 'Cancioneiro', in *Gedichten*. Amsterdam: De Arbeiderspers.

ten Bos, R. (2005) 'Agamben and the community without identity', in C. Jones and R. Munro (eds) *Contemporary Organization Theory*. Oxford: Blackwell.

ten Bos, R. (2006) 'The ethics of business ethics', in S. Clegg and C. Rhodes (ed.) *Business Ethics: Contemporary Contexts*. London: Routledge.

Chapter 12

Double-crossing the landscapes of philosophy

Conjoining the transparency of 'things' with the veil of language

Rolland Munro

INTRODUCTION

In this chapter I touch upon what I call the 'landscaping' view of language. Language can be regarded as either subjective or ostensive, with words held alternatively to re-present either ideas or objects. And there is much to be said for either view. Yet it seems as important to grasp language also in terms of *affect*. This is to say speech and gesture do not only point outwards to the transparency of 'things', or inwards to the veil of 'meanings'; they also 'body forth' (Merleau-Ponty, 1962) our relations with others.

It is in understanding these relations to be 'ordered' by language that our ideas of philosophy and organization might be altered. Ordered, that is, in the double sense of being arranged *and* demanded. Motherhood and duty to nation do not just move us about; such matters are themselves motile, being there one moment and gone the next (Munro, 2004). Yes, what we say *elicits* responses. But what is being understood also *evokes* the very 'worlds' that shapes these responses. So as well as being represen-tative *of* things or meanings, words are deployed as much *for* representation. In this way language helps to make visible 'who we are' as much as it is simultaneously helping shape the worlds we construct.

Ahead of setting out this thesis, I pick up two tropes of language. First, 'the veil', in which the meanings of words are imagined as existing in a kind of shroud, the 'cloud of occlusion' wherein we live out our lives. And second, that of 'transparency', whereby words point directly to objects of the real world like a chair. But not to valorize one over the other. It seems unarguable that the phenomenology of each is to be taken seriously. Yes, language provides the dazzle of 'things' that are to be seen on the one hand, and the perspective of 'meanings' crafting the view on the other. Yes, one minute when we *see* something; and language appears to go backstage so to speak. But the next minute language is then 'frontstage'; the very attempt to say what we see or think comes to block our sight and create its own labyrinth of problems and issues. One minute language appears to be no more than a medium of representation; after which it then has us cascading, head over heels, in answer to its call. One moment language has nothing to do with philosophy; then the next it is everything.

In an effort to get out of the horns of this dilemma, the chiasm of our everyday experience with words, I go on to suggest how language is also, and always, 'doing' social relations: gathering us this way; and then the other. Language is not only uncircumventable, as Heidegger insists. In our questing after identity and community, language turns out to be instrumental in all our consequent stratifications and exclusions of others *as* Other. What complicates an understanding of the organizational issues here is that language is forever giving us more than voice and meaning. As much as it grants perspective and position, it also helps organize and advertise our relations and belongings. At its heart, language is central to an endless privileging of 'us'.

My aim here is to go further than merely asserting a 'pragmatics' of language over its 'semantics' or its 'syntactics'; by augmenting, say, a communitarian view of language familiar to sociologists and anthropologists. Yes, as the oldest technology, the expressions of language require to be 'mastered' and, as the most public, its meanings insist on being 'shared'. But language in its excess is also ahead of us. It is always 'going on before' in ways that both jump ahead of it being fully grasped *and* prohibit it ever being entirely shared. Yes, in its elicitation of relations, language helps make some 'things' present and others absent. Yet as an evocation, language also can shift about and move the very worlds being composed and recomposed.

SHIFTING THE LANDSCAPE

But first to 'things'. 'Why are there things, rather than nothing?' In posing this question in his *Introduction to Metaphysics*, Heidegger (1959: 1) is doing more than attempting to escape from the Western tradition; what Foucault (1980) has called a 'regime of truth'. He is also getting ready to 'double-cross' the philosophical community in which he has been brought up.

In asking 'Why are there things?', Heidegger is first 'crossing over' ground established by the method of doubt. He is able to re-create a sense of mutual territory because he fully understands the conventions of the metaphysicians who have gone before. The question is recognizable – and repeatable – as a valid question. It is not only understandable in itself – 'Why *are* there things?' It is also to be understood to be a question that is entirely open for the asking, at least *within* the tradition of metaphysics. Indeed, this is a question that could be asked only by someone brought up within this particular tradition. Only someone fully conversant with the conventions of metaphysics would formulate their question in this way.

But, equally, Heidegger is also 'crossing out', so to speak, this familiar ground. He is negating the traditional method of doubt as a 'way' by going on to show its path leads nowhere. By *questioning* the question, he is intensifying the doubt in the method of doubt. In putting 'under erasure' ground that has previously been taken-for-granted, he thus breaks with the community that has succoured him.

So how is this 'double-crossing' of crossing over and crossing out made possible? Which convention is Heidegger actually breaking? Top of the list appears to be the convention, the ritual of being sceptical about the existence of any single entity being posited. To each 'thing', Kant's X, must be raised what Heidegger calls the 'ontic' question: does X exist? Or does it not exist? Please tick. Heidegger's question still echoes this formulation, even though such questioning adds nothing – the idea of existence in Heidegger's view having become over the centuries too degraded and no longer worthy of the term ontological. And in going on to repeat the question again and again and yet again – until the bankruptcy of this line of questioning is exposed to all – Heidegger is clearly breaking ranks.

Next, in insisting on deploying the blank form of 'something', rather than filling in the X, Heidegger is deliberately leaving open the nature of essence as general rather than specific. Here he is breaking a second convention, one that acts as the corollary of the first. This is the convention that organizes the world into a roll-call of putative entities, one at a time, and subjects each – fire, water, earth, air – in turn to the microscope of scepticism. Thus, in ticking the boxes of existence for one entity – it is necessary to pass onto the next. A kind of on-tic ticking: yes/no; yes/no; yes/no. So that, gradually, and securely, it is only those entities considered worthy of the idea of existence that are included within the metaphysics of reality. But Heidegger eschews all this. Instead of building up the putative existence of one entity on top of the other, in the tradition of the Systematics, Heidegger simply asks: 'Why *is* there something?' And then adds, with faultless logic, 'Why are there entities at all?'

It is this third break with convention that is particularly startling. In adding the seemingly redundant and unnecessary clause '. . . rather than nothing' to his question, Heidegger is reversing the focus of earlier scepticism. He is shifting the landscape of doubt from one remaining within its originating framework – the doctrine of substance – to a questioning that *includes* the possibility of nothing. And *permanently* includes this possibility. Not just admitting doubt to one or other of the million or so ideas floating, randomly as it were, inside a person's mind (Sterne, 2003; cf. Munro, 2005); but going on to install nothingness as integral to the very *possibility* of presence.

So not just the idea of one or another specific thing being nothing – whatever this could mean! As if things could be a kind of non-thing, an absence of matter by default. But, instead, the more general idea of thinking about things in the *horizon* of time. This is to say that what may give meaning to the notion of time is not just the possibility of the absence of something, but an ever-present potential for something to be absolutely nothing at all. Here Heidegger is not merely speculating on origins, as with the opening words of Genesis. And he is far from going down the route, favoured since the Greeks, of treating 'nothingness' as a kind of single essence on which to begin to build the world. Heidegger is seeking another way.

THE REINTRODUCTION OF TIME

Heidegger is clearing a path in order to reintroduce time. Unlike representation, in which sign and objects coexist, the 'gathering' of language needs duration not petrifaction. In simply asking whether something exists or not, traditional metaphysics has unthinkingly perpetuated visions of a world that is organized by being completely static. Their world might as well run backwards as forwards, for all it is made to run at all. Either things exist, or they do not? Well, no longer. After Heidegger, it is the conditions of possibility for 'things', their very conjunction with their conditions of possibility, that becomes important.

Yet if Heidegger is breaking so many conventions, the rituals of doing philosophy, why is he not ostracised from the community for breaching the conditions of his membership? The scandal is that Heidegger has, irrevocably, done something to philosophy itself. Specifically, as already discussed, he has broken traditional understandings of the method of doubt by picking up the (unquestioned) presumption that the question of existence applies to particulars. He exceeds this convention by gathering all the particulars together and making the question general. Why is there (always) something (i.e. anything), rather than nothing? Not why is there X, or Y, or even Z? *But for everything together.*

So why is there *always* something? This is a question that exceeds all previous limits. And this is the question that makes previous philosophers, even Descartes and Husserl, seem hidebound by convention. Yet the true impetus of Heidegger's question comes into force when he adds his rider – 'rather than nothing' – to a question that he has already generalized. He thus *defers* the doubt, the negative option, until he has the difference in play. First, he recognizes the phenomenology of all thinking involving 'things' (even if it seems that certain things get proposed only so that others can doubt them). Then, and only then, does he generalize doubt and, devastatingly, offer the possibility of nothing.

Unlike Descartes, who radicalizes all doubt into a pre-emptive strike, Heidegger's insight is to resituate nothingness as a *horizon*. Nothingness need not be treated as an empty term, the mere obverse of existence. It can be taken seriously and brought alive by being contrasted with the possibility of Being. This is what is to be contemplated: that *every* something might have been nothing, or may even return to being nothing. Being is temporary, it is never for ever. And it can vary. So even birth and death is possible. All this opens up the possibility of a dynamic world of presence and absence, not the static world of universal truths.

So Heidegger *delays* the method of doubt. Heidegger's gambit is not to weigh in, simply criticizing traditional metaphysics over its fetish for existence. Does X exist? Does Y exist? Does Z exist? The method of doubt seems interminable. Is every single thing to be put to the question? Just how *do* you oppose this roll call of the object world? So far from attempting a blank slate by dismissing all prior ideas (an impossible gesture in any case since this Cartesian gesture must escape what it announces),

187

Heidegger is ready to be banal. He sticks with the obvious: that there always *is* something. Yes, yes! We can go along with this; this much is obvious. There *is* always something. And this strategy of deferral is one Derrida might recognize.

Heidegger's form of deconstruction works instead through a slowing down of the reader. Why is there something rather than nothing, he asks? And plays with the question. Relentlessly. People want to know whether something exists or not. Okay. So be it. Let's admit the doubt. But let's not do it too precipitately. So Heidegger asks instead: why *is* there something? 'Why is there something, rather than nothing?' and on and on, warming to his theme until this repetition becomes – oddly – no longer meaningless. Its evocation echoes around our brain until – eventually – its echo begins to recover something of the ground – the landscape – that there might have been for philosophy *before* the ontological reduction of the world to 'things'.

HANGING LANGUAGE OUT TO DRY

In his essay 'Signature, Event, Context', Derrida (1982a) takes up J. L. Austin's ordinary language philosophy to explore an equally radical shifting of the landscape in philosophy. This is a shift within ordinary language philosophy, from words being used to represent things to words becoming things in themselves. Shifting the landscape in this case, however, requires a little extra help. Austin's (1962) writing, as Derrida explicates, is rooted in the 'communication' assumptions of the analytical tradition. And, indeed, are so deeply rooted that Austin misses the force of his own insights.

Language for Austin is indisputably a medium of communication. And, yes, it is for him more or less 'transparent'. It is just that he, Austin, is about to draw our attention to some uses of language that depart from this idea of transparency, as well as noticing various 'infelicities' that also get in the way. However, unlike those who have gone before, Austin is sufficiently intrigued with 'ordinary' language not to simply write off all these infelicities to ambiguity and error.

Austin (1962, 1970) is about to explore how to *do* things with words. In investigating the minute detail of this mundane aspect of life, he notices certain conventions in language that appear to become activities in their own right. For example, someone launches a ship with the words 'I name this ship . . .'. Or a couple recites together the words 'I do' and they are married. Suddenly, then, words are no longer to be taken as just representative, words are now to be recognized as transformative. *They change things*. And where they change things, words can no longer to be considered as a mere medium of representation.

But if there are forms of words that, in turn, become part of the world of 'things', what are we to make of such utterances? Are the examples to hand just anomalous, a kind of polluting hybrid, neither pure object, nor pure language?

Perhaps. But Austin is not ready to abandon the firmament that splits the world between language as the intention of subjects, on the one hand, and reality as the

188

extension of 'things', on the other. What Austin (1962, 1970) does, instead, is to recognize conventions as specific occasions, rituals and rites, where subjects effectively turn their speech into objects. And in particular he finds a category of speech called promises, conventions in which people not only say what they might do but go on to bind themselves to doing it. Promises are defined by Austin as belonging to a class of utterances he calls *performative*.

Like other kinds of 'performative utterances', which can include naming, betting, welcoming, censuring, congratulating and apologizing, statements made by way of promising in the form of 'I promise' are understood to be 'doing something rather than merely saying something' (1970: 235). As he adds:

> We must distinguish between the function of making explicit what act it is we are performing, and the quite different matter of stating what act it is we are performing. In issuing an explicit performative utterance we are not stating what act it is, we are showing or making explicit what act it is.
>
> (Austin, 1970: 245)

It is clear that, for Austin, the form 'I promise' is not of the same order as a descriptive statement 'I am sitting'.

At this point it is evident that Austin is doing something more than working with words. He is doing something *to* philosophy. Which is of course precisely what Austin must deny. To do his painstaking, almost pedantic work, he must subscribe to the tenets of analytical philosophy, particularly in terms of observing Frege's distinction between sense and reference. Yet by more or less installing this particular class of utterances *as* objects, Austin is close to admitting that the boundary between words and 'things' cannot hold.

CHANGING THE GROUND

Austin is doing things to philosophy. Suddenly 'things' of language are taking place; they enter reality *as* objects. This of course immediately puts the transparency view, as Austin notes, under threat. Words and things, it seems, can no longer be held apart.

Yet Austin is wary of admitting language into the object world. So he adds back these 'oddities' very restrictively, drawing attention mainly to what he calls 'speech acts'. These are in his view a limited group of linguistic phrases. So he is far from thinking he is being radical here. Only those speech acts sufficiently conventional and stable to be regarded *as* objects – marriage, investiture, etc. – can be installed in the object world. Or so he implies. But Austin, intentionally or not, is not just setting out a new set of objects for view when he, self-consciously, adopts the neologism 'performative' (Austin, 1970: 235).

Austin, in Derrida's (1982a) terms, is turning to the oldest ground. Against Plato,

Austin is reinstating language over *logos*. Thus, instead of just leaping in every time to 'see' whatever an argument is telling us is there to be seen, Austin is slowing things down until it is the *instructions* about 'what to see' that come themselves into view. Indeed, Austin slows things down, so much so that eventually we begin to see the actual language in which events are 'taking place'. Thus we don't just see a ship named, we register the very words that name it. We don't just see a couple being married, it is the words each say to the other that sticks.

Unlike previous philosophers, Austin is not thinking principally from his own meditations, searching for, and working from, the clear and distinct idea. Instead, he is dwelling on the kind of phrases that are *iterated* in everyday life. Well, perhaps not quite 'everyday' life. More those that echo conventions within the life lived by an Oxford philosopher, the good life extolled by Socrates, a world in which the breaking of a promise is something that would have everyone involved 'rounding' in on one:

> when I say 'I promise', a new plunge is taken: I have not merely announced my intention, but, by using this formula (performing this ritual), I have bound myself to others, and staked my reputation, in a new way.
>
> (Austin, 1970: 99)

In the case of statements that appear in the form of 'I promise' etc., the phrases are so stock that they typically no longer point 'outwards' to the petrified world that they evoke. Rather such phases typify the conventions they gather as they go.

And we can assume that this is what Derrida notices: this doing things *to* philosophy. And Austin, as Derrida demonstrates, is too good a philosopher to rely entirely on his strategy of turning to 'conventions' to hold the ground. The best he can do is *deferral*. As Austin himself notes in passing: 'Philosophers at least are too apt to assume that an action is always in the last resort the making of a physical movement, whereas it's usually, at least in part, a matter of convention' (Austin, 1970: 237). And, really, conventions in speech can act as forcibly as conventions in action. So, whereas Derrida has been busy making pronouncements, valorizing for example writing over speech, in order to wake up philosophy, Austin has already, if almost invisibly, changed its very *ground*.

Although he never says as much, Austin wants speech acts to be 'things' on a par with objects, objects as 'transparent' as any other. But here's the problem. In so far as any set of words – 'I am sitting' as much as 'I promise' – may elicit a response from others, it is not clear that there is any firm boundary between descriptive and performative statements. Only if Austin can insist that there are a very *limited* amount of phenomena that can travel over the frontier might the boundary between 'words' and 'things' be held. So the tag *Limited Inc.* (Derrida, 1988) exactly captures Austin's dilemma over how to stop the contagion.

STICKING TO THE REAL

In their very different ways, Heidegger and Austin might both be understood as demonstrating something of the truth of the veil theory of language. Yet neither, for very different reasons, might have been happy with this idea. Heidegger was out to change Western metaphysics and Austin himself seemed content merely to extend a peculiarly English version of analytical philosophy. It is true that both mastered language, albeit in very different ways. However, while Austin made language central to his methodology, he stuck with his cloistered vision of the real.

To see the real, it seems then you don't have to attend to language all that much. But to see *all* the real, you sometimes have to attend very closely to the language itself, particularly when it doesn't work, or when it – so to speak – has to double up and be both medium *and* object. So much for Austin. Heidegger, by contrast, wants to go more real. The language game of ostension is just not real enough for him. Ostension is merely a pointing, a device that ultimately is concerned only to restitute language from its imminent ruin. 'What is an orange?' asks Wittgenstein. 'This [points] is an orange.' 'What is an apple?' 'This [points] is an apple.'

As witness his later turn in style, language for Heidegger becomes more and more undecidable. In *Being in Time* the early Heidegger (1962) faces us with an exhaustive lexicon of new terms. These are designed to imprint a new ontology of Being and turn us away from empty old metaphysical questions. For example, in terms of his ideas of being-in-the-world, we notice language for the most part only when it fails to work. Almost like when the hammer we are swinging hits our thumb; only then do we wonder what this funny object is doing in our hand! So, too, with words. These, too, we barely notice; at least when we are happily chatting away. Again, it is only when these 'fail' us that words come into presence. Whenever a tool becomes present-to-hand, we can be sure that it is also out of place. Words come into view at the moment in which the very world they are helping to construct starts to fall apart.

By the time of the later essays, especially those on technology and art, Heidegger has all but abandoned the precision of the earlier work. No longer does he try to rewrite language to bring it more in line. Essays, like that of 'Building, Dwelling, Thinking' (1978a), become exercises in the powers of evocation; they play endlessly with the iteration of word roots and with the assonance of poetry. The language is Wagnerian in its reach, echoing the hills with the sound of Thor while painting a vision of peace.

Do these later essays fail the real? No. To the contrary, it is almost as if the wilder the language, the clearer Heidegger's vision becomes. For, by reminding philosophy of its poetical roots, he is forever doing something to philosophy. What he wants to do to philosophy is join the world all up again, language and all. What counts is no longer a 'correctness' in language, using the right word to point to the right object. What matters to Heidegger now are moments of *unconcealment*, moments when truth slips through the veil (see Heidegger, 1978b).

191

So in summary of what has been said so far, both Austin and Heidegger changed the ground of philosophy. In noticing the power of words to make an *elicitation*, Austin admits certain parts of the world as 'cultivated'. But he stops short of Heidegger, who is explicating the *worlds* language helps to install. That such 'constructions' also always involve his making an *evocation* is now discussed.

BRIDGING THE LANDSCAPE

In discussing language as a built thing, as something constructed rather than culti-vated, Heidegger confronts us with the idea of the bridge as granting a crossing. The bridge takes us over, so to speak, from one side to the other.

> The bridge swings over the stream 'with ease and power'. It does not just connect banks that are already there. The banks emerge as banks only as the bridge crosses the stream. The bridge expressly causes them to lie across from each other.
>
> (Heidegger, 1978a: 354)

So this is what the bridge does: it *crosses*. Streams, gaps, chasms, fissures.

In order to cross, Heidegger argues, the bridge must first bring into focus the existence of banks; that is, in order to join, the bridge also *separates*. Although there may be many possibilities for building along the stream, this separation – in which one side opposes the other – happens only at the site where the bridge is built: 'One of them proves to be a locale, and does so because of the bridge. Thus the bridge does not first come to a locale to stand in it; rather the locale comes into existence only by virtue of the bridge' (Heidegger, 1978a: 356).

The consequence of building a bridge is that the banks do not just go on as before, side by side, they also come into a confrontation with each other. But, critically, he adds, they do so *after* the building of the bridge.

Any utterance, I argue, commits us in a similar way. It doesn't necessarily matter if I say 'I promise' or 'I am sitting'. Like the bridge, the semantics may be predictable, but the *affect* is not. A word, a phrase, and we are already across. We have made our crossing, even before we can ask: Why this word? Why now? We have already been transported.

It is not therefore the 'transparency' that matters, or even the technical meaning of a word. Rather the power of words lies in their being able to transport us into different landscapes, different worlds. Thus a novel turn of phrase may 'lift' us – taking us 'out of ourselves'. While a conventional phrase, consecrated and hallowed by ceremony and precedent, can put us into a new life: 'I do', says the bridegroom and he steps anew into life as a married man.

THE CHIASM OF PLACE

A repeated phrase acts as a 'bridge' between two distinct periods of clock time. It can rewind us, so to speak, transporting us back to 'places' where we heard the phrase before. This is what Alice discovers in Nicci French's genre novel *Killing Me Softly* (2000) at the moment when she has been unable to convince the police that she is not mad in thinking her husband, Adam, is a murderer. Having discovered that Adam may have killed seven people, including two previous lovers, Alice now finds her husband has arrived at the police station in the company of a doctor, another previous lover, to arrange for his wife to be sectioned.

It all seems so easy just to give up. Maybe she, Alice, has just got it all wrong? After all she still desperately loves him and, for a moment, there 'was nobody in the room except me and him, everything else was just blur and noise'.

> 'Alice, my darling,' he said, soft against my ear, hand on my hair, 'didn't I promise I would look after you? *For ever and ever.*'
>
> He held me close and it felt wonderful. *For ever and ever.* That was the way I thought it was going to be. Maybe it could still be like that. Maybe we could turn the clock back, pretend he had never killed people and I had never known. I felt tears running down my face. A promise to look after me *for ever and ever.* A moment and a promise. Where had I heard those words? There was something in my mind, blurred and indistinct, and then it took shape and I saw it. I stepped back out of Adam's arms and I looked clearly at Adam's face.
>
> 'I know,' I said.
>
> (French, 2000: 320, emphasis added)

What Alice suddenly 'knows' is where Adam has put the body of Adele Blanchard, his former lover. She even carries a photograph of the woodland spot where she is most likely buried. For this is the same spot where Adam asked Alice to marry him and made her swear the marriage vows that they would be together 'for ever and ever'. The words now echo like a citation and revive the landscape from whence they came.

Alice has made a *double* 'crossing'. As the words 'for ever and ever' resonate through her, she first follows wherever the words take her, 'crossing over' the ground of loyalty and commitment. Only then to 'cross out' all this as she finds herself transposed into an entirely different landscape from that of the world of incarceration within which she found herself a moment before. One moment she is binding herself back with Adam, her lover, back into the wonderland of love and eternity. The next she is transmuted to the same landscape in which her future husband asked her to marry him. Except that, in now knowing that she was once standing on the grave of his former lover, it is no longer the same place.

Here is the point. The elicitation and the evocation work together. Had she not responded to Adam's call to come back to him, been tempted to cross over to the offer of unity, she could not have then 'crossed' to same spot where he first promised this ever-ever land. It is only by virtue of her 'double' crossing here – this momentary fusion of landscapes – that has Adam revealing himself to be a serial murderer; as the person who killed not only his best friend but also his former lover.

This dynamic tension between what goes before and what comes after is partly what Heidegger means by his idea that the bridge 'admits' and 'installs' the landscape (Munro, 2002; cf. Miller, 1995). The bridge admits what goes before and it changes what is about to come after. And, as with built objects like bridges, then so too with words. Put a word in a certain place and the world is different. It no longer looks or feels the same; the very atmosphere as well as the view is changed. So there never is a single landscape – a single language – to be communally shared. There are a myriad of landscapes waiting to appear, each wrought around a single 'instance'. Let's consider another, possibly more familiar example of 'double crossing'.

HOW TO RE-CITE THE LANDSCAPE

Bernard Stiegler, on the basis of a reading of *Of Grammatology* (Derrida, 1976), argues that the history of the human is nothing other than that of the exteriorization of 'memory'. This sentence is lifted wholesale from Timothy Clark's (2000) chapter on 'Deconstruction and technology' in *Deconstructions: A User's Guide*, edited by Nicholas Royle. I have merely repeated, without addition, Clark's words. As it happens, the addition of this second sentence not only avoids the charge of plagiarism, but also can be expected to act as a stop on the 'crossing' being elicited by the first sentence. The reader, ready to follow up the idea of 'the exteriorization of memory', is arrested in mid-flight. What is being 'crossed over' is suddenly 'crossed out'.

We are, quite specifically, discussing here not the meaning of language, but its *movement*, its literal mobility. Once uttered and now repeated, it seems that within discourse it is the very words that are beginning to travel.

> This citationality, duplication, or duplicity, this iterability of the mark is not an accident or an anomaly, but is that (normal/abnormal) without which a mark could no longer even have a so-called 'normal' functioning. What would a mark be that one could not cite? And whose origin could not be lost on the way?
>
> (Derrida, 1982a: 320–321)

So rather than lightening up the 'things' of the world, or even moving us about with a word or phrase, it is the words and phrases themselves, in their citation and iterability, that take on momentum.

As words and phrases become mobile, it is *their* repetition and iteration that starts to move us (always remembering we are never sure about who this 'us' is), *across* communities and into different 'worlds'. We might just pause here to consider the different landscapes within which words might reverberate anew in the inky breath of the author. I had intended, for example, to juxtapose Bernard Stiegler's (1998) idea about memory with Plato's story of Thales, the inventor of writing. Puffed up with pride, Thales boasts to the King about all the benefits of his new technology. But in Marshall McLuhan's (1962) telling of the tale, the King replies that writing will not help men remember, so much as it will help them forget. On the basis of this last narrative, the field would then be open to positioning the invention of writing as merely an early example, say, of the 'outsourcing' of work to the built environment, an early stage perhaps in what Heidegger (1978a) sees as our continuing shift from dwelling to building.

In this respect of writing being understood as an 'outsourcing' of memory, it might seem important to resurrect also the context of Clark's (2000) own citing of Stiegler (1998). The latter comes after a discussion of memory and technology as one of the relation between interiority and exteriority, in which he quotes Derrida: 'This amounts to saying that the exteriority of the division, the dis-junction, *is the relation*, the essential juncture between thinking memory and the so-called techno-scientific, indeed literary outside' (Derrida, 1986: 109–110, emphasis in original). Now this is an odd kind of relation! A veritable 'no-thing'. If we read this aright, in an echo of Heidegger's ambulation between something and nothing, Derrida is imputing the relation between interiority and exteriority not to the conjunction of things, but to their dis-junction.

Not for the first time, Derrida is proposing a link – a hinge – where there would appear to be none. And not just any link. *The relation*. Things can turn out to be most joined precisely where they seem most apart. For, as Clark (2000: 246) interprets Stiegler (1998), 'memory' becomes such only through exteriorization, constituting qualities and capabilities that become 'human' only in this same originary supplementation and prosthesis. The effect is thus to radically rethink all philosophy. And indeed, much organization theory, as has been explicated elsewhere (Munro, 1997a, 1997b).

CONJUNCTION AND CITATION

Citation is a serious matter. Within just one sentence I establish a genealogy: I quote Clark, who is actually drawing on Stiegler, who is in turn interpreting Derrida. The question is in the air is whether I intend to augment this Royal line, quibbling with some of its pieces, but not threatening the hierarchy or the heritage of the deconstruction community. Or whether, indeed, I might be more concerned to rock the boat in ways that seek to overthrow the lineage itself? But since the chapter itself is drawing to a close, time is also pressing.

So perhaps the final word should go to Derrida on conjunction. This too is a serious matter. A matter, he suggests, of love. Conjoining, as he points out, includes the copula as well as the conjugals:

In Arabic, the 'and', the *wa* (or *waw*), the linking letter, which can mean 'also' also, along with 'with', or at the same time 'at the same time', and simultaneously a sort of simultaneity, well, *waw* can also be defined, I am told, as the 'letter of tenderness', as if, through this very linkage, through this grammatical magnet, a gathering, some gesture of bringing together, a loving movement always left in it the trace of an affect, a communitarian connotation, in the very place at which it would seem to be the opposite (opposition, contradiction, disjunction, incompatibility, privation: 'to the exclusion of', 'against', 'without' or 'for want of', for 'without' always signifies, you guessed it, 'without-with' or 'with-without', 'and-without'. This is a general law of formal logic: a conjunction slips and insinuates itself into every disjunction, and vice-versa).

(Derrida, 2000: 291)

In the note to this passage, we are told that Derrida's informant, one Mounira Khemir, has also told him that this letter is apparently also the 'travellers' letter'. The implication is that those who are away from home, otherwise out of place, need to swear, or 'give oath', to 'what one invokes and by which one commits oneself' (Derrida, 2000: 303). Each of us says 'I do' and we are married. Just like that!

So should we stay with Derrida and give credence to his one word 'and'? I don't think so. As indicated in the previous examples, almost any set of words can act as a conjunction. One moment Alice is in wonderland, the next she finds herself standing over the body of the woman who has 'gone before'. One moment one engages with a history of the human (via Stiegler), the next, as the acknowledgement of one citation leads to another, the reader is transported to the 'technics' of the field of deconstruction.

All words make a gathering, not just 'and'. This is what we learn about citation, the iterability of the word. A word, any set of words when run together, is so promiscuous that anybody can be saying anything. Or, indeed, be made to say anything. In this respect it is hard to resist adding here that current work calling itself 'deconstruction' is hardly facing up to the pervasiveness of this problem of citation. As pointed out by Derrida, citation – as a possibility of its *own* functioning – is 'cut off, at a certain point, from its "original" meaning and from its belonging to a saturable and constraining context' (Derrida, 1982a: 320).

As an evocation as well as an elicitation, language is, at heart, still part of the crafting of each of us as self or other. What is usually missing from analysis is just this performative side of language, the 'conjugals' of the 'conjunctions' which philosophy (as we have been told) can never grasp. Philosophy has its infinities and is engrossed in these. Too engrossed to ever care for the everyday, which is to say that philosophy – when it is turned towards this 'exteriorization of memory' – has never anything to say to life itself. So we find thinking is already organized in ways that have it always slipping outside of what we want to do and slipping past the words we want to say. Whether it wants to make sense of 'things', or systematize 'meanings' into the form of a dictionary, language is always slipping from our own hands into the hands of others.

DISCUSSION

The aim of this chapter has been to open up understandings about the *place* of language in philosophy, a matter I have pursued elsewhere to explicate the idea of a 'motility' of language games (Munro, 2001a), whereby some moves in a language game *alter* the language game itself; and in ways that can shift the landscape entirely. Here, in contrast, I am gesturing to the organizational issues of time in language. But just to say that time is both an issue *and* at issue hardly takes us forward.

It is all too easy to admit that language is indeed special, particularly since it is internalized as 'mine'. All other technologies are kept apart – in the prosthetics of identity and extension (Munro, 1996) – as mere supplementary 'parts'. This is the difference. Riding the air we breathe, language becomes but second nature. Indeed, we are so mesmerized by the 'power' for language to make 'present' other things, that we have overlooked its own ontology as the very *absence* of 'presence'. We have failed to register how to interpret both the 'thinness' of reference and its supplementary retreat of meaning into 'context'.

If language, metaphorically, is the bridge that creates the 'banks', there will always be objects or 'things' on one side and ideas or 'meanings' on the other. Derrida's contribution in this respect is to help us read the *presences* of absence. To be clear, this is not a guidance to begin listing merely what is 'absent'. Yes, often, clues are given by noticing in a text what is simply not mentioned. But Derrida can hardly be accused of simply attempting to make the world more politically correct, so that everything and everybody must be included in a litany of evasions, additions, caveats and extenuations. His gift is rather to suggest how we can see past the 'bridge' of words and read across the fissures of language.

Yet in attending to language only as a technology that can make 'things' present and absent, we can overlook what I have called a 'disposal' of the world (Munro, 2001b) in which language is the key to making relations that otherwise would always be *disjunct*. Language indeed intrudes itself between what we think of *as* us, in all our various forms of identity and belonging, and the 'things' of the worlds that we are constructing. But, consequently, in acting both as hinge *and* horizon, bridge *and* landscape, language ends up as much more than a veil separating cause from effect. Acting through what is called 'affect', language might be better understood to act like a second skin – a skin so scrumpled that its closest literal analogue is perhaps the 'tympan' of the ear (Derrida, 1982b).

For all his displays of a love of language, I worry that Derrida has failed to follow through on a language of love. In so far as Heidegger has already pointed to how the 'banks' are highlighted by the bridge, it seems all too easy to be seduced by Derrida's focus on difference and get lost in the divisions language creates for itself. This would be to 'forget' what is specific and important in language, namely the 'conjoining' that is accomplished by the landscaping nature of language. But this is not to be mistaken for a claim that communities are actually born from this endless conjoining of 'things' and 'meanings'. The powers of language to both create the perspective of 'meanings' *and* bring 'things' into view are irremediably tied to its intrinsic disjunction of cause and effect. The point then is that all we have then is affect; and that affect, by virtue of this very disjunction, is always *nomadic*. So communities, as Anderson (1991) has anticipated, are always being 'imagined'. What is granted to us by language is a sense of place; but, in reality, as an effect of the 'veil', we are nowhere.

CLOSING NOTES

Unless philosophy takes seriously the social study of organization, broadly understood, matters like language and time continue to elude it. Language, I have argued, is always a 'doing' of social relations. It 'gathers' us; bringing together those who are conjoined, but who might otherwise fall apart.

What remains is to understand better the *organizing* of this 'gathering' and 'ungathering'. This is not just to say, with Roland Barthes (1982), that there is no exit from language. Rather it is to admit that with the 'transparency', the dazzle of what we see, comes the 'veil', the second nature of living in language. Cut off by language from any immediacy with 'things', all we can do is appreciate the nomadic nature of the 'bonds' being installed from moment to moment through the pyrotechnics of identity work and our endless professions of belonging.

This said, it might seem as if it is 'division' itself – of which class, gender, religion and species are only some of the more prominent versions – that we are being mobilized to stand against. Far from gathering 'things' in their ontological fullness, as Heidegger would have us do, we are perhaps too ready to fall back onto a new kind of 'ontic' tick whereby an ever-multiplying supply of 'divisions' are treated as real. Here we might appreciate the extent to which deconstruction, when applied without love and without curiosity, currently aids and abets these diasporas.

And yet it is surely in attending closely to what is being positioned as 'irreconcilably different' that we grasp that opposition is always a politics and, often, a failure of imagination. Briefly, we may say there is always, whether we register it or not, an *elicitation*: some are called and some are excluded. Yes language 'gathers' the world, bringing things into view and revealing what otherwise might be concealed. Yet, as an *evocation*, language is not simply a making of things present or absent. However tentative and fragile its workings, language is also a 'landscaping' of our sense of relative presence and absence in the hearts of others.

REFERENCES

Anderson, B. (1991) *Imagined Communities: Reflections on the Origin and Spread of Nationalism*. London: Verso.

Austin, J. L. (1962) *How to Do Things with Words*. Oxford: Oxford University Press.

Austin, J. L. (1970) *Philosophical Papers*. Oxford: Oxford University Press.

Barthes, R. (1982) 'Inaugural lecture, Collège de France', in S. Sontag (ed.) *A Barthes Reader*. London: Cape.

Clark, T. (2000) 'Deconstruction and technology', in N. Royle (ed.) *Deconstructions: A User's Guide*. Basingstoke: Palgrave.

Derrida, J. (1976) *Of Grammatology*, trans. G. C. Spivak. Baltimore, MD: Johns Hopkins University Press.

Derrida, J. (1982a) 'Signature, event, context', in *Margins of Philosophy*, trans. A. Bass. Chicago, IL: University of Chicago Press.

Derrida, J. (1982b) 'Tympan', in *Margins of Philosophy*, trans. A. Bass. Chicago, IL: University of Chicago Press.

Derrida, J. (1986) *Memoires for Paul de Man*, trans. C. Lindsay, J. Culler, E. Cadava and P. Kamuf. New York: Columbia University Press.

Derrida, J. (1988) *Limited Inc*, trans. S. Weber. Evanston, IL: NorthWestern University Press.

Derrida, J. (2000) 'Et cetera', in N. Royle (ed.) *Deconstructions: A User's Guide*. Basingstoke: Palgrave.

Foucault, M. (1980) *Power/Knowledge: Selected Interviews and Other Writings, 1972–1977*, ed. C. Gordon. New York: Pantheon.

French, N. (2000) *Killing Me Softly*. London: Penguin.

Heidegger, M. (1959) *An Introduction to Metaphysics*, trans. R. Manheim. New Haven, CT: Yale University Press.

Heidegger, M. (1962) *Being and Time*, trans. J. Macquarrie and E. Robinson. Oxford: Basil Blackwell.

Heidegger, M. (1978a) 'Building, dwelling, thinking', in D. F. Krell (ed.) *Basic Writings*. London: Routledge.

Heidegger, M. (1978b) 'On the essence of truth', in D. F. Krell (ed.) *Basic Writings*. London: Routledge.

McLuhan, M. (1962) *The Gutenberg Galaxy: The Making of Typographic Man*. London: Routledge & Kegan Paul.

Merleau-Ponty, M. (1962) *Phenomenology of Perception*, trans. C. Smith. London: Routledge.

Miller, J. H. (1995) *Topographies*. Stanford, CA: Stanford University Press.

Munro, R. (1996) 'A consumption view of self: Extension, exchange and identity', in S. Edgell, K. Hetherington and A. Warde (eds) *Consumption Matters: The Production and Experience of Consumption*. Oxford: Blackwell.

Munro, R. (1997a) 'Connection/disconnection: Theory and practice in organization control', *British Journal of Management*, 8(special issue): 43–63.

Munro, R. (1997b) 'On the rim of reason', in R. Chia (ed.) *In the Realm of Organization: Essays for Robert Cooper*. London: Routledge.

Munro, R. (2001a) 'After knowledge: The language of information', in S. Linstead and R. Westwood (eds) *The Language of Organization*. London: Sage.

Munro, R. (2001b) 'Disposal of the body: Upending postmodernism', *ephemera: critical dialogues on organization*, 1(2): 108–130.

Munro, R. (2002) 'The consumption of time and space: Utopias and the English romantic garden', in M. Parker (ed.) *Utopia and Organization*. Oxford: Blackwell.

Munro, R. (2004) 'The remains of the say: Zero, double-crossing and the landscaping of language', *Journal for Cultural Research*, 8(2): 183–200.

Munro, R. (2005) 'The aesthetics of disposal: From the succession of ideas to the stream of consciousness', paper presented at the Aesthetics of Listening conference, Creuzberg, Germany, April.

Sterne, L. (2003) *The Life and Opinions of Tristram Shandy, Gentleman*. London: Penguin.

Stiegler, B. (1998) *Technics and Time, 1: The Fault of Epimetheus*, trans. R. Beardsworth and G. Collins. Stanford, CA: Stanford University Press.

Chapter 13

After power

Artaud and the theatre of cruelty

Steven D. Brown

> Where there is power there is also resistance, and yet or consequently, this resistance is never in a position of exteriority in relation to power.
>
> (Foucault, 1979: 95)

> I would not go so far as to say that philosophical systems ought to be directly or immediately applied, but we ought to be able to choose between the following:
>
> 1 Either these systems are a part of us and we are so steeped in them we live them, therefore, what use are books?
> 2 Or we are not steeped in them and they are not worth living. In which case what difference would their disappearance make?
>
> (Artaud, 1974: 1–2)

INTRODUCTION

The first of the opening two quotations will be familiar to many readers. It comes from the notorious 'method' section of the first volume of *The History of Sexuality* where Foucault presents 'a certain number of propositions' in relation to power and power relations. The first four propositions map out his now well-known immanentist conception of power as 'manifold relations of force that take shape and come into play in the machinery of production' (Foucault, 1979: 94). Power is entirely of a piece with the social field, it subsists within and lends shape to every conceivable relationship. As such, power is neither external to the social, nor has itself any 'outside'. But at the very moment that Foucault leaves his readers stunned with the implications of this dramatic conceptual hyper-inflation, in proposition five he performs a no less dramatic about-face. Yes, power is everywhere, but so too is resistance. It may be meaningless to consider an 'exit' from power, but resisting power does not require such an illusion in any case.

A generation of authors in organization theory have received and promoted the content of these five Foucauldian propositions as the default theory of power in organizations (see Burrell, 1988; Clegg, 1989, 1994; Deetz, 1992; Fleming, 2002;

201

Knights and Vurdbakis, 1994; Knights and Willmott, 1989; McKinlay and Starkey, 1998). It is perhaps not too grand a claim to make that Foucault's gnomic fifth proposition on 'resistance' has taxed this same generation who have wanted, beyond all reason, for it to be *true*. For what Foucault tantalizingly offers here is a way to think to the very limits of power and to find, right at the limit, that all that opposes power has been there all along, at every step – 'Where there is power there is also resistance'. But how can this thought be properly articulated? How can it be made to pass for truth? An immanentist definition of power already skirts with nominalism inasmuch as the term 'power' now becomes a redundant modifier to the word 'relation'. To speak of relations is already to have invoked questions of influence, control, domination, freedom, association. Summing this up as a matter of 'power' adds very little. To then add, almost as an afterthought, that 'resistance' is immanent to what we mean when we speak of power is to risk lapsing further into the purely arbitrary. The would-be critic of power is then faced with an almost insoluble task – how can this unruly and inchoate term be fitted onto actual empirical instances? And how on earth does one divine where and when 'resistance' becomes part of the picture? Small wonder that many critics rediscover the strategy of Lewis Carroll's Tweedledum and Tweedledee – the words 'power' and 'resistance' mean whatever I want them to mean, they are out there in the world exactly where I say they are.

It is precisely this strategy that the second quotation appears to mock. It appears in the preface to Antonin Artaud's 1933 series of texts published as *The Theatre and its Double* (Artaud, 1974). In this collection, Artaud is also concerned with power and with resistance. He wishes to define a role for the theatre as a critical force in social life, as a space for the exploration, formation and performance of a very different kind of modern humanity. In order to do so, one might consider it necessary to provide some theoretical basis on which to prioritize the role of the theatre, some 'philosophical system'. But if such a system exists, then it is either already constitutive of the very conditions against which theatre seeks to protest, or else it is so radically external to the field in which theatre operates that it provides no assistance whatsoever to the critical ambitions of Artaud's envisaged theatre-to-come. Thus Artaud's conclusion: philosophy is either part of the problem, or else it is so removed from the liberation project envisaged for theatre that it is entirely irrelevant.

One cannot then, Artaud appears to suggest, overcome power relations through formal theorizing. After all, as Artaud writes later in the same text – 'the present state of society is iniquitous and ought to be destroyed. If it is theatre's role to be concerned with it, it is even more a matter for machine-guns' (Artaud, 1974: 29). Even allowing for the deliberately provocative tone of these comments, it is difficult not to hear the resounding irony in these words written by an author who aspires to stage a major theatrical spectacle, and who will go to extraordinary lengths to create social and financial networks as a means to this end (see Brown, 2005). To liberate theatre from the 'iniquitous' relations of power in which it is embedded, it is of course necessary to theorize, for how else is one to authorize, to recruit commitment to *what must be done*. But this theorizing is ultimately, of itself, useless. Artaud recognizes the futility of the words he writes as an integral part of the act of writing itself: 'Writing is all pigshit. People who leave the realm of the obscure in order to define whatever is going on in their minds, are pigs' (1968a: 75). These lines serve as a kind of auto-condemnation of writing, mocking both the reader and liquidating the authority of the author. What remains is simply the gesture of writing and immediate erasure, of assertion and elision. Artaud demonstrates in his writing that thinking the limits of power leads to the discovery that there is no exit from power relations. To write is to make oneself over into the 'trash' that power desires, and in so doing to utterly exhaust whatever is vital ('obscure'). All writing (and all speech) is then destined to fail, leaving behind only a gesture that has no means of recording or inscribing itself on the world.

I want to contrast these two attempts, by Foucault and Artaud, to think the limits of power. In a sense both attempts are failures. It is now clear to us, especially after the publication of the Collège de France lecture series, contemporaneous with the writing of *Discipline and Punish* and volume one of the *History of Sexuality*, that Foucault's journey into the origins of modern governance led him to doubt his fidelity to a post-Nietzschean conception of 'relations of force' (see Foucault, 2004a, 2004b, 2004c; also Marks, 2000 for critical commentary). And despite Foucault's legendary attempts in interviews (for example Foucault, 1989a) to fashion a consistency between his work in the mid-1970s and the unexpected classicist turn taken in the final two volumes, greatly influenced by Pierre Hadot (see Case, Chapter 5 in this volume), the fifth proposition on 'resistance' now seems ever more tenuous, more of a blind alley off the road to the direction taken in the final works.

ARTAUD'S FAILURE

In Artaud's case, his own personal biography, which has acquired a near iconic status, seems to speak of an even greater failure. In brief, that biography runs a little like this (see Barber, 1993; Esslin, 1976 for proper details). Between 1920 and 1937, and again in the eighteen months preceding his death in 1948, Artaud was involved in a succession of theatrical and literary projects, most notably his planned 'Theatre of Cruelty', which was thematically linked around the problem of expression and representation. Artaud envisaged a revolution in theatrical production, which would do away with the privilege accorded to author and script and thereby liberate a pure performativity in the form of 'spectacle' (Bermel, 2001). In the intervening years, Artaud was incarcerated in a series of asylums, most notably Rodez, where he produced a series of artworks (see Rowell, 1996 for reproductions of the works and Derrida and Thévenin, 1998 for critical engagements). Artaud's oeuvre is voluminous (stretching to twenty-six volumes in French) and is composed of published books, essays, criticism, lectures, manifestos, letters, poetry, graphite and crayon works on paper and 'spells'. To which can be added his cinematic acting work (much of which was performed for financial gain and subsequently disowned by Artaud himself), surviving records of the few theatrical performances he managed to stage, and the audio recording of a banned 'obscene' radio performance (see Artaud, 1995a; also visit www.ubu.com/sound/artaud.html).

During the course of this extraordinary productive life, Artaud managed to acquire the status of a poet whose legacy was a series of letters to a literary editor (Jacques Rivière) justifying why his poetry was unsuccessful (Artaud, 1968b), the Surrealist who was expelled by the Surrealist movement and who later used a police guard to have members expelled from his production *The Cenci* (Breton, 1969), the theatre practitioner who managed to alienate the greater part of the Parisian theatrical community (Brown, 2005) and whose rare productions either closed early or created more drama off-stage than on (Bermel, 2001), the intellectual whose lectures descended into farce and apparent madness (Barber, 1993), the actor and would-be scriptwriter who infamously participated in disrupting the premiere of the sole film adapted from his work (Germaine Dulac's 1928 *The Seashell and the Clergyman*) and ultimately the lunatic who attempted to send 'spells' on burned, symbolically inscribed paper to friends, former colleagues, and, most perplexingly, Adolf Hitler (see Rowell, 1996: 50–51).

Put simply, this certainly seems to amount to a life consisting of continuous failure, of an incessant production with neither proper aim nor realizable objective (for more on this, see Böhm, 2005). What value can then be placed on the 'work' of an author who is so completely unreliable? Worse yet, what to make of texts which seem suspended between the categories of the 'critical' and the 'clinical'? As Jacques Latrémolière, the psychiatrist who supervised the electro-convulsive therapy given to Artaud at Rodez, puts it:

> Screaming [as performance] was all he could do and I believe that someone who can't control himself has nothing to offer anyone else. I have his complete works here. I have the first editions of his works. He gave them to me . . . and I read them bit by bit. Well, when you read the totality of what he says, you see that there is very little that's intelligible. It contributes nothing to civilization. Nothing at all.
>
> (Lotringer, 2004: 23)

What Latrémolière is partly alluding to here is a now legendary public lecture given by Artaud on 13 January 1947 which descended into 'wild improvisation, constantly shattered by cries, screams and savage gestures'. This event has been central to what Scheer (2000) calls the 'Artaud Question': in which frame of reference ought Artaud's work be situated? Should he be understood as author, theatre practitioner or madman? And how does Artaud's oeuvre problematize or disrupt these categories? The critical commentary on Artaud since the 1940s suggests various answers (see Scheer, 2004 for a useful summary). The most relevant, for our current purposes, is

204

undoubtedly the uptake of Artaud in the substantive philosophical work of Deleuze (1990, 1998; Deleuze and Guattari, 1984, 1988), Derrida (1978a, 1978b; Derrida and Thévenin, 1998) and, in particular, Foucault (1995, 2005). I will seek to touch upon some of this work as we proceed. Much of it takes as its point of departure the claim made by Maurice Blanchot in 1959 (reproduced as Blanchot, 2004) that it is precisely Artaud's apparent 'failure' to produce adequate poetry that is at issue.

In his correspondence with Jacques Rivière, who had recently rejected his poetry for publication in *Nouvelle Review Française*, Artaud bemoans his weakness as a poet at length, which he attributes to a mental inability — 'a sickness affecting the soul in its most profound reality, poisoning its expression. Spiritual poison. Genuine paralysis. Sickness robbing us of speech and memory and uprooting thought' (Artaud, 1968b: 41). Rivière notes the contradiction between the elegance with which Artaud expresses himself in these letters, with his 'extra-ordinarily precise self-analysis' (Artaud, 1968b: 34), and the relative failure of the poetry, and proposes to publish instead their correspondence. Blanchot argues that while Rivière's sensibilities are worthy in noting the contrast, he fails to notice the significance of Artaud's cries to be defeated by poetry:

Common sense immediately poses the question why, if he has nothing to say, does he not in fact say nothing? We may reply that one can content oneself with saying nothing when nothing is merely almost nothing; here, however, we are apparently confronted with such a radical nullity that, in the exorbitance it repre-sents, the danger of which it is the approach, the tension it provokes, it demands, as if it were the price to be freed from it, the formulation of an initial word which would banish all the words which say something.

(Blanchot, 2004: 112)

Although Artaud professes (and would continue to do so in his final writings) that he has 'nothing to say', that he suffers from a 'powerlessness', an 'unpower' that interrupts his work, Rivière is wrong to assume this 'nothingness' is a crisis suffered by thought. Rather it is a 'radical nullity' that is itself 'thinking', or rather an image of thought as withdrawn from speech. What Artaud experiences as a 'void' is the 'tension' or the 'danger' which arises as speech confronts the absent traces of the thinking which serves as its conditions, and which correspondingly must be effaced in the act of speech. Blanchot hails Artaud's poetry as an attempt to think the 'impossi-bility of thinking'. That is, to confront thought as it absents itself from the formal, rational organization of expression (of which poetry is emblematic). It is this absence that Foucault (1989b) would later famously refer to as 'the thought from outside' in his well-known essay on Blanchot. It is then important for Blanchot to distinguish the character of this struggle from 'madness' as such:

We must not make the mistake of reading as analysts of a psychological state the precise, unflinching and detailed descriptions of this which Artaud offers us. Descriptions they are, but of a struggle. This struggle is in part imposed on him. The 'void' is an 'active void'. The 'I cannot think, I cannot manage to think' is an appeal to a deeper thought, a constant pressure, a forgetting which, unable to bear being forgotten, none the less demands a more complete forgetting. Thinking now becomes the step back which is always to be taken.

(Blanchot, 2004: 114)

Artaud's struggle is to evacuate language in such a way that it is adequate to the task of going after 'the void'. Blanchot uses the language of forgetfulness to describe the trace-like character of thought as both perpetually absenting itself from expression, and yet making that absence felt within whatever is expressed. To go after the void is then to turn expression back on itself so there is nothing left but the traces of absenting thought (a 'complete forgetting'). Blanchot also hints that indirection, taking a 'step back', is the method Artaud begins to apprehend in the correspondence with Rivière, since the object of the struggle is not 'forwards' into a finely honed expression (successful poetry, well-received plays), but rather 'backwards' pursuing thought by collapsing the expressions which stand in between the subject and thought's perpetual elision.

If we follow Blanchot, two points become immediately clear. If Artaud's struggle with thought was pursued by a constant 'stepping back', then it would never have given rise to an integrated oeuvre, a 'life work', which would be in any way comparable to that bequeathed by Foucault. Correlatively, the lack of cohesion within such a work need not indicate a complete failure, since the purpose of each individual component (letters, poems, theatrical productions) would be to serve as yet another site for ruining expression in the struggle to confront thought. Thus if both Artaud and Foucault can be said to have 'failed' in their theorization of power then there is a real qualitative difference between these two failures and the meaning of 'having failed'.

OVERCOMING THE RATIONAL

Let us pursue the contrast between Artaud and Foucault by turning to a common concern – the rule of reason. Betraying orthodox Weberian roots, much contemporary organization theory regards 'rationalization' as simply the 'crush space' of modern modalities of governance. The order of formal reason, in all its various manifestations, is a strategy deployed within power relations to provide the illusion of reflection. 'Reason' is a way for organizations to enjoy the last gasp of those they will then proceed to press the life from. It is a warrant, a licence to kill. Seen in this way, reason is inevitably polluted and must be subverted by any means possible, such as through recourse to critiques which self-consciously offend reason (for example Burrell, 1997), by uprooting the epistemic wellsprings of faux-rationality (for example Calás and Smircich, 1999), through exploring aesthetic alternatives to formal reason (for example Linstead and Höpfl, 2000), directing effort to revalorize the body and its powers (for example Hassard et al., 2000) or by invoking Otherness (for example Cooper, 1983; Willmott, 1996).

These reactions to formal rationality occupy the space opened up by Foucault's (2005) monumental excavation of reason and its Other. Foucault concerned himself with how 'madness' receives its determination as 'unreason' from reason itself, and in so doing offered up an alternative origin story for organized rational modernity. Unreason is welcomed, is tamed, when it takes up the definitions and axioms afforded it by the generalized rationalization of conduct (i.e. as that which deviates from normative 'mental health'). But in hearing this story, the reader cannot but feel a longing for the time when madness was itinerant, before it was recruited into the role of staking out the borders of the rational. Foucault certainly encourages such a longing, not only by way of the narrative framing of his 'history' but also by pointing to modern examples of madness beginning to find its own voice within the very heart of reason.

One of the voices that Foucault identifies is that of Artaud. It is worth hearing a little of the kind of speech Foucault is pointing toward. Take the following open letter drafted in April 1925 by Artaud as part of his activities as director of the Surrealist Bureau de Recherches, and addressed to the *Chancellors of the European Universities*:

> Gentlemen, In the narrow tank you call 'Thought', the mind's rays rot like old straw . . . Europe is becoming set in its ways, slowly embalming itself beneath the wrappings of its borders, its factories, its law-courts and its universities. The frozen Mind cracks beneath the mineral staves which close upon it. The fault lies with your mouldy systems, your logic of 2 + 2 = 4. The fault lies with you, Chancellors, caught in the net of syllogisms. You manufacture engineers, magistrates, doctors, who know nothing of the true mysteries of the body or the cosmic laws of existence. False scholars blind outside this world, philosophers who pretend to reconstruct the mind. The least act of spontaneous creation is a more complex and revealing world than any metaphysics.
>
> (Artaud, 1968c: 179)

Although it is Chancellors who are directly addressed, Artaud's target is what these 'Gentlemen' embody: the capturing of thought in the form of abstract logic. Thought – that power of expression which for the Surrealists surged forward from the great inexhaustible reservoir of unconscious being – is bound up by the manifold wrappings of syllogisms and logical precepts, like a mummified body sealed within strips of viscous cloth. And beneath this wrapping which becomes denser everyday, thought, and with it the whole of Europe, is slowly putrefying.

Although the Surrealist Revolution with which Artaud was briefly and ultimately unhappily associated was to be a revolution in thought itself (Esslin, 1976), Artaud here conceives of thinking as a work of the *body*: 'I do not separate my thought from my life. With each of my tongue's vibrations I retrace all the paths of my thought through my flesh' (Artaud, 1968d: 165). Considered as a 'total organism' (which includes those aspects of being which we moderns are apt to call 'mental processes' or 'cognition') the body, by virtue of its very existence, is that which apprehends the world and acts within it. The body *thinks* as it *acts*. Thus doctors and engineers, whose expertise is based upon a premature and superficial grasp of embodiment, are numbered among the accused. All fail to understand what is really at stake: 'the true mysteries of the body'. It is the body *qua* thinking-thing, with its miraculous powers of creation which should be the proper object for investigation and which suffers so greatly from the constriction of formal metaphysics. Chancellors, magistrates and physicians are all complicit in enacting a system which sets upon the body, which 'usurps' and locks thought up into sterile, vapid rationality, leaving 'all the forces of being' trapped by a maze of 'ever-changing walls' or else 'lost in its own labyrinth'. Logic is a system for suffocating life, whose fetid corpse Artaud disdainfully sniffs:

> In the name of your own logic we say to you, Life stinks Gentlemen. Look at yourselves for a moment, consider your products. A whole generation of gaunt and bewildered youth is passing through the sieve of your diplomas. You are a plague upon the world, Gentlemen, and so much the better for the world, but let it consider itself a little less in the vanguard of humanity.
>
> (Artaud, 1968c: 179)

It is in the midst of this stench that Artaud seeks to wallow. In an image which would recur in his later writings on *Theatre and the Plague*, Artaud casts himself as a vagabond taking his pleasure among the rotting waste of a great scourge. For it is only in the very presence of death that life seems most vital, where one is brought within the full presence of 'an extreme force' where all the 'powers of nature are newly rediscovered the instant something fundamental is about to be accomplished' (Artaud, 1974: 17). At seemingly the very moment when existence is most threatened by the brute abstraction of Logical Europe it is possible to re-encounter the primal force which animates all beings. But at what cost! A certain 'unlevelling' of thought is required, and since thought is proper to the entire 'living animal' rather than the deified 'conscious aggregate' of metaphysics (Artaud, 1968e: 186), this unlevelling finds its coefficient in a deterioration of the 'physical organization' of the body.

For Artaud, the organization of life under the sign of reason can be opposed only by attacking what then passes for life itself. There is no question of simply recovering some raw living unorganized matter – or *bios*, as Foucault (1984) has it – from the clutches to rationalization, since the very organization of the body participates in and augurs the modern dominance of reason. In a small essay written to accompany a display of his Rodez portraits, Artaud (1995b: 277) argues that the human face itself bears 'a kind of perpetual death on its face', from which it is the painter's task to save it. By this he means that the physical organization of the face acts as a barrier to the expression of the vital forces which are obliged to pass by way of it. It is as though, throughout history, the face has breathed and spoken without yet starting to 'say what it is and what it knows' (1995b: 277). The human face is then a screen, emitting deathly signs denuded of all vitality. Artaud's own portraits seek to recover these vital forces by staging focused and concentrated attacks on the faces in various ways (see images in Rowell, 1996: 98–132). His 1946 works concentrate on distorting a single feature – Roger Blin's nose appears as a giant fold of flesh, Jacques Prevel's face is split in two with the right side sliding away, a dancing figure appears across Colette Thomas' pursed lips (Rowell, 1996: 103, 108, 113). By 1947 this gives way to wholesale assaults – Paule Thévin's entire head chained by tiny figures, Henry Pichette's neck erupts with spikes and thorns and in a self-portrait completed four months before his death, faces appear to erupt everywhere from a blurry stem like body and torturously erect fingers, all of which dissolves into scratched lines of graphite (Rowell, 1996: 115, 124, 128).

The body is, for Artaud, always and already an abortive attempt at organization. From the moment of birth, one is forced to endure a botched and impoverished physical form, a set of 'conditioned reflexes' and organs which are 'badly correlated' with the directions in which thought needs to press. In a short note 'On suicide', Artaud imagines humanity as simply badly designed:

> Life was not an object or form for me, it had become a series of rationalisations. But these rationalisations never got off the ground and only freewheeled, they were like possible 'diagrams' within me which my will-power could not light on.
>
> (Artaud, 1968f: 158–159)

To live under such circumstances is to accept the fate of a 'walking automaton' which is 'kept alive in a void of denials and furious disavowals' (Artaud, 1968f: 158). The alternative, to commit suicide, is then not an act of despair or self-destruction, but rather the rejection of a flawed design and the submission of a new set of plans:

> If I kill myself, it won't be to destroy myself, but to re-build myself. For me, suicide would only be a means of violently reconquering myself, of brutally invading my being, of anticipating God's unpredictable approach. I would reintroduce my designs into nature through suicide. For the first time I would give things the shape of my will.
>
> (Artaud, 1968f: 157)

This extraordinary image of rejecting the human form as inhospitable to thought, to will, is continued in the macabre imagery of 'Toxic knuckle bones' (1968g). The 'free man' (*sic*) lies as a bloated body stretched before the gaze of attending physician/ judges. He is 'dead', but yet 'conscious', at some threshold of existence where these apparently (logically) opposed states achieve an 'imperceptible cohabitation'. Having 'touched danger', the free man now finds himself released into the breath of 'All-life'. Artaud hectors the assembled observers:

> What does he feel? He has lost any feeling of himself. He escaped you through thousands of openings. You think you have hold of him, yet he goes free. He does not belong to you.
>
> (Artaud, 1968g: 190)

The 'free man' is finally beyond the limits of the rational. He slips into the 'thousand tiny openings' between the nets of syllogisms. But in doing so he enters a state of perpetual undecidability, where pronouncements of 'madness' or 'sanity', or even 'dead' or 'alive' have little purchase. To 'touch danger' is to not merely court non-existence, but to actively pass over into a state of disfiguration that is the complete other of organization.

What are we to make of courting death itself as the only conceivable form of resisting organized rational modernity? Artaud appears to be promoting 'death' – and we must inevitably add 'madness' – as a political programme of total critique to be played out in direct opposition to the powers which subject us to our own individuality, which provide us with the forms of denomination that we are obliged to live out. For so corrupted are our own bodies that we have, in effect, to become still madder than the utter insanity of unrestrained technological-rationality, less 'civilized' than the rampant barbarism of organized modernity itself. She or he who seeks to resist power finds themselves ultimately in the position that Artaud claimed for Van Gogh as 'suicided by society', that is, finding their own personal destruction to be the only plausible response to a lifeless form of living. Artaud then appears to rob organizational theory of every resource that it might muster to overcome reason. There is no hope in stylistics, epistemology, art, 'the body', or Otherness. The relentless ordering of reason proceeds before the moment of our own birth. It can be neither resisted nor overcome, Artaud seems to suggest. If this is madness finding its voice, as Foucault insists, then the voice utters only a two word suicide note: 'design refused'.

But before reaching such a conclusion we would do well to observe a note of caution expressed by Deleuze (1990) in *The Logic of Sense*. Commenting on Artaud's half-hearted attempt to translate a 'fragment' of Lewis Carroll's poem 'Jabberwocky', Deleuze observes that the difference between Artaud and Carroll is that the latter prodigiously maintains a gap between expression and denotation in language – that is between what language does, in its transformation and movement, and that to which it ostensibly refers. Artaud collapses any such gap by treating language in purely physical terms, as that which directly strikes the body (see also Munro, in this volume). For Deleuze, treating language in this way creates the impression of endless depth:

> Things and propositions have no longer any frontier between them, precisely because bodies have no surface. The primary aspect of the schizophrenic body is

that it is a sort of body-sieve. Freud emphasised this aptitude of the schizophrenic to grasp the surface and the skin as if they were punctuated by an infinite number of little holes. The consequence of this is that the entire body is no longer anything but depth – it carries along and snaps up everything into this gaping depth which represents a fundamental involution. Everything is body and corporeal . . . Every word is physical, and immediately affects the body.

(Deleuze, 1990: 86–87)

If we leave to one side the rather problematic use of the term 'schizophrenic', Deleuze's claim is that Artaud envisages a 'language without articulation' consisting of 'breath-words' and 'howl-words' in which 'all literal, syllabic, and phonetic values have been replaced by values which are exclusively tonic and not written' (Deleuze, 1990: 89). We may see this as the inevitable conclusion of the double operation of treating speech and writing not as expressive acts but as occasions for struggling with absenting thought and the simultaneous rendering of such thought as entirely co-extensive with embodiment. If this is so then 'speech acts' are to be regarded as the small change of rationality, wounding and insulting the body, with words themselves taken as physical entities that swarm around the porous body-seize, which is at the same time thought contorted into the most painful and exposed configuration (i.e. thought locked into the poorly designed 'diagram' of the human form).

To avoid this conclusion it will be necessary to demonstrate that Artaud does actually have an account of language that restores a surface between words and things, however thin and porous that might be. We may begin to recover this account by making a series of sidesteps from his manifestos to his other work with Breton and Surrealists, and from there to his writing on theatre, and on towards the final performance for radio *To have done with the judgement of God*.

THE EXQUISITE CORPSE

In a superb demonstration of deconstruction as fidelity to the interiority of text, Derrida's (1978a) essay 'La parole soufflée' re-marks the tension at the heart of Artaud's writing. To write, to speak is to have failed, to have negated the expressible in the very act of its articulation. First, because to even begin to speak is to place oneself in relation to a field of possible expressions that will have to be appropriated in some way in order to afford reasoned discourse. This is exemplified best in Artaud's fundamental opposition to the form of theatre that sets itself the task of performing, as faithfully as possible, the scripted words of the author ('let us do away with this foolish adherence to texts, to written poetry. Written poetry is valid once and then ought to be torn up. Let dead poets make way for the living': Artaud, 1974: 59). Second, because speech, having been first stolen (or 'spirited away' as Derrida has it), becomes subject to a second form of theft once it is passed on and rendered as an object for critique, commodification, or simply as no longer belonging to the speaker. On the basis of this double movement of 'theft', Derrida reads the Artaudian consciousness as fragmented by this undecideability about 'who speaks':

> I am in relation to myself within the ether of speech which is always spirited away [*soufflé*] from me, and which steals from me the very thing that it puts me in relation to. Consciousness of speech, that is to say, consciousness in general is not knowing who speaks at the moment when, and in the place where, I proffer my speech.
>
> (Derrida, 1978a: 176)

The speaking subject is riven with a fissure. To be conscious of one's own speech is to not know with any certainty 'who speaks'. Speech is dominated by the figure of theft, or as Derrida will have it, rather the stealing of language from our mouths by 'the thief who has always already lost speech as property and initiative' (1978a: 178) is itself the exemplary scene of theft from which all other instances will borrow their determination. Moreover, for Derrida, Artaud's scorn for the poorly designed body is not primary in relation to his disdain for language, but rather both betray a more general distrust of the organized:

> Organization is articulation, the interlocking of functions or of members, the labor and play of their differentiation . . . Artaud is as fearful of the articulated body as he is of articulated language, as fearful of the member as of the word.
>
> (Derrida, 1978a: 186)

The question Derrida then asks is whether this fear ultimately leads to a kind of complicity with the metaphysics that Artaud denounces (i.e. of self-presence, of capturing thought itself etc). Perhaps unsurprisingly Derrida (1978a: 194) argues that such complicity is a 'necessary dependency of all destructive discourses: they must inhabit the structures they demolish, and within them they must shelter an indestructible desire for full presence, for nondifference: simultaneously life and death'.

Derrida's text then serves as a useful reminder that Artaud's own texts are 'duplicitous'. They pose as suicide notes, promising the destruction of the botched body and the overcoming of the order of reason, but do so carefully, strategically, experimentally, in the spoken and written medium that they denounce so furiously. If Artaud demonstrates that language is spirited away in its articulation, then he is also an adept thief himself, able to purloin meaning in unexpected ways. Consider the following extracts from a short text written with the participation of Breton. *Dialogue in 1928* (Artaud, 1968h) is a series of texts produced by what was termed 'Exquisite Corpse'. The procedure is based on an old parlour game – the first participant writes a phrase on a piece of paper which is then folded up and covered leaving a space for the next participant to make their addition. The whole is then revealed by unfolding the paper at the end, with the final text treated as an 'accidental' or 'chance' production. Here are two instances:

> Artaud: 'Does Surrealism still hold the same importance in the organisation and disorganisation of our lives?'
> Breton: 'It is all mud, almost entirely composed of flowers.'
> Artaud: 'Is death of any importance to you in organising your life?'
> Breton: 'It is time to go to bed.'
>
> (Artaud, 1968h: 189)

The interest in these randomly produced texts lies not so much in the wild juxtapositions between the subject matter, but rather in the apparent ease through which the basic machinery of language affords some kind of meaning to the paired questions and responses. For example, in the first couplet, Breton's response is clearly nonsensical in any ordinary sense, but it is not unintelligible. Breton uses the classical form of predication 'it is' followed by a wildly implausible predicate 'all mud, almost entirely composed of flowers'. And yet since the response conforms to the basic structure of grammar, it is still possible for a reader to construct some form of meaning, however far-fetched, from the couplet. Moreover, Breton's random answer does actually fit with Artaud's question inasmuch as it *performs* something of the qualities of Surrealism, it demonstrates Surrealism-in-action as a force for the organization and disorganization of lives.

Similarly, the second couplet can be rendered intelligible by focusing on its basic grammatical features. By 'it is time to go to bed', Breton may well be producing a kind of response to how one should organize one's life in response to death, or else he may simply be expressing his fatigue with the conversation. The crucial phrase is 'it is time'. Usually such a formulation would serve the deictic purpose of tying the utterance to the time and place of its articulation. Deixis is a basic and ubiquitous means of invoking an extra-linguistic context of utterance. Used in this way, practically any statement following 'it is time' might conceivably be heard as relevant to the prior conversational term. Is this a conversation between luminary Surrealists or a drowsy chat before bed? We do not know, but we are able to make such readings because the deictic formulation automatically renders the statements as plausible in some way.

What this experiment demonstrates is how it is possible to subvert speech, to open up unexpected and wildly inventive meanings by merely tinkering with the basic grammatical structure of ordinary language. For, as Michel Serres (1995) so elegantly notes, the Lilliputian-like character of the basic machinery of language – prepositions, deixis predication – labours constantly beneath our everyday affairs. Language is then disorganized, or at least twisted into unexpected shapes, not so much by refusal or by complete disruption (as in screaming) but rather by setting that miniscule machinery off into novel directions. In this sense, the wildly uneven character of Artaud's oeuvre can be seen as a kind of programme aimed at hollowing out, within language, spaces which bend formalism back on itself to create unpredictable singularities – chance 'events' in language. Artaud does his poetry through exchanging letters with an editor, he achieves his theatre through reviews and critiques. In both cases the form of the text is completely different in nature to the performative act that is accomplished within and insinuated into that form. Or put another way, the performance, the 'doing' of the poetry or theatre is always off to the side, conducted through other means, such that the supposed 'poem' or 'play' appears a failure when it is artificially separated from these sidesteps.

In an early essay, Foucault (1995) identified precisely this disruptive experimentation with language, and claimed this as evidence for a new form of communication between madness and literature. The basis of his claim is that one form in which madness has been classically understood is that of:

> subjecting an utterance, which appears to conform to the expected code, to another code whose key is contained within the same utterance so that this utterance becomes divided within itself. It says what it says, but it adds a silent surplus that quietly enunciates what it says and according to which code it says what it says.
>
> (Foucault, 1995: 294)

Such utterances would then necessarily take the form of singularities, since they would not entirely obey existing codes for the formation of discourse (despite broadly resembling such codes), but would rather contain within themselves the keys to the articulation of a second code which have the effect of not only transforming the utterance but also rendering the utterance entirely unique. Foucault points to Artaud, Nerval and Roussel as having made this technique 'the place of literature'. But in so doing, this gesture – which, for Foucault, brings literature and madness into close proximity – means that literary criticism assumes a new importance, for it becomes essential to handling the singularity of texts and the distribution of codings, and that, perhaps even more importantly, it now becomes impossible to consider the authors of such work as endowed with an 'oeuvre' in the classical sense. Crudely put, if each text is singular, there can be no overarching code – the 'life work' – under which these texts can be gathered. Their power resides instead in the 'empty form from where this work comes, in other words, the place where it never ceased to be absent, where it will never be found because it had never been located there to begin with' (Foucault, 1995: 296).

Foucault gave the term 'the absence of work' (more properly the 'absence of the life work') to this emerging practice, of which he saw Artaud as one principal exemplar. Now this absence, or rather deliberate attempt at absenting the work from subordination to a given set of codings, certainly captures one other key aspect of Artaud's theorization of language. Namely that language 'works', that is, it is at its most efficacious, precisely when it appears to be 'not working', giving rise to a body of texts which gain their standing not through which they appear to affirm, but through the avoidances, sidesteps, omissions and 'failures' that they perform. In this respect each text is to be judged in terms of the 'silent surplus' of meaning it hollows out in its carefully constructed apparent misfiring. But the question that Foucault leaves us with is how could such a series of 'absences', of convoluted utterances be assembled into a life that both overcomes the power of formalization while maintaining some kind of internal consistency? Or put slightly differently, how can one aspire to live 'after power' when each successive act of resistance offers neither guarantees nor lessons for the next act?

BETWEEN CARE AND CRUELTY

Both Foucault and Artaud are driven through their thinking of power toward asceticism. In his final works, Foucault famously moves from a description of subjectivity as emerging in continuous dialogue with relations to power to a more sombre, classical view of the aesthetics of selfhood. Here it is the unswerving concern for self, the 'taking charge of life' through positing the question of self-being within all one's relations to the world that defines 'care' (cf. Foucault, 1984, 1987, 1988). Care, as the relentless interrogation of one's own actions in relation to the codes one assumes as necessary for living, is a form of strictness imposed by the self in order to form it-self:

> The idea of the *bios* [life] as a material for an aesthetic piece of art is something which fascinates me. The idea also that ethics can be a very strong structure of existence, without any relation with the juridical per se, with an authoritarian system, with a disciplinary structure. All that is very interesting.
>
> (Foucault, 1984: 348)

This separation of ethics as 'a very strong structure of existence' from the disciplinary matrix of power represents something akin to a 'starting over' in Foucault. Accompanied by an historical shift, from the proto-modernity of the eighteenth and nineteenth centuries towards the more remote social practices of classical Hellenic and Roman culture, Foucault's exploration of care and the associated 'arts of living' conveys a sombre tone at odds with the strident speech of proposition five. Perhaps in this turn Foucault really did find a means to situate himself outside of power, but that is constituted by a giving up of the terms of proposition five rather than its fulfilment.

Artaud similarly becomes concerned with the ascetic demands that must be made in order to form one-self. His word of choice to capture this demand is 'cruelty':

> I use the word cruelty in the sense of hungering after life, cosmic strictness, relentless necessity, in the Gnostic sense of a living vortex engulfing darkness,

in the sense of the inescapably necessary pain without which life could not continue.

(Artaud, 1974: 78)

In both cases, what is at issue is the placing of demands upon oneself, demands which must be experienced and endured as both inflexible and without end. In this way, Foucault and Artaud equally stress that living constitutes a project of going after *life itself*, and that it is through this pursuit and taking charge of the vital in an unremitting, painful manner that one forges 'a life'. What makes for the difference between 'care' and 'cruelty'? It is not immediately obvious, since there is a certain kind of arbitrariness between the terms. In the same way that Artaud clearly did not intend 'cruelty' to be read as the literal inflicting of pain, so Foucault equally clearly did not intend 'care' to be taken as unconditional regard for self. At their root, both terms imply the self-imposition of a non-negotiable obligation ('strictness'). One difference is that, as we have seen, for Artaud life, or at least the form in which the human body interns life, is beyond redemption. As *bios* the body is currently very poor material which can produce only the worst kind of 'art'. But a more important difference is the nature of the codes to which one must submit. For Foucault, these remain recognizably discursive. Selfhood emerges by way of the grid of meanings that one chooses to submit oneself to. But as described above, Artaud's conception of language proposes that it is not a medium for the constitution of meaning, but rather for the generation of affects. Artaud suggests not only that utterances contain their own codings, which divide speech in the moment of its appearance, but moreover that words themselves are physical beings with their own particular affective force. Words and the human voice itself literally 'strike us', and in so doing establish connections, an ordering between things in the world. Our apprehension of the world is always initiated by the 'shock' or 'tension' that language engenders within us.

Considered in this way, language is akin to a physical gesture made by members of an 'active culture' to one another. But it is precisely this force of gesture that has been forgotten. In order to recover its power, Artaud compares the experience of life in an active culture to situations of extreme anxiety and confusion:

Just like the plague, it [language in the active sense] reforges the links between what does and does not exist, between the virtual nature of the possible and the material nature of existence.

(Artaud, 1974: 17)

Because language is able to literally push people around and generate intense emotions – 'sudden silences, fermata, heart stops, adrenalin calls, incendiary images surging into our suddenly awoken minds' – it brings about a confrontation with 'living powers' (Artaud, 1974: 17, 65). In short, it is by realizing that language is primarily affective – a call to action – that we recover our full powers to act upon ourselves.

216

Artaud's conception of language as affect drew a great deal, whether reliable or not, from his encounter with a Balinese theatrical production (Artaud, 1974: 38–55; cf. Bermel, 2001). In such productions the precision of ritual gestures is critical, such as certain movements of the eyes or lips, which produce 'studiously calculated effects' (Artaud, 1974: 39). Staging is used not in support of words, but as part of the symbolic coding of activities wherein a gesture, a visual symbol or a particular mask may be combined together, without differentiating 'word' from 'image', in order to form complex expressions:

> In fact the strange thing about all these gestures, these angular, sudden, jerky postures, these syncopated inflections formed at the back of the throat, these musical phrases cut short, the sharded flights, rustling branches, hollow drum sounds, robot creaking, animated puppets dancing, is the feeling of a new bodily language no longer based on words but on signs.
>
> (Artaud, 1974: 38–39)

The Balinese theatre showed Artaud that a radical distinction between 'discourse' and 'language' is possible. Taken in its broadest sense, language is any system of codified elements, a broad grammar constituted by heterogeneous materials, whose fundamental operation is to order space through the assembling of intricate spatial forms. Language does not 'signify' anything, that is, it does not point outside of itself to worldly referents, since it is the things themselves that are being put into play to construct a complex lived space. And as part of that language – since there is no external 'God's eye' position from which to observe the proceedings – we apprehend what comes to pass through the affects which arise as we are ourselves put into play and moved about.

Artaud's notion of the theatre as the 'double' of life then has renewed importance. Organization theory has made much of the metaphor of 'theatre', suggesting that if organizations are treated as spaces for performance, something of the creativity and complexity of organizational life as narrative enactment without end becomes clear (Boje, 1995; Mangham and Overington, 1987). But to treat organizations in this way is to miss what is at stake in invoking theatre. Artaud insists on the following steps. First, we must see that theatre as it is traditionally understood reproduces the crushing futility of the order of reason, which enshrines the absent Author and The Work as central and renders performance as merely the speaking of the words (it is in this sense that indeed organizations are theatres, if by that one means to draw attention to the living death of repeating the gesture of the already said in as many different ways as possible). Second, we must understand that the theatre provides a supposed guarantee for reason, since it purports to reflect life and its vicissitudes in all its glory. Patrons then attend the theatre for 'purely digestive reasons', Artaud sneers. Third, that as a sheltered space off to the side of mundane affairs, theatre can actually provide an opening, a 'crack', where life can be seized upon, taken unawares, in performances which trap expression in a mesh of gestures and affects. Words no longer repeat The Work, but become a swarm of physical objects that the performer engages with, struggles with and submits themselves to experimentally. It is in this sense that theatre can propose models for life as it ought to be pursued outside the order of reason. Fourth, the translation of this model outside of the theatre, to make life over along the experimental lines that the Theatre of Cruelty demands, is what finally makes life over as the double of theatre.

What would it be to take this fourth step? In Artaud's (1995a) infamous radio performance, *To Have Done with the Judgement of God*, the final step in the doubling of life and theatre is outlined. The piece closes with the much discussed scene of humanity placed on an autopsy table where the 'sickness' of God is removed. As Deleuze (1998) makes clear, 'God' is here cipher for the ultimate guarantee of reason in and by itself, the projection of transcendent values which will secure perpetual judgement. It is the constant withdrawing, or rather deferment of the basis on which judgement is made that constitutes God's will. By having reason emanate from elsewhere, life is turned into a perpetual waiting for ultimate judgement by God, a deferment and debt without end which will make up the business of living. But through the use of the doubling effect of theatre, Artaud demands a reversal of terms. Rather than accept life as that which is judged by God, life will be turned inside-out as the process of putting God, putting reason itself on trial. The Theatre of Cruelty is also the staging (perhaps the 'show trial') of a process conducted against reason. And to the extent that such a process will involve dragging the traces of reason from our own bodies themselves, that trial will become a forensic autopsy. Hence the significance of the following lines:

> Man is sick because he is badly constructed.
> We must decide to strip him in order to scratch out this animalcule
> > which makes him itch to death,
>
> > > god
> > > and with god
> > > his organs.
>
> For tie me down if you want to,
> but there is nothing more useless than an organ.
>
> When you have given him a body without organs,
> then you will have delivered him from all his automatisms and restored
> > him to his true liberty.
>
> Then you will teach him again to dance inside out
> as in the delirium of the dance halls
> and that inside out will be his true side out.
>
> > (Artaud, 1995a: 307)

To 'have done with judgement' it is necessary to have done with God, with the notion of a prior organization that already determines the vitality of human life. Rooting out this organization, wresting 'life' from the 'badly constructed' designs which force us to embody a prior judgement in our very embodiment, is essential to achieving 'true liberty'. As Deleuze puts it 'judgement implies a veritable organization of the bodies through which it acts: organs are both judges and judged, and the judgement of God is nothing other than the power to organize to infinity' (Deleuze, 1998: 130). Here we have the final confrontation with power, where the disorganizing and affective power of language is turned back on the body, within the experimental space provided by the theatre as the 'doubling' of life, to make living into the trial of reason, which will strive to have done with judgement (that is, with power, with organization) when a new organ-less living is realized. That is, the vitality of life ripped away from the apparent strictures of given designs, and treated as a site for the play of affects and intensities – 'a nonorganic vitality' as Deleuze (1998: 131) puts it. Living without judgement, beyond power, is the final object of 'cruelty', through the making over of life as 'theatre' ('the delirium of the dance halls'). It may well be that here, as elsewhere, this confrontation is yet another grandiose failure on Artaud's part – perhaps the attempt to live without judgement can only ever end in the 'mis-trial' of reason – but in Artaud's layered descriptions of experimentation, affect, doubling and the judging of judgement, what it means to 'resist power' is significantly reworked.

'AFTER' POWER

The title of Marilyn Strathern's (1992) study of reproductive technologies, *After Nature*, contains a marvellous pun (see also Jones and Surman, 2002; Royle, 1995). To intervene in reproduction is to both to track nature down, 'going after' or going 'head to head' with the natural world, so to speak, and also to situate human affairs in what follows 'after' the order of nature has receded. In this piece I have argued that this dual sense of 'going after' power has exercised a considerable hold over much organization theory since the mid-1980s. My claim has been that this hold stems from the conceptual promise that proposition five in volume one of the *History of Sexuality* offers. And yet, as I have described, albeit all too briefly, Foucault's ultimate failure to resolve the double gesture of 'confrontation' and 'passing over' renders the project of deriving a liberation theory of power in organizations untenable. The hermeneutics of the subject that Foucault develops in his final works might then be best understood as Foucault authorizing himself to 'take his leave' of 'power' as a core analytic; this sidestep being cut short by his untimely death.

The contrast I have drawn is with Artaud's own confrontation with power, which takes the various forms of an attempt to 'go after' thought through the disruption of expression, freeing vital powers by rejecting the diagram offered by the order of reason, the subversion of the orderability of language, and finally turning life itself into the endless 'trial' of Reason/God. But in Artaud's case, the failure of the double gesture was inscribed in the very formation of 'going after' power. From the rejection of his poetry by Rivière through to the cancellation of the broadcast of *To Have Done with the Judgement of God* by Wladimir Porché at the very end of his life, failure is the defining feature of Artaud's fragmentary and uneven oeuvre. But this failure is not merely a matter of having been unable to situate the work with respect to an audience who would hail and define it as such (although doubtless this was a concern for Artaud). It is the convoluted acknowledgement that the work will have to 'fail', will have to dismantle itself in order to make the sidestep that, paradoxically, brings it into the greatest possible proximity with power, and simultaneously displays, through its own auto-erasure, glimpses of what it will be/will have been to come 'after' power.

If organization theory has gone after Foucault with such vigour, it is in pursuit of the dream of making proposition five real. What would this be? To have confronted power as it is and not as it passes itself off (i.e. in labour process theory). To have theorized, stylized, written, performed and proclaimed a reflective space outside of power. To have created a whole school, nay, an entire *discipline* of 'critical' studies of management and organization! To parody Artaud, 'if it is organization theory's role to be concerned with it, it is even more a matter for machine-guns'. Yet, all of us, as readers of this book to some extent share these dreams. I confess they are my dreams too. However, I want to close with the suggestion that it is Artaud rather than Foucault with whom we ought to engage to feel something of the impossible but necessary confrontation with power. In demanding that the 'event' or the taking place of the work be accorded greater importance than its completion, or its anointment as 'the work' (qua finished fetish object), and in rendering the work as perpetually unrealized or as only realizable in the form of fragments and traces, wherein thought is pursued through sidesteps, Artaud makes his work into a singularity, which receives its own determination, which cannot be categorized or exemplified as anything other than the event that it constitutes. Is that after power?

> Who am I?
> Where do I come from?
> I am Antonin Artaud
> and if I say it
> as I know how to say it
> immediately
> you will see my present body
> fly into pieces
> and under ten thousand
> notorious aspects
> a new body

will be assembled
in which you will never again
be able
to forget me.
(Artaud, 1995c: 323)

ACKNOWLEDGEMENTS

Audiences in Leicester, Essex and Limberg have endured versions of this chapter, enlivened only by a brilliant dramatic contribution from Simon Lilley. Several generous readers have assisted with the slow and painful progress of the written version. Thanks to Bob Cooper, Campbell Jones, Nick Lee, Jean-Luc Moriceau, Rolland Munro and René ten Bos.

REFERENCES

Artaud, A. (1968a) 'Nerve scales', *Collected Works: Volume One*, trans. V. Corti. London: Calder & Boyars.

Artaud, A. (1968b) 'Correspondence with Jacque Rivière', *Collected Works: Volume One*, trans. V. Corti. London: Calder & Boyars.

Artaud, A. (1968c) 'Letter to the Chancellors of the European universities', *Collected Works: Volume One*, trans. V. Corti. London: Calder & Boyars.

Artaud, A. (1968d) 'The situation of the flesh', *Collected Works: Volume One*, trans. V. Corti. London: Calder & Boyars.

Artaud, A. (1968e) 'Further letter about myself', *Collected Works: Volume One*, trans. V. Corti. London: Calder & Boyars.

Artaud, A. (1968f) 'On suicide', *Collected Works: Volume One*, trans. V. Corti. London: Calder & Boyars.

Artaud, A. (1968g) 'Toxic knuckle bones', *Collected Works: Volume One*, trans. V. Corti. London: Calder & Boyars.

Artaud, A. (1968h) 'Dialogue in 1928', *Collected Works: Volume One*, trans. V. Corti. London: Calder & Boyars.

Artaud, A. (1974) 'The Theatre and its Double', *Collected Works: Volume Four*, trans. V. Corti. London: Calder & Boyars.

Artaud, A. (1995a) 'To Have Done with the Judgement of God', in *Watchfiends and Rack Screams: Works from the Final Period*, trans. C. Eshleman and B. Bador. Boston, MA: Exact Change.

Artaud, A. (1995b) 'The human face', in *Watchfiends and Rack Screams: Works from the Final Period*, trans. C. Eshleman and B. Bador. Boston, MA: Exact Change.

Artaud, A. (1995c) 'Here lies . . .', in *Watchfiends and Rack Screams: Works from the Final Period*, trans. C. Eshleman and B. Bador. Boston, MA: Exact Change.

Barber, S. (1993) *Antonin Artaud: Bombs and Blows*. London: Fontana.

Bermel, A. (2001) *Artaud's Theatre of Cruelty*. London: Methuen.

Blanchot, M. (2004) 'Artaud', in E. Scheer (ed.) *Antonin Artaud: A Critical Reader*. London: Routledge.

Böhm, S. (2005) 'Fetish failure: Interrupting the subject and the other', in A. Linstead and S. Linstead (eds) *Organization and Identity*. London: Routledge.

Boje, D. M. (1995) 'Stories of the storytelling organization: A postmodern analysis of Disney as "Tamara-land" ', *Academy of Management Journal*, 38(4): 997–1035.

Breton, A. (1969) *Manifestos of Surrealism*, trans. R. Seaver and H. R. Lane. Ann Arbor, MI: University of Michigan Press.

Brown, S. D. (2005) 'Collective emotions: Artaud's nerves', *Culture & Organization*, 11(4): 235–246.

Burrell, G. (1988) 'Modernism, postmodernism and organizational analysis 2: The contribution of Michel Foucault', *Organization Studies*, 9(2): 221–235.

Burrell, G. (1997) *Pandemonium: Towards a Retro-Organization Theory*. London: Sage.

Calás, M. B. and L. Smircich (1999) 'Past postmodernism? Reflections and tentative directions', *Academy of Management Review*, 24(4): 649–871.

Clegg, S. (1989) *Frameworks of Power*. London: Sage.

Clegg, S. (1994) 'Social theory and the study of organization: Weber & Foucault', *Organization*, 1(1): 149–178.

Cooper, R. (1983) 'The other: A model of human structuring', in G. Morgan (ed.) *Beyond Method: Strategies for Social Research*. Newbury Park, CA: Sage.

Deetz, S. (1992) 'Disciplinary power in the modern corporation', in M. Alvesson and H. Willmott (eds) *Critical Management Studies*. London: Sage.

Deleuze, G. (1990) *The Logic of Sense*, trans. M. Lester. New York: Columbia University Press.

Deleuze, G. (1998) 'To have done with judgement', in *Essays Critical and Clinical*, trans. D. W. Smith and M. A. Greco. London: Verso.

Deleuze, G. and F. Guattari (1984) *Anti Oedipus: Capitalism and Schizophrenia*. London: Continuum.

Deleuze, G. and F. Guattari (1988) *A Thousand Plateaus: Capitalism and Schizophrenia*. London: Athlone.

Derrida, J. (1978a) 'La parole soufflée', in *Writing and Difference*, trans. A. Bass. London: Routledge.

Derrida, J. (1978b) 'The theatre of cruelty and the closure of representation', in *Writing and Difference*, trans. A. Bass. London: Routledge.

Derrida, J. and P. Thévenin (1998) *The Secret Art of Antonin Artaud*, trans. M. A. Caws. Cambridge, MA: MIT Press.

Dulac, G. (dir.) (1928) *Coquille et le clergyman*, 41 mins, black and white film.

Esslin, M. (1976) *Artaud*. London: John Calder.

Fleming, P. (2002) ' "Lines of flight": A history of resistance and the thematic of ethics, death and animality', *ephemera: critical dialogues on organization*, 2(3): 193–208.

Foucault, M. (1977) *Discipline and Punish: The Birth of the Prison*, trans. A. Sheridan. Harmondsworth: Penguin.

Foucault, M. (1979) *The History of Sexuality, Volume 1: The Will to Know*, trans. R. Hurley. Harmondsworth: Penguin.

Foucault, M. (1984) 'On the genealogy of ethics: An overview of work in progress', in P. Rabinow (ed.) *The Foucault Reader*. Harmondsworth: Penguin.

Foucault, M. (1987) *The History of Sexuality, Volume 2: The Use of Pleasure*, trans. R. Hurley. Harmondsworth: Penguin.

Foucault, M. (1988) *The History of Sexuality, Volume 3: The Care of the Self*, trans. R. Hurley. Harmondsworth: Penguin.

Foucault, M. (1989a) 'An aesthetics of existence', in S. Lotringer (ed.) *Foucault Live: Interviews 1966–84*. New York: Semiotext(e).

Foucault, M. (1989b) *Maurice Blanchot: The Thought from Outside*, trans. J. Mehlman and B. Massumi. New York: Zone Books.

Foucault, M. (1995) 'Madness, the absence of work', *Critical Inquiry*, 21: 290–298.

Foucault, M. (2004a) *'Society Must be Defended': Lectures at the Collège de France, 1975–1976*, trans. D. Macey. Harmondsworth: Penguin.

Foucault, M. (2004b) *Sécurité, territoire, population: Cours au Collège de France, 1977–1978*. Paris: Seuil.

Foucault, M. (2004c) *Naissance de la biopolitique: Cours au Collège de France, 1978–1979*. Paris: Seuil.

Foucault, M. (2005) *History of Madness*, trans. J. Murphy. London: Routledge.

Hassard, J., R. Holliday and H. Willmott (eds) (2000) *Body and Organization*. London: Sage.

Jones, C. and E. Surman (2002) 'After organization studies', *ephemera: critical dialogues on organization*, 2(3): 186–192.

Knights, D. and T. Vurdubakis (1994) 'Foucault, power, resistance and all that', in J. Jermier, D. Knights and W. Nord (eds) *Resistance and Power in Organizations*. London: Thompson.

Knights, D. and H. Willmott (1989) 'Power and subjectivity at work: From degradation to subjugation in social relations', *Sociology*, 23(4): 975–995.

Linstead, S. and H. Höpfl (eds) (2000) *The Aesthetics of Organization*. London: Sage.

Lotringer, S. (2004) 'Interview with Jacques Latrémolière', in E. Scheer (ed.) *Antonin Artaud: A Critical Reader*. London: Routledge.

McKinlay, A. and K. Starkey (eds) (1998) *Foucault, Management and Organization: From Panopticon to Technologies of Self*. London: Sage.

Mangham, I and M. Overington (1987) *Organizations as Theatre: A Social Psychology of Dramatic Appearances*. Chichester: Wiley.

Marks, J. (2000) 'Foucault, Franks, Gauls: *Il fait defendre la société*: The 1976 lectures at the Collège de France', *Theory, Culture & Society*, 17(5): 127–147.

Rowell, M. (ed.) (1996) *Antonin Artaud: Works on Paper*. New York: Museum of Modern Art.

Royle, N. (1995) *After Derrida*. Manchester: Manchester University Press

Scheer, E. (ed.) (2000) *One Hundred Years of Cruelty: Essays on Artaud*. Sydney: Power Publications.

Scheer, E. (ed.) (2004) *Antonin Artaud: A Critical Reader*. London: Routledge.

Serres, M. (1995) *Angels: A Modern Myth*, trans. F. Cowper. Paris: Flammarion.

Strathern, M. (1992) *After Nature: English Kinship in the Late Twentieth Century*. Cambridge: Cambridge University Press.

Willmott, H. (1996) 'Recognizing the other: Reflections on a "new sensibility" in social and organizational studies', in R. Chia (ed.) *In the Realm of Organization: Essays for Robert Cooper*. London: Routledge.

223

Index